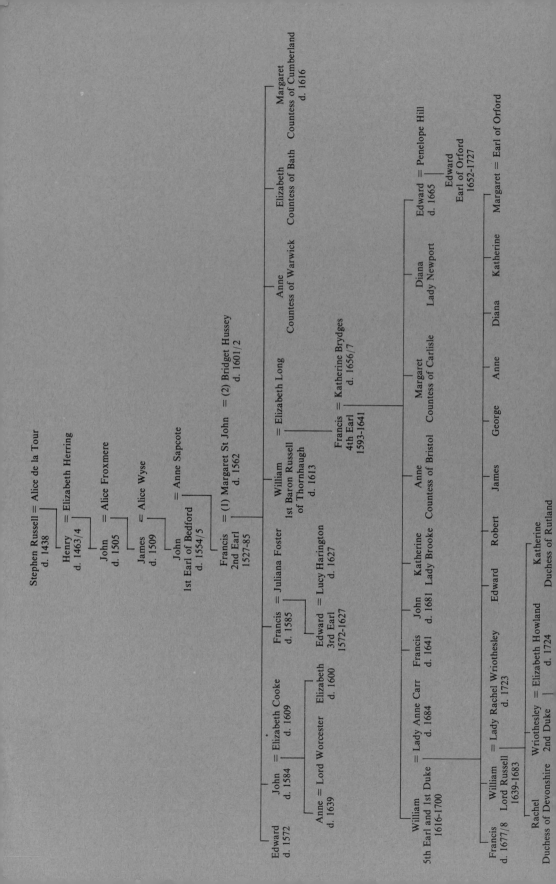

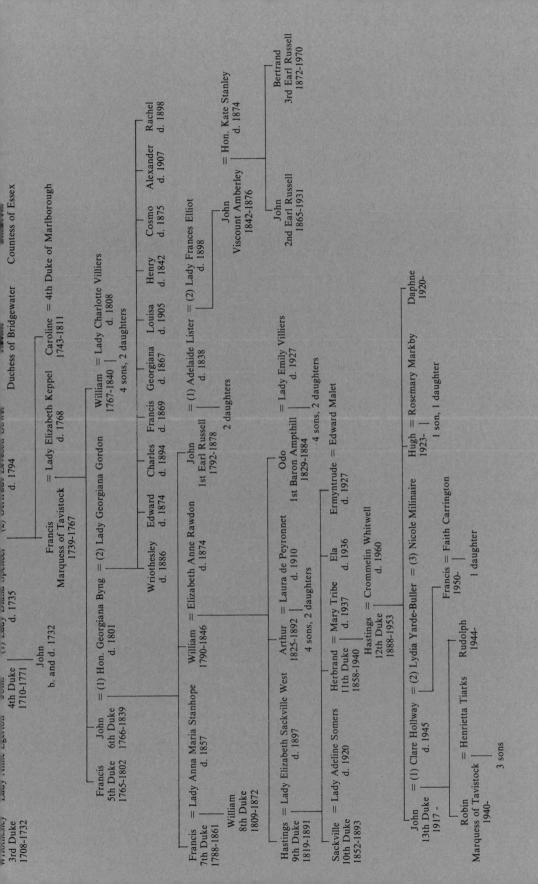

WOBURN AND THE RUSSELLS

Books by the same author

Lord William Russell and his wife
(John Murray)

WOBURN
AND
THE RUSSELLS

Georgiana Blakiston

Constable London

First published in Great Britain 1980
by Constable and Company Limited
10 Orange Street London WC2H 7EG
Copyright © 1980 by Georgiana Blakiston
Set in Monotype Bembo 12 pt
Printed in Great Britain by The Anchor Press Ltd
and bound by Wm Brendon & Son Ltd
both of Tiptree, Essex

British Library cataloguing in publication data
Blakiston, Georgiana
Woburn and the Russells
1 Russell family
I Title
929'.2'0942   DA28.35.R8
ISBN 0 09 461210 2

Foreword and acknowledgements

I have chosen to end this book with the death of Herbrand, eleventh Duke of Bedford in August 1940. It brought to a conclusion a way of life that had been carried on at Woburn for more or less three hundred years. England was engaged in a struggle for survival and it would not have been possible to continue any longer the lavish formality of the past, even had the old Duke's son wished to live in the family home on the same scale – which being a Socialist he did not. At the end of the war, when the Government Department that had occupied the house withdrew, it was discovered that dry rot had invaded part of the Abbey and rather than undertake expensive repairs the twelfth Duke decided to demolish the whole of Holland's east front – about one third of the house. He has written of his own childhood and youth at Woburn, describing the experiments made with keeping wild animals in the park, an interest that he had in common with his father, though there were not many others. His concern for the art collection was limited. The loss of wall space after the east wing had been pulled down was followed by a regrettable sale of pictures in 1951, when portraits of people who had been associated with Woburn Abbey were dispersed. The present Duke, his son, has given in his book an account of his relationship with his father and grandfather, and his own energetic efforts, after his succession to the dukedom, to rehabilitate the Abbey, to open it to the public, and to live there with his wife and children. He has now made way for his son, Lord Tavistock, to carry on the tradition that Woburn Abbey is a family home as well as a much visited show place.

I owe a debt of gratitude to the Duke and Duchess for their hospitality while I studied at leisure the fascinating collections in the house, and Lord Tavistock has been generous in letting me illustrate this book with photographs of the portraits. The Trustees of the Bedford Settled Estates gave me free access to the papers in the Bedford Office, and Mrs Marie

v

Draper, their archivist, was unfailingly helpful, patient and encouraging.

I would like to thank the Duke of Marlborough for letting me see the correspondence between Sarah, Duchess of Marlborough and the third Duke of Bedford, while those papers were still at Blenheim. I am grateful to the Governors of Somerville College, Oxford, for allowing me to examine the papers of the late Gladys Scott Thomson which are deposited there, and to make use of her draft for a life of the fifth Duke of Bedford. In the Library of the Royal Botanic Gardens, Kew, I met with kindness from Miss Sylvia Fitzgerald and Miss Irene Smith.

Mr C. W. H. Rawlins and Mr Cosmo Russell have allowed me to draw on their memories of the eleventh Duke, and Mr Robert Cecil has let me quote from the letters of Arthur Russell to Lady Derby, which are in his possession. Mr R. E. Latham's erudition helped me to clarify Lady Bacon's peculiar Latin. For the patient forbearance of my publisher I cannot say enough.

While the Russell family still prefer the old-fashioned pronunciation of Woburn as though the first vowel were doubled (and so it often was written in the past) it has not been universally adhered to; but to show the wide latitude in sound and orthography I have appended at the end of this book a list compiled by the Woburn postmaster in 1840 of the many different ways in which that place was spelt on the letters that passed through his office.

TO MY GRANDCHILDREN

Contents

Illustrations

Illustrations

Illustrations

꧁ᰮᬀᰮᬀᰮ꧂

Quest for ancestors

THE collection of family portraits at Woburn Abbey is one of the most interesting and remarkable in the country. From the time of the first Earl of Bedford until today the Russells have had their portraits painted, and if in recent times the artists chosen have not been always among the first masters, their work may be taken as representative of the taste and talent of their day.

As tributaries swell a great river, so marriages have made their contribution to the collection, bringing from fresh sources pictures as well as new blood to the heritage. Sovereigns have bestowed a regal portrait on a faithful subject; noblemen were once happy to present their own likeness to a friend. The currents of the accumulation are fascinating. But contemplating the pale or ruddy faces, meeting the gaze that is stern or doubting, frank or elusive, how hard it is to detect the character behind the face. Baffled by the eyes which outstare or evade, the observer shifts to easier ground – an inspection of the garments that clothe the men and women portrayed: that gown of Flemish cloth, fur-trimmed; the slashed velvet doublet, closely buttoned; the silks and satins adorned with ribbons and lace. Profuse jewels, meticulously depicted in the early portraits, make a footnote to the history of dress, and a picture can be dated by the form of a fan.

Between the windows of the state rooms reconstructed by Flitcroft for the fourth Duke of Bedford, there hang magnificent gilded looking-glasses in which once were fleetingly reflected the images of those later Russells and their friends who frequented the great house. The little bouncing Duke himself must often have encountered his own eyes in one of them – the living confronting the transient – and in the mirror's pair his Duchess may have assessed the fit of a new dress. Before another, did Charles James Fox, on his way for a snooze in the gallery after dinner, perhaps pause and recognize the intolerable strain of his figure on his waistcoat buttons? Young men, arm-in-arm, moving towards the whist table, may have laughed and smirked, or cut a caper before their reflection. Other tenants of the house were captured too – a child chasing through the rooms a leaping dog; a housemaid leaning briefly on a broom, pleased to view her ordinary face in the glass that she must dust. An alert imagination will reach forward and people the rooms with figures from the less distant past who were domesticated here. The dedicated hunting men in pink coats, ready for the chase; the diminutive and fragile figure of Lord John Russell passing on his way to a Riesener writing-table on which the red boxes of his office are awaiting his attention; the fringed and bustled daughters of the house of a later generation; the Flying Duchess in her airman's fur helmet, or in the uniform of a Red Cross nursing sister. What a variety of movement and appearance has been momentarily held in the great looking-glasses; nothing now remains on the mirrors' surface of those brief and insubstantial images – it is to the portraits that we must turn and make what we can of the vanished men and women.

For anyone who attempts to write about a particular family there must be a presumption that some members of it and their way of life can claim the interest of the world generally, and it becomes the business of the writer to indicate without bias those characteristics which have contributed to the survival of a family that for more than four hundred years has held a steady place in the annals of the nation.

It would be easy to assume that the continuous distinction of the Russells has been based only on wealth early acquired – prudent marriages thereafter augmenting great possessions – but it was discreet good sense that promoted those marriages; firm characters and capable hands have taken care of the wealth, while cool heads have steered a safe and enlightened course through the fluctuating currents of the centuries.

Fuller tells us that the first Earl of Bedford 'brought himself in by what humoured and kept himself there by those things that did oblige himself'; a compound of altruism and self-interest that was a sound receipt for success. Integrity coupled with a love of country and a natural acceptance of service to the state initially kept the name of Russell to the fore. A martyr in the family helped to fan the embers of youthful pride and gave a whiggish direction to latent patriotism. From the security of settled wealth and power an independent and liberal outlook developed, manifested by a stubborn opposition to the power of the Crown. Strong and stable characters have been much in evidence, and where strength has been lacking, obstinacy has sometimes helped conceal its absence. Yet Russells are generally cautious and mild, and the slave of passion makes but a rare appearance. As individuals they tend to show in divers ways a disregard for accepted attitudes, each pursuing his course in his own way with no timid apprehension of being thought different from his fellow-men. Two recent members of the family whose births separated them by only fourteen years, and who had little in common except their Russell blood, may be taken as examples – Herbrand, eleventh Duke of Bedford (1858–1940) and Bertrand Russell (1872–1970). The Duke, a military man, was in many ways conventional, but he held acute and independent views on public affairs, playing a constant and unostentatious part in the business of the House of Lords, while recognizing that effective personal management of his estates could not be combined with a political career. He undertook without pleasure the duties he thought were demanded from a person of his position, acting for thirty-three years as chairman of the Bedfordshire County Council, and serving for some time as the first Mayor of Holborn. As President of the Zoological Society for thirty-seven years he found an occupation nearer his heart. A lifelong interest in animals and natural history was not a taste he shared with many of his equals. He maintained with a quaint exaggeration the material standards of the past, and his adoption of uncreased trousers and a white tie for daily use made his appearance quietly unusual. While in his letters he expressed his ideas with astonishingly fluent clarity, he was shy and uncommunicative in society and he had an almost pathological desire for privacy. His favourite plant was *Heracleum giganteum*: the giant hogweed.

His cousin Bertrand Russell, mathematician and philosopher, showed no fear of being in the public eye. As a socialist he rejected his inherited title of Earl Russell; as a pacifist in the first world war he went to prison. His unconventional attitude towards marriage, his brilliant intellectual powers, and the clarity of his literary style made his name widely known. During the last thirty years of his life he campaigned against nuclear armaments and the H-bomb, and was often photographed sitting grimly protesting on a London pavement, or marching in procession to Aldermaston with mothers pushing babies in prams; his white hair and stubborn expression became familiar all over the world. A black sheep in the family, he was not invited to Woburn Abbey until he was over seventy, when his position as the second best-known living Englishman was recognized.

On a slight eminence in the park at Woburn there stands not far from the house an ancient oak, which by tradition served as the gallows for Robert Hobbes, the last abbot of the Cistercian monastery which was founded in 1145 by thirteen monks from Fountains Abbey, who chose near the little town of Woburn a secluded and delectable site for their new house. The crabbed and meagre branches of that tree are evidence of its antiquity; in 1539 it must already have been more than a sapling. 'Generations pass while some trees stand and old families last not three oaks', wrote Sir Thomas Browne. The life of an oak may be half a millennium and few families can claim survival or trace their history through fifteen hundred years. The stock may fail from divers causes; feeble procreation can hinder its continuance; misfortune and violent death may obliterate a line, while fine hereditary qualities – like Shakespeare's circle in the water – with 'too much spreading will disperse to naught'.

The old families of England destroyed each other during the Wars of the Roses, and oaks were felled in their prime to build the ships of Queen Elizabeth's navy. New men rose into the ranks of the nobility under the early Tudors, while some oaks escaped the Elizabethan woodman's axe.

When Sir Thomas Browne was writing *Urn Burial* the new men had been established long enough to feel confident of a settled future; stress was being laid on the importance of birth and they were beginning to take a practical interest in their origins and progenitors. Queen Elizabeth in the early years of her reign had accepted a descent from Adam and Eve, Methusaleh and Seth, and James I is said to have studied with interest and amusement pedigrees prepared for him by loyal subjects – and those who wished to ingratiate themselves with the new monarch – that traced his ancestry back nearly to the Flood.

The study of genealogy and pedigrees was ever an interest shared in common by the higher ranks of society. William Cecil, the first Lord Burleigh, during the course of his busy life, laboured to construct pedigrees for his friends; in the eighteenth century Horace Walpole (who considered that little ability but much perseverance was required by the genealogist) was ready to busy himself with reference books and tables to oblige a friend with the details of an intricate relationship. The slips of paper that fall out of old books and turn up in bundles of family manuscripts, covered with names and dates of births and marriages, are witness to the industry of leisured and interested persons intent on proving kinship with a cardinal, or truth in a legend of descent from Genghis Khan.

In the summer of 1821 the sixth Duke of Bedford engaged a Quaker named Jeremiah Wiffen to be his librarian at Woburn. It was for both of them a satisfactory appointment, and their happy relationship lasted until the death of Wiffen fifteen years later. During eight of those years he was engaged in writing a lengthy history of the Russell family.

Wiffen was the son of an ironmonger in the town of Woburn and was largely self-educated. As a boy he had been a pupil with John Bright and William Howitt at a school in Yorkshire, where he had the reputation of inventing exciting romances to amuse his school-fellows. For a time he kept a small school in his native town, and during those years he studied to become conversant with French, Spanish, Italian, Hebrew and Welsh. In 1819 he visited the Lake District and met Wordsworth and Southey, the latter telling him that he had been at Woburn Abbey when the news of the battle of Leipzig was brought. He was regarded by James Hogg as the best scholar among the Quakers. He had wide literary interests and when he came to the notice of the Duke of Bedford he had already published a volume of verse.

One of his merits in the eyes of his employer was his preference for working in an unheated room in the basement of the Abbey; the Duke, who was personally extravagant, appreciated frugality in others, and this economical peculiarity endeared Wiffen to him, although after his librarian's early death he expressed fear that the circumstances of working in a stoveless room may have hastened that excellent man's end.

Among the Woburn Abbey manuscripts of which Wiffen was the custodian was a beautifully illuminated pedigree roll of the Russells that had been compiled by Le Neve, the York Herald, in 1626 for the third Earl of Bedford. It traced the Earl's descent from Hugo de Rosel, one of William the Conqueror's knights, and the roll carried at its head a figure of this ancestor: a sturdy ruffian with drooping moustaches, gilt spurs, broadsword and a wide green cloak.

A study of the pedigree set fire to the gentle Quaker's imagination. He had a natural aptitude for research, and he examined ancient rolls and records that were within his reach in England. A glance at a map of France showed him that le Rosel lay near Caen in Normandy, and thither he betook himself, meaning to stay four weeks, but, supported by the generosity of the Duke, he remained four months. It was a heady time for so romantic an investigator, whose self-appointed task was to outdo Le Neve. Examining abbey charters, unrolling cartularies, blowing the dust from deeds and documents preserved in the muniment rooms of the province, he planned *The Historical Memoirs of the House of Russell*.

Gibbon noted that 'the proudest families are content to lose in the darkness of the middle ages the tree of their pedigree', but Wiffen's industry traced the lineage of the Russell family to Olaf the Sharp-eyed, king of Rerik, who flourished in the dark forests of the north in the seventh century.

When later two substantial volumes appeared from the press, the Duke of Bedford had reason to see that his liberality had not been dispensed in vain. It was history written in a suitably flattering style; few warts were to be detected in the portraits Wiffen drew of his patron's ancestors, and his diligence could not be denied.

In time the quality of his adulation and his lively imagination came to be ridiculed, and the sharp-eyed Norseman was scoffed out of his pre-eminence in the pedigree, but the figure of Hugo de Rosel, the Norman knight, was comfortably accepted in the family until early in this century. In 1895 the figures of two saints were acquired from the curé of the church at le Rosel, and installed in the chapel at Chenies. In a letter to his aunt at this time, Duke Herbrand humorously proposed 'that it would be well to retire to Rozel and establish the contents of Woburn Abbey in a château in that vicinity' to avoid the penalties of English taxation; and in 1944 a young Russell, serving on General Montgomery's staff in Normandy, was greeted with warmth in le Rosel when he made known his name; for a tradition remained in the village that the family of the Duke of Bedford had come from there, and it was recorded that Lord John Russell in about 1850 had visited the area to see if any members of the family remained. Had not the victorious army been moving forward rapidly the young British officer fancied he might have been given a civic reception.

It fell to the late Mr J. H. Round to demolish 'the too ingenious Mr Wiffen's' story of the ancestry of the Dukes of Bedford. Castigating the zealous and well-meaning Quaker for failing to show the evidence for much of what he said, Round poured scorn on him for making errors in deduction from old pedigrees, and while acknowledging the existence of one Henry Russell (an important link in Wiffen's chain) he wrote of him with contempt because he owned a barge. It was demolition without construction, and a later scholar – Gladys Scott Thomson – showed that Wiffen by his industry had uncovered grains of truth.

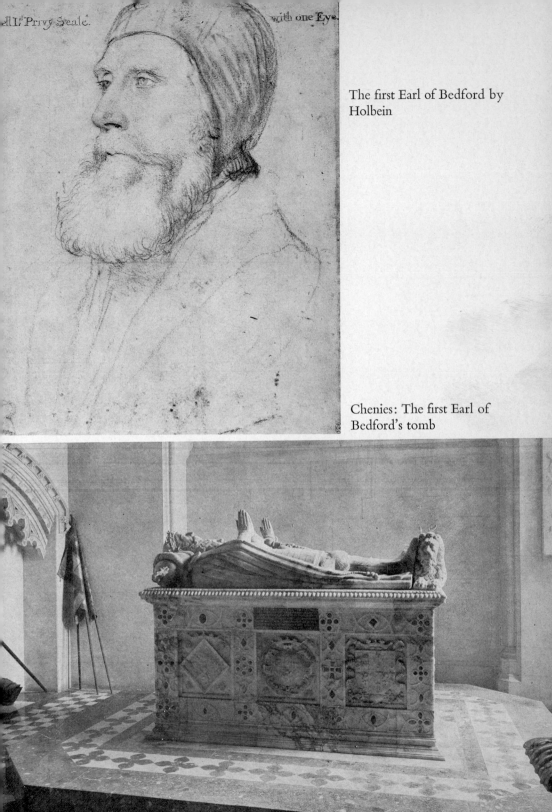

The first Earl of Bedford by
Holbein

Chenies: The first Earl of
Bedford's tomb

The second Earl of Bedford by
Zucharo

Edward, Lord Russell by an
unknown painter

2

The Gentleman from Dorset

JOHN, sixth Duke of Bedford, and Jeremiah Wiffen might well have been astonished had they heard it stated contemptuously that the family of the Duke descended from a bargeman living in the fourteenth century. The Duke, we may believe, would in his rational and good-humoured way have been interested and amused, the librarian mortified and incredulous that Olaf the Sharp-eyed and Hugo de Rosel must no longer figure in the pedigree that he had so carefully concocted.

In the use of the term 'bargeman' there was perhaps some desire to shock, for it suggested a very humble calling, whereas in fact five hundred years ago a barge was a sea-going vessel of eighty tons, and might carry as many men. The first ancestor of the Earls and Dukes of Bedford proven by documentary evidence was Stephen Russell, who flourished at Weymouth at the end of the fourteenth century. He may have owned a barge; his son Henry certainly did, and other ships as well. Very little is known about Stephen, and that which is derives from the records of the lawsuits in which he engaged, sueing successfully for recognition of his wife Alice's claim to parcels of land in scattered parts of Dorset; she being, as she contended, heiress of the de Blynchesfield and de la Tour families, long established in that county. It was through her that the property of Berwick by Swyre came into the possession of the Russells. The manor house still stands, though much changed, and is regarded as the cradle of the family, for it was the home from which John Russell set out in 1506 on his fortunate career to become first Earl of Bedford; in time receiving from the Crown large grants of land in other parts of England.

It can be assumed that Stephen Russell was a person of some consequence – since he had been able to make a match with a woman of fortune – and that he was respected as a citizen, for he was sent to Westminster as member for Weymouth in 1394, and he polled at other elections. During a time of trouble and disturbance that heralded the outbreak of the Wars of the

Roses, he and his son Henry appeared together as men '*potentes*' and '*valentes*' before the Chancellor of England at Dorchester, to take an oath to keep the peace and to see that others did the same.

Stephen was a merchant by calling; prosperous, perhaps, although he had his losses. When a notorious pirate carried off from Weymouth harbour a barge containing seventy-nine tuns of white wine, besides iron and other commodities, it appeared at the inquiry into these nefarious doings that Stephen Russell had a part interest in the merchandise on board, though the barge, the *La Marie* of Bordeaux, was owned by a Frenchman. Weymouth's trade with the western seaboard of France, like that of other south coast towns, flourished while Gascony was a province of England. The vessels that undertook the dangers of tempest and rough seas, and the hazards of attack from pirates, both French and English, carried wool and fleeces in their cargoes, returning laden with the Gascon wine that was almost a staple drink of England at that time. Commerce was lively and profitable; traffic flowed between the countries, and there was a constant migration of men both ways. A Frenchman would have been no unfamiliar sight on the quayside of Weymouth or Dartmouth, and the naming of a street in Bordeaux, rue de Russell, which appears in contemporary records, is an echo of the dealings of a Dorset family with that town.

It was, perhaps, his connection with south-western France that gave Stephen Russell his alternative name of Gascoigne. The use of an alias was not uncommon and was generally derived from some personal peculiarity or from a geographical association. As Stephen Garsquen, Gascon or Gascoyn, or Stephen Russell Gascoigne, he appears in wills and deeds relating to his affairs; he may indeed have been a Gascon settled in this country, in which case the family of the Duke of Bedford can again put forward that claim to French ancestry that was denied them when Hugo de Rosel was scoffed out of their pedigree. It would be easy to assume that Stephen came from a line of Russells established since the thirteenth century at Kingston Russell in Dorset, but of this there is no proof, and that male line failed long ago. No parentage has been found for him; his origins may lie hidden in Dorset or in Gascony, but the alternative name of Gascoigne, that he shared with his son, and its occurrence in documents having reference to both father and son, distinguishes these two men from any other of the Russells who abounded in Dorset at that time.

Stephen's son, Henry, was perhaps the principal ship-owner in Weymouth, and he was, as his father had been, engaged in trade. 'Henry

Russell of Weymouth, otherwise called Henry Russell of Weymouth merchant, otherwise called Henry Gascoigne Russell of Weymouth gentleman or by whatsoever name he may be styled', runs a contemporary document. He must have been a familiar figure on the quays watching his boats nose their way out of the harbour to the open sea, setting off on their long voyage down the Channel and beyond to western France. The perils attendant on legitimate seafaring were recognized by Parliament, and in 1442 an order went out to Weymouth that the owners of ships were to furnish help between Candlemas and Martinmas in patrolling the Narrow Seas, for which payment was made by the Crown. Henry Russell provided one barge and one pinnace of the sixteen that were demanded from Weymouth for this service, and his name headed the list of those who were required to contribute aid in keeping the sea free from pirates, smugglers and the King's enemies. Respected men were called on to undertake the duties of their position, and Henry Russell shouldered his. He served as bailiff for Weymouth, and as a commissioner to levy money for the King, activities that kept him near the port, but being sent three times to Westminster as one of the burgesses for Weymouth, a service that entailed long absences from home, his commercial interests must have suffered frequent interruptions. A worthy, perhaps ambitious man, his employments multiplied; but when he was appointed King's customer for Exeter and Dartmouth to see that ships did not slip out of those ports until proper dues had been paid on their cargoes, he was already acting as bailiff in Weymouth. Unable to be in two places at once, he failed to do the work he should have done in the west country. A jury of inquiry at Exeter found him guilty of neglecting his duties, by which the King had lost money, but none the less so generally sound a public servant was granted a pardon.

The temper of this active and capable man may be seen in his threat to kill an abbot with whom he had a dispute about land at Shaftesbury. Since he continued to hold the property and it passed to his descendants, it may be presumed that he had right on his side, and that it was his piety, rather than an act of amendment for the threat, that prompted him to found a guild within the chapel of St Nicholas overlooking the harbour at Weymouth, and to establish a chantry of one priest to celebrate mass daily for the King, the founder, and the brothers and sisters of the guild.

An inhabitant of the seaport, he owned a house in Dorchester as well. He settled this on his daughter and her husband, who held the tenement by the rent of a red rose, payable each year on the Feast of St John the

Baptist. It was to Dorchester that Henry was carried when he died in 1464; he was buried in the church at the top of the town that was dedicated to the Holy Trinity, and the Russell arms of a lion rampant and three scallop-shells were emblazoned on his tomb.

He was succeeded by his son John and his grandson James, who became the father of that other John, the first Earl of Bedford. John the elder, and James, who lived at the manor house at Berwick, were buried within sound of the sea at the church at Swyre, where two brasses commemorate them and their wives.

Every legend is said to contain at least one grain of truth, and the seed may be discovered when the chaff has been winnowed from it. John Russell, the great-grandson of the merchant Henry, steps into the clear light of historical fact from the shadows of tradition that surround his origins. His youthful years are obscure, his schooling unknown, but he had the reputation of being a good linguist when he joined the stream of history; it was a skill he may have acquired from voyages in those ships in which his family had an interest, that left Weymouth on a south-westerly course for France, and that were now extending their trade with the ports of Spain.

It is well known that in January 1506 the Archduke Philip, son of the Emperor Maximilian, was returning from the Low Countries to Spain with his wife Joanna, the daughter of Ferdinand and Isabella, and that while passing down the Channel their ship was driven by a great storm on to the coast of Dorset near Weymouth. The predicament of such distinguished persons made an urgent call on the resources of the neighbourhood. Sir Thomas Trenchard, the most important landowner at hand, received the royal pair into his house while messengers carried the news of the shipwreck to the court of Henry VII. Tradition has it that Trenchard sent to fetch his young cousin John Russell from Berwick Manor to act as interpreter to his guests. Joanna's sister, Catherine of Aragon, was living impecuniously in England since the death of her husband Prince Arthur, but was receiving attentions from her widowed father-in-law, who was undecided whether to marry her himself or to engage her to his surviving son, Henry. When at length the messengers returned to Trenchard at Wolfenden Hall they brought the King's commands that the Archduke and his wife should proceed forthwith to Windsor. Henry was quick to seize the chance to act as host to a person of such diplomatic consequence as the Emperor's son.

Necessary to the Archduke as an interpreter, and perhaps by now a favourite with him, John Russell may have been in that small party of not more than a dozen persons who, clad in 'sad tawny black', set out with Philip to Windsor, whence the King came to meet them at Clewer with a glittering company; or he may have ridden in the large suite that followed later with Joanna.

Henry VII chose his servants personally and with discrimination. His discerning eye fell on the young man from Dorset who, fluent in French, Italian and Spanish, had made his appearance at the Court, and he made sure that during the last three years of his life he had the services of Russell as a Gentleman Usher – one of those men who in turn kept the door of the room where the King dined, stood by while the royal bed was made, undertook the care of strangers at the Court and saw that all sat down to meals according to rank – no trivial task when claims to precedence were firm and men stood upon the order of their going. It was a busy life, close to the King, full of ceremonial, and one in which great opportunities were offered to the able and the adaptable. Russell had these qualities, and when the old King died and Henry VIII succeeded his father he kept his place at Court, to become in time of even greater use.

Clever, high-spirited, violent, cruel, and disloyal, the new King was a formidable and merciless master; the men who served him learnt that if they ceased to lay their whole duty at the King's feet they might be required to lay their heads upon a block. 'They need to be slow and wary in that place where there is no failing the second time, the first error being irremediable.'

Russell learnt to be discreet and to know the King's mind by his countenance. Alternatively courtier, diplomat and soldier, he never put a foot wrong during the thirty-eight years he served four successive Tudor sovereigns; but for being cautious he has been called cold, and for being adaptable, a trimmer. Having seemingly little desire for power, he never engaged in politics, plots, or other schemes of personal ambition, but went about the King's business doing the best he could. There was a steadiness and an integrity in his character that bound his master to him. In moments of turmoil, tantrums and despair, Henry found support in a man not much older than himself, who put the King's well-being before his own, and dared to speak his mind and honest thoughts, even if his words went unheeded. The time came when John Russell appears to have been constantly at the King's elbow to calm, to comfort, and to advise.

When at Rochester Henry had his first view of Anne of Cleves, and, overcome with disappointment, exclaimed in despair: 'Do you think the lady so fair and of such beauty as report hath been made of her?', Russell was by his side and, adroitly evading the question, murmured: 'Your Grace, I took her not for fair but to be of a brown complexion.'

'Alas,' cried the King, 'who should men trust? I promise I see no such thing in her as hath been showed unto me of her, and I like her not.'

'I saw', said Russell, a witness later in the divorce proceedings, 'his Highness was sore troubled at the time.' He had been close to the King at the time of a previous matrimonial adventure. After the beheading of Anne Boleyn he seems to have accompanied Henry to Wolf Hall, the home of the Seymours, where the betrothal to Jane took place. Eighteen months later, at Hampton Court, he witnessed the King's extreme grief when the Queen died after the birth of their son. Lord Herbert of Cherbury recorded Russell's equivocal judgement of the two women, Anne and Jane: 'that the richer Queen Jane was in cloaths, the fairer she appeared, and that the other, the richer she was apparell'd the worse she looked.'

But before John Russell, Gentleman Usher, entered into that intimacy which he enjoyed with the King as Comptroller of the Royal Household and Lord Privy Seal, much water was to flow under London Bridge. In an age when men contrived to be poets as well as soldiers, and being courtiers were also diplomats, action and adventure were an habitual part of life. Russell wrote no verses but he had a good share of hazardous activity. His use of *Plus que jamais* as a motto, and his favourite saying '*Sans l'ayde de Dieu je ne puis*', express both vigour and humility. Forsaking after a few years the silken dalliance of the palace and the courtier's bended knee, he adopted rougher clothing and a more military stance. At the request of the King he was placed as a 'spear' in the garrison at Calais, and when Henry landed there with his army in 1513 Russell saw warfare at the battle of the Spurs and, following the capture of Tournai, received for his services a grant of forfeited land there. It was his first, and was not to be his last, experience of royal bounty.

The fluctuation of English relations with France between the stormy and the amicable found him, during a period of peace, in the train of the King at the Field of the Cloth of Gold, where he witnessed all the extravagance of human and material display. Two years later he was fighting the French in an assault on the coast of Brittany. Before Morlaix he was wounded, and he was one of those knighted after the battle by the Earl of Surrey. 'Indeed he was a man of spirit, carrying a badge of valour (not a blemish but a beauty) in his face. The loss of an eye.' Already noticeable for 'a moving beauty that waited on his whole body', he was now to be conspicuous for his wound. Holbein, drawing him in profile at a later age, concealed the injury but marked the picture: *The Lord Privy Seal with one eye*.

The devious policy pursued by Henry VIII and Wolsey when dealing with continental affairs, wavering between an alliance with Francis I or with the Emperor, was the cause of a visit to England in 1522 from Charles V. After six weeks of negotiation and junketing he was escorted to the coast and returned to Spain. Russell was among those who accompanied him to Southampton, and twenty years later the Emperor recollected him as a man of 'singular good qualities'.

During the war that ensued between the Emperor and France, England supported Charles, it being her aim to detach the Constable of Bourbon from his shaky allegiance to Francis I. Sir John Russell was chosen by Henry in 1523 to meet Bourbon and convey to him twelve thousand pounds, hoping to promote his defection and help maintain the army he led against the French King. Enriched by the profits from a newly granted licence to import three hundred tuns of woad and French wine, and receiving two hundred pounds for his expenses before he set out, Russell embarked on an expedition of danger and adventure. When he reached the Low Countries it was arranged that the money should be carried by some merchants travelling to Besançon, Russell and a servant accompanying them in disguise. The journey was safely accomplished but, no contact with Bourbon having been made, he spent the winter at Besançon, moving to Geneva in the spring, where he was plagued by spies. Feigning to cross the Alps by the St Bernard pass, he doubled on his tracks and went over the Mont Cenis to Turin. His adventures, and the information he acquired during the journey, he detailed at length to Henry and Wolsey. His style was vigorous, and in his letters to the King he sometimes allowed himself a wry joke. His precious charge, he told Wolsey, he caused 'to be packed in bales trussed with baggage, as oats and old clothes, to make it bulky and nicked with a merchant's mark, as merchants accustomably doth use to convey merchandise into Italy upon mules, for other carriage is not to be had.' A meeting near Chambéry with the Duke of Savoy helped him on his way, since that prince agreed to take the money into his own coffers, and had it carried into Piedmont labelled as though it were the furnishings for his chapel.

'Pleaseth your highness to understand . . . there hath been divers enterprises and ambushes set for to attrap me,' wrote Sir John to the King from Turin, and he described how his bales 'continued still trussed as though the money continued therein to the intent that none otherwise might be thought but that the said money was still in my company.' Ten months after leaving England he found Bourbon and the imperial army besieging Marseilles, but the town being obstinately defended by the French, the Constable was compelled to withdraw his forces into Italy. Another consignment of money to subsidize these troops having been despatched from England, as though it were intended for the use of the Grand Master of the Order of St John in Rome, Russell's business now was to find the band of travellers who carried it, and he wandered from one town to another in the north of Italy until he at length fell in with them at Viterbo. In Rome he had conversations with the Pope, and he went as far as Naples to buy himself a new horse. This roving period ended when he was recalled to England by Wolsey. He wrote that as he journeyed homewards he had at times to assume a false character, or leap in a moment on his horse and leave a town by one gate as the French entered by another. He was in the prime of life and his letters rang with confidence.

Two weeks after the battle of Pavia, when French military power was overthrown and their King captured by the imperial army, Russell was writing to Henry from Milan: 'When I heard the battle was given I in diligence did post thither thinking it necessary one should be near the said duke [Bourbon] at this time.' It seems doubtful if he was actually engaged himself in the slaughter of the French nobility on that bloody occasion, but he remained long enough at Milan to report on the negotiations for peace that followed.

His marriage to the heiress of the Cheneys took place in England the following year. Ann Sapcote had been twice widowed. Russell would have known her at Tournai when he served under her second husband, Sir Richard Jerningham, who was Deputy there; and at the Field of the Cloth of Gold Lady Jerningham had been in attendance on Queen Catherine. The King may have been eager to forward a marriage that had such obvious advantages for a man with whom he was well pleased, who had rendered good service, and whose worth had been proved. As a person of substance, well equipped with the necessaries of life, Russell could cut a figure in the world when acting for the King. Promoted to be a Gentleman of the Privy Chamber (two of whom slept each night in the King's chamber), Sir John needed a home within easy riding distance of Westminster, and this his wife provided in the old manor house on her estate at Chenies in Buckinghamshire. By her he had one son. Her talents were domestic, and her character worthy of his own. The cambric shirt she offered the King as a New Year's gift, 'wrought with black work', was doubtless embroidered in silk with her own hands, and of a pattern to be seen in countless Tudor portraits. It must have been appreciated, for she gave him another two years later. We have a description of the King accepting these traditional gifts 'smiling and leaning against a cupboard, receiving all things. Behind his Grace stood Sir John Russell.' The King in his turn gave presents at that season, and the Russells and other courtiers received gilt vessels, pomanders and jewellery, according to their rank.

Charles V's victory at Pavia changed the balance of power in Europe, and Wolsey's policy of friendship with him veered towards an alliance with France and the Pope. In 1527 Sir John Russell and Sir Thomas Wyatt were despatched to Rome to urge Clement VII to pursue his intention of putting himself at the head of a league against the Emperor – England giving financial help but no more. The envoys being held up for horses at Civitavecchia, the Pope courteously sent 'a Turkey horse, on which he rides himself' for Russell to make his entry into Rome in a style proper for the ambassador from England. 'They would have lodged me in the palace but I declined as the ambassadors of other princes were not so lodged,' wrote Russell modestly to Wolsey.

Meetings with the Pope were conducted very much as Russell's descendant Odo Russell, three hundred and fifty years later, was to carry on his diplomatic interviews with Pius IX. The echo is unmistakable. Russell advised; he cautioned; he cajoled. He suggested the Pope should excommunicate the Emperor; he shamelessly pointed out that cardinals might be created for cash to raise funds for defence. But his holiness demurred; he raised objections, he spoke of scruples. A liberal historian has described Clement as a 'charming, cultivated Tuscan gentleman who exhibited the parochial perspective of an Italian princelet and the nervous indecision of a fussy invalid'. The forceful English ambassador transmitted to his superiors his exasperation with this hesitant would-be leader of a Holy League.

Russell's name was everywhere on men's lips while he was in Italy and the outcome of his negotiations was uncertain; and his movements were noted and reported by the agents of other powers. But time was running out; news was received and passed on to Henry and Wolsey of the savage behaviour of the unpaid and undisciplined imperial forces advancing on Rome, shortly to join up with those under the command of Bourbon. 'If

God does not punish so much cruelty and wickedness we shall infer that he does not trouble himself about the affairs of this world', wrote Sir John. 'Never were infidels more cruel than the imperialists.' He wrote at last with mistaken confidence that he had overcome the Pope's timidity, and set off on another diplomatic enterprise; but, his horse falling on him, he broke his leg. While Clement sent him a mule and litter, Andrea Doria, the Genoese captain, offered him one of his own galleys to convey him wheresoever he pleased. But for this accident Sir John Russell would have been in Rome rather than in Savona when disaster overtook the Eternal City. In May 1527 the dreaded Lutheran Lanzknechts reached the walls of the town, and while Clement took refuge in the Castle of St Angelo the imperial troops sacked Rome. And so, too, it happened that in 1870, when the forces of newly united Italy marched into Rome and Pio Nono shut himself up in the Vatican, Odo Russell, absent on leave, was, like his ancestor, not present at a moment of crisis in the history of the papacy.

The question of the King's divorce and Wolsey's disgrace was prominent in the two years following John Russell's return to England. He was himself in high favour with Henry. Compelled to listen while the King read aloud to him his letters to the Cardinal, each communication carrying a sting, he was further used as a go-between. He had always been on good terms with Wolsey, and while the King's feelings towards his Chancellor blew hot and cold, Russell was steady in his friendship for the prelate, writing him from wherever he might be in attendance on the King, letters of gentle intimacy, venturing sometimes a joke, passing on a royal message intended to raise the spirits of the fallen statesman. While the Court was at Ampthill he wrote Wolsey a letter of good advice, expressed in mild, wise and compassionate terms:

Pleaseth it your grace that I have received your letter, wherebye I perceive that your grace is good lord unto me, which is great comfort and rejoicing to me. I can recompense your grace with nothing but my poor heart and service which is at your commandment, and shall be while I live. The king is merry, thanked be God; and I am sure that his grace would that your grace were so likewise. Your grace must comfort yourself and be of good cheer, assuring your grace that the king is well appeased and satisfied in his mind, as I well perceive when he speaks of you. And doubt you not that you shall have him as good to your grace as ever he was in his life; for his grace is a prince of so many good qualities and of so good remembrance that he will remember the great service and pains that your grace has taken for him, and also the great familiarity that has been by times gone. Wherefore your grace may be of good comfort, and take the matter well, for you shall have no other cause. Sometimes the father and son be in displeasure, and brother by evil report, as may fortune has been now between your grace and the king.

Methink it should be well done that your grace should come more unto the king, that your grace mote speak with him which should be greatly to your both contentations. And thus Jesus preserve your grace.

There is an account by Cavendish, Wolsey's gentleman usher, of Russell acting as a messenger from the King. After Wolsey had been deprived of the Great Seal and had retired to Esher, John Russell arrived there one night soaked to the skin, bearing 'a great ring of gold with turquoise for token', and a message from the King bidding him be of good cheer, and protesting his love. It was but a false token of royal affection, and John Russell earned the hatred of Anne Boleyn, who refused to have converse with him because he had spoken to the King in favour of the Cardinal.

Deprived of the revenues from Winchester and St Albans, Wolsey begged that out of them a fee of twenty pounds a year be settled on Russell as a testimony of his regard, which was accordingly done by act of parliament for term of life.

As Wolsey's star set that of Thomas Cromwell rose. His introduction to the Cardinal has been attributed to the early recommendation of Sir John Russell, who may have known him in Italy. In Thomas Heywood's apocryphal play *The Life and death of Thomas, Lord Cromwell* there occurs a scene in which the young Cromwell helps John Russell to escape from captivity in Italy, by changing clothes with a servant. In view of Russell's adventurous early life, it is not impossible that this is a story founded on fact that had become a legend nearly a hundred years later.

The year in which Henry VIII put to death his second wife and married his third saw also the demise of his first. Catherine of Aragon died at Kimbolton and her obsequies were arranged by Sir John Russell at Peterborough cathedral early in 1536. At midsummer he was a witness of the King's extreme happiness with Jane Seymour. With no love for the former wife, Anne Boleyn, Russell conveyed his satisfaction with the King's new marriage to Lord Lisle. 'The King', he wrote, 'has come out of hell into heaven for the gentleness in this and the cursedness and unhappiness in the other.'

In the autumn of that same year the northern rebellion broke out in Lincolnshire. Cromwell's cold and capable hands had accomplished the first stage of the dissolution of the monasteries, but the Pilgrimage of Grace was a symptom of the disunity among the people created by the Reformation. As one of the commanders holding land in the district who were charged to put down the rising, Russell – who held Thornaugh in Northamptonshire by right of his wife – carried out operations with the Duke of Suffolk. From their headquarters at Stamford he was reported to be going among the rebels in disguise and sending back information. 'God never died for a better couple,' declared John Williams to Thomas Cromwell at this time, bracketing the names of Russell and Sir Francis Bryan.

Masques had been introduced into England from Italy at the beginning of the sixteenth century, and these poetical and allegorical entertainments, which became immensely popular with the nobility and Court, offered a welcome opportunity for the ladies to let down their beautiful hair, and for men and women equally to indulge in all the paraphernalia of fanciful clothing and thin disguise. Henry VIII's taste for dressing up was manifested in the preposterous garb he wore for the launching of a warship – a sailor's jacket and trousers of cloth of gold – and his adoption of a canary-yellow outfit when he heard of the death of Catherine of Aragon; fantastic clothing that was, indeed, not intended to disguise his burly form, but was an expression of his innate flamboyance.

In the diversions of the Court the young Russell must sometimes have assumed a dress concealing his identity, but it is surprising to find the staid and gentle man of fifty courting danger by going disguised among the rebels, even if the habit he adopted was but a rough cloak thrown over armour with a staff substituted for a sword. He was renewing, perhaps, the excitement he had experienced in the tricks and adventures of his early years. The sober figure of Russell standing with three others clad in aprons and holding towels by the font at the christening of Henry's infant son, Edward, is more recognizable.

Distinctions and honours came thick and fast to the man who had now been thirty years at Court. He had 'brought himself in by what humoured, and kept himself there by those things that did oblige him'.

A beautifully precise account book bears witness to his term as Comptroller of the Royal Household. Delicate provisions were obtained for the King's table from France where then, as now, fruit and vegetables came into season a few weeks earlier than on this side of the Channel. Lord Lisle, the Deputy of Calais, could be depended on for a steady supply of quails and *primeurs*. Russell, when desiring him to send twenty or thirty dozen quails for the Queen, stipulated that they must be fat, and should there be none that were fat at Calais he must send into Flanders for them; they were to be despatched alive and not to be killed until they reached Dover. He intimated the King's approval when two dozen arrived which, he said, the royal couple had divided between dinner and supper. Peascods and cherries were welcome when none could be had in England before midsummer; and by the King's special command all the artichokes produced at Calais were to be kept for him. Russell resigned this responsible and possibly trying post (for it involved the management and discipline of the whole Court) when he was created Baron Russell of Chenies and a Knight of the Garter in 1539; dignities that were soon followed by his appointment as President of the Council of the West. Although he had continued to hold property in Dorset there is no evidence that he ever returned to the home at Berwick from which he had set out on his fortunate career. A grant of the dissolved abbey and lands of Tavistock now gave him the status of an important landowner in the west; from this time to the end of his life he wielded immense authority in the western counties, where he was treated in all respects like the King, kneeling excepted.

About this time he exchanged a house he owned in Chiswick for one in the Strand to facilitate attendance on the King, but his new employment in the west of England meant that Bedford House in Exeter was in the future to see more of him than the London mansion, or the manor house on the steep hill above the river Chess. It was however at Chenies that Lord and Lady Russell were hosts to Henry's fifth queen, Catherine Howard, during her brief reign, and, as it appeared at her trial, her lover Francis Dereham was there in attendance on her. During the dreadful period before the Queen's execution, Lady Rochford, deeply implicated in the Queen's disgrace and doomed to suffer with her mistress, became insane. She was sent by the King to be with 'the Admiral's wife', and he sent his own physician to visit her: Russell had been Lord High Admiral since the previous year, an office he held until he was made Lord Privy Seal three years later.

With his fellow veterans the Dukes of Norfolk and Suffolk, he took the field for the last time against the French in the summer of 1544, and, no longer young, he found a great deal to grumble about. Detained at first at Dover by a 'contrarious' wind, he declared that he would be forced to row over to Calais. Reaching France, he wrote to the King that there was a deplorable lack of victuals. The soldiers, he pointed out, had drunk no beer for ten days, 'which is strange for Englishmen to do with so little grudging'. They could not live on their wages, since everything in the market was very dear. 'I think never an army lay so rawly as we do.'

The campaign was carried on in league with the Emperor, but Russell complained that the allies 'care not much whether we do win it or not, so that we may lie there and be as a defence and a buckler for their country'. It pleased him to observe that these allies were eating horseflesh, 'and some of their soldiers, gentlemen Italians, glad to eat of a cat well-larded, and call it dainty meat'.

Henry VIII's arrival in person at Calais, and his obstinate direction of strategy, exasperated his generals and his allies. Norfolk and Russell got bogged down in front of Montreuil, and while the King triumphantly took Boulogne, the Emperor quietly made peace on his own with the French. Hungry and thirsty, and anxious for his troops, Russell gave his frank opinion of the campaign in a letter to Sir Anthony Browne:

> I must declare unto you, as my very good friend, my foolish opinion what I do think in this. I have seen the king's majesty make four sundry voyages into France, sith the beginning of his reign, with this journey: and for all these charges his majesty hath not in France one foot more than he had forty years past. And in case we should after this wander, as I may well call it, in a wild war, dispending so much, to the king's no little charge, the same cannot sound so much to his highness' honour.

It was the complaint of a man who had kept accounts and knew what he was talking about. Henry had dissipated the riches of his father in futile wars with France, and England was only to have possession of Boulogne for the next six years. Lord Russell's task the following year was to secure the coastal defences in his presidency of the west of England against a threatened invasion, and having inspected the seaports from Poole to Plymouth he was able to assure the Council that the French would 'find it a hot coming unto'.

Henry VIII died in 1547. Lord Russell was an executor of his will and one of the moderate party among the sixteen councillors chosen by the King to advise his young son. Before his death Henry had spoken of an earldom for Russell, and expressed a wish that he should be granted lands to the value of one hundred pounds a year. He received the reversion of the abbey lands of Woburn, a lease of which at the dissolution had been given for twenty-one years to Sir Francis Bryan, Russell's neighbour in Buckinghamshire. It is doubtful if he ever went to Woburn, or had anything to do with it; its significance for his family lay in the future; but as he passed up and down England on his missions for the King at the time of the Pilgrimage of Grace he may have had a glimpse of the old monastery buildings from the road leading to the north; and when the court lay at Ampthill and there were hunting parties, he must sometimes have ridden across tracks leading to the Abbey.

He had to wait until 1550 for his earldom. With it other favours were showered on him; he received grants of land in Devonshire and Cornwall, in Northamptonshire and Buckinghamshire and Bedfordshire, and a large part of the domain that had belonged to Thorney Abbey in Cambridgeshire. Covent Garden and the seven acres of Long Acre – part of the estates of the Duke of Somerset – were granted to him after the attainder of that nobleman. It was to be an area of great significance in the fortunes of the Russell family, and the bestowal of it followed the culminating labour of the Earl of Bedford's military activities. In the previous year the Council had chosen him, as a person having a good name and great authority in the west, to put down an insurrection that started in Cornwall as a protest against the use of the new Book of Common Prayer and the abolition of the Mass. Exeter was seized by the rebels and weeks passed before the Lord Privy Seal was able to overcome them with the help of German and Italian mercenaries. It was the first time an English ruler had used foreign troops against English subjects, and there were bloody encounters between half-armed Devonshire peasants and trained Lanzknechts and Italian arquebusiers. Miles Coverdale, the translator of the Bible, was with Russell as his chaplain, and preached a thanksgiving sermon among the fallen soldiers. The Lord Privy Seal's savage treatment of the rebel prisoners earned him a reprimand from the Council for exceeding his instructions. He was getting old; he had sat the whole of one night on horseback in preparation for battle; his sympathies were, perhaps, with neither one religious party nor the other. He had received commands to stop the rebellion from spreading to other parts of the country, and he belonged to an age when punishment by death was an everyday affair.

The last years of the Earl of Bedford's life were marked by events that were bloody, but no more so than what had gone before. 'In the faction between the Seymours and the Dudleys he was neuter', we are told. Seymour heads fell; the young King died, limiting the crown in his will to the Protestant, Lady Jane Grey. Bedford at first supported her, with many of the Council, but when it was apparent that the people wished for a Tudor to rule over them, he changed his mind, gave his allegiance to Mary, and was reconstituted Lord Privy Seal. He was not the only one to turn about.

Nearly thirty years before, Russell's friend, Sir Thomas Wyatt, had given his son, aged fifteen, advice on the conduct of his life:

Think and ymagine alwais that you are in presens of some honist man that you know, as Sir John Russell, your father-in-law, your unkle, parson, or some other such, if at ony time ye find plesur in naughty touchis, remember what shame it wer afore thes men to doo naughtily.

Young Wyatt's rebellion cost Lady Jane Grey her head; he lost his own and no few others lost theirs. This wild attempt to raise the country against Queen Mary was a 'naughtiness' not envisaged by his father. The Earl of Bedford and his son, Francis Russell, rode side by side to put down the revolt, and it was the last time the Earl drew his sword on behalf of the Tudors; he had, however, one more mission to perform in the service of that family: it was to fetch a husband for the Queen from Spain. A Spanish chronicler described the scene at Santiago de Compostela when Philip worshipped at the shrine of St James before leaving the country, watched from an upper window by the English ambassadors, the Earl of Bedford and Lord Fitzwalter, 'their faces shrouded in their cloaks'. Lord Bedford, the writer believed, was heard to say: 'Blessed be God who has given us as good king as this.' It is no surprise therefore that, hearing such flattering words, the Spaniards thought the Earl 'a great gentleman and a good Christian'. Philip's comment was less generous when, next day, the English attended Mass: 'which God grant may continue, for they need it badly enough'. The chronicler described the rich presents distributed by the King, Bedford receiving a piece of gold plate 'more than three feet in height, exquisitely chased with classical and grotesque figures'.

Philip, the grandson of that other Philip who, fifty years before, had

Giles, Lord Chandos by
Jerome Custodis

The Countess' Pillar, from a
sketch by Flora Russell

*That modest stone that pious
  Pembroke reared
Which still records beyond the
  pencil's power,
The silent sorrows of a parting
  hour.*

Samuel Rogers

William, Lord Russell of Thornhaugh by an unknown painter

been wrecked on the Dorset coast, was known to be a bad sailor, and should the voyage be a stormy one, it was not likely that he would endure to go further than Plymouth, though Southampton was the port where preparations had been made for his arrival. Bedford recognized that a landing in Devonshire would fall hard on his good friends at Exeter, who would be put to the unlooked-for expense of receiving the King and some six hundred attendants. He wrote from Santiago to the Mayor at Exeter that he would do all in his power to keep the King on board until he reached Southampton, 'but', he added, 'we are all at the mercy of the tide and winds'. It was July, the wind stood fair, and Philip landed at Southampton. His marriage to Mary took place a few days later in Winchester Cathedral, and the Earl of Bedford and four other peers gave the middle-aged and faded Queen away.

Less than a year later, John Russell, first Earl of Bedford, died at Russell House, near Ivy Bridge, in the Strand. He desired in his will that his funeral might be conducted without pomp or vainglory, but it was carried out with splendour, and the people who watched it pass along the route to Chenies, where he was to lie (the first of the long line who would follow him there), had the satisfaction of seeing a procession that in its length and magnificence, did justice to the honoured name of the 'good' old Earl of Bedford.

Good, gentle, discreet, sad – that is, serious – were adjectives coupled with John Russell's name by his contemporaries, yet how hard it is to form a clear picture of the man who, for fifty years, steered an even course through the dangerous currents of a period when no length of service could make a man certain of the King's favour. One of his friends, William Paulet, when asked in his old age how he had survived so many storms and changes, answered: '*Ortus sum e salice, non ex quercu.*' (By being a willow and not an oak.) There was more of the oak in Russell's fabric, yet he was not laid low by the gales that levelled other men. If integrity, loyalty and compassion are his most conspicuous qualities, wisdom must be added, for he eschewed all faction and had no enemies – but neither had he many intimate friends. The biographer Lloyd commented a century later that Russell's comeliness 'exacted a liking if not a love from all who beheld him'. Were his good looks frosty? Did he lack warmth in a passionate age? It is a want remarked in Russells to this day. Records bear witness to his kindness of heart, his love for his wife, and his pity for the weak and fearful. Generous in his praise of younger men, he was quick to pay honour where honour was due, and urged that thanks given to one who expected none would encourage others. He was tender when excusing the fault of a simple man, pleading once that what a poor erring fellow had done was but for lack of discretion. He spoke plainly to persons with whom he disagreed and he hated Jews, whom he found, so he said, no better than Spaniards or Portuguese. His testy comments on Sir Anthony Browne may be attributed, perhaps, to his jealousy of Browne's great intimacy with the King. When campaigning in the west, he wrote to Paget:

I understand the good cheer you have had at Cowdreye, where I doubt not but that you have found Mr of the Horse [Browne] a man most unreasonable, and as one whose words and deeds do not agree together (for he will speak in such kind of fare more than I am sure he hath performed), and one that will blame every man for that fault and yet will do worse himself. I would he were here, where he should have want of both good meat and drink.

Forgetful of the day when he had urged the Pope to create cardinals for cash, he expressed in middle age his disapproval of buying posts for money, saying: 'The King will never be well served so.' His great power as Comptroller of the Household made lesser men appeal to him for places, sending him gifts of wine, game and fruit, but they quickly found they had taken the wrong pig by the ear – there would be no preferment without merit.

Like the majority of Englishmen, the Earl of Bedford probably remained a Catholic at heart while accepting the new forms of worship; there is a tradition that his wife leaned towards the reformed religion, influencing their son, who adhered firmly to the Protestant persuasion. Although the Earl employed Miles Coverdale, a Lutheran, as his chaplain, and succeeded in getting him made Bishop of Exeter, we know from Chapuys that Bedford more than anyone advocated a reconciliation with the Holy See in 1540, but the King would not listen to him. Like many Russells since then, he was perhaps lukewarm in religious matters, and had a simple preference for the faith in which he had been raised.

When Edmund Burke heaped obloquy on the fifth Duke of Bedford for his enormous wealth, he insisted that the Duke's ancestor John Russell, 'a prompt and greedy instrument of a levelling tyrant', took a hand in the plunder of the monasteries, from whence came those riches. Burke's invective bears no weight; the distribution of Church lands allowed the

Crown, with no expense to itself, to reward serviceable men, and there is no evidence that Lord Bedford was a more shameless beggar than others; ten peers received larger grants than he did.

Bedford had a trenchant epistolary style, and from his writings we are sometimes able to infer what he thought about the King, whom he had seen grow from a silent stripling, cowed in the presence of his father, to be a boisterous, gifted, handsome man, his lustiness betrayed by a voice more woman-like than male. On Henry at the end of his life – the gross, infirm, and cruel egoist, who liked cream cakes, and was not averse to bloodshed – Bedford left no comment, save, as we have seen, his critical assessment of the King's useless wars with France. He approved of the high spirits that could dominate a hunting party, when Henry used himself 'more like a goodfellow than a King', and he was always glad when he saw him merry. He had compassion for the dejection that was so often the companion of his master's brief periods of wedlock, but he had no patience with his parsimony. While acting as Keeper of the More [Moor Park], he told Thomas Cromwell that if the King would only give six-pence a day for a gardener, he would find that he could get no one at that price – the place was going to rack and ruin; there would be no deer left, for the rotten paling would let them all escape – and that he himself had never received a penny for his services. Impatiently he wrote again: 'I get no answer from you. If the King will give eightpence, I will give six-pence a day out of my own purse.' In the end he sent his wife to see the Chancellor, and she pleaded with effect, having an interest in the More herself, for it was there she kept a bear – no doubt for the sport of baiting it. Her husband, while he was in the west country, kept for his amusement a fool named Joll.

Ann Sapcote survived her husband four years. Her effigy lies beside his on the tomb in the Bedford chapel at Chenies. Her features have no aristocratic distinction, and they have been called stern. The low brow, broad cheeks, and large blunt nose make it probable that it is a likeness done from life of the capable woman with strong family affections, who took a practical interest in her still-room and her conserves, rode up and down the country with her third husband, cherished him during his bouts of ague and after his death commissioned the beautiful monument that perpetuates their memory in rosy alabaster.

3

Protestant Father and Warrior Son

THE continuance of the Russell line was dependent on the life of the Earl of Bedford's only child, Francis, and at the accession of Mary it was in some jeopardy, for Lord Russell was seized and confined to the Fleet with other reformers, his attachment to the Protestant faith being well known. Soon released from prison (no doubt by the influence of his father) he fought against Wyatt to save the crown for a Catholic queen; but he kept in touch with the reforming party and sent money to Underhill, the 'hot gospeller' with whom he had been intimate at Cambridge, who was still in captivity. As with the first Earl, his loyalty to the Tudor succession was paramount. Nevertheless, when his father died he found it judicious to leave England for a while. The Queen and Philip, making no difficulties, both signed his passport, and the gift of their joint portrait, now hanging at Woburn, points to royal favour. Though he travelled as far as Venice and Naples it was at Zürich and Geneva that the second Earl found a truly congenial society among the sober Swiss theologians and the Protestant exiles who gathered there and who were as deeply committed as himself to the reformed religion. Confirmed in his puritan cast of thought, he corresponded with Beza, Bullinger and Gualter to the end of his life, slipping easily into the pious phraseology distinctive to that group of persons, and in striking contrast to the style in which his letters to Queen Elizabeth and William Cecil were written. Despite the religious persecutions of Mary, he returned to England before her death and appeared as one of her captains at the battle of St Quentin. He was enlisted in Elizabeth's first privy council and was among those who debated the revision of the prayer book; he helped to draw up the new liturgy. He held a number of responsible posts under the Crown and, being like his father gifted in languages, he was employed by Elizabeth as a diplomatic envoy. At Fontainebleau, whither he was sent to congratulate Charles IX on his accession, his knowledge of Italian and his affable

26

manners made him agreeable to Catherine de Medici. 'The eyrle hath the Italian tonge verie well,' wrote Sir Nicholas Throckmorton to Cecil, 'and the quene mother hath pleasur yn hyr owne tonge.' But Bedford retained no very happy memory of his sojourn at that court, for part of his mission had been to get an assurance from the late King of France's widow, Mary Queen of Scots, that she would abstain from using the royal arms of England. He found her a cunning match in diplomacy and his interviews with the young woman left him baffled and displeased.

As Lord Lieutenant of the northern counties and Governor of Berwick, he was to have further acquaintance with her and with the turbulence of Scottish affairs. Sir James Melville asserted that 'the good earl ... was one of the surest and most affectionate friends she had in England'. Nevertheless, Bedford himself wrote that he found her doings 'abominable and to be detested'. Indeed his attitude towards the Scottish Queen shifted at one time and another, almost as much as Elizabeth's policy towards her did, and his change of opinion was not always concurrent with his sovereign's. The veerings of the Royal Weathercock in London confused him and made him anxious and impatient. 'If her majesty will openly declare herself uncertain hearts will be determined again and all will go well,' he wrote hopefully to William Cecil. He was often made to feel in the wrong by the Queen and his worries were only partly lessened by the confidence he had in Cecil's friendship and goodwill. During the three years that he lived on the frontier of England and Scotland he promoted an intensive strengthening of Berwick's fortification, and his authority restrained the confusion of Border warfare.

He was one of the commissioners in the sterile negotiations for Mary's marriage with Lord Robert Dudley, and when she chose Darnley his despatches declared his distrust of the match, and stressed the offence given to his Protestant convictions by her headstrong ways. 'The Lord Darnley and this queen fall still to popery; for on Candlemas day last they carried their candles, and since that time seek further to advance it.' He was perhaps reminded of his annoyance and alarm when his own queen, while being courted by Charles of Austria, had given orders that the crucifix should be restored to the altar of the Chapel Royal. Bedford had protested bitterly at the time to Cecil, and the order had been suspended, but only for a day or two. Failing to reassure the Catholics of her kingdom, Elizabeth managed to exasperate the Protestants. The long and graphic account of Rizzio's murder sent to Secretary Cecil, with comments on the intimate relationships of the Queen and her husband, Bedford had from the lips of the conspirator Lord Ruthven himself, who fled across the Border after the affair at Holyrood. Later that same year Mary's child was born, and the Earl of Bedford was sent by Elizabeth to represent her at the christening of the infant prince, her godson. Bearing her gift, a font of gold weighing 330 ounces, he travelled with a large retinue to Stirling and was graciously received by the Queen of Scots. 'She saluted my Lord of Bedford with a kiss, whether he would or no', and the Earl jested amiably when he saw how large the baby was and how small the font. But the northern climate did not suit him, he complained to Cecil of rheums and catarrhs, and in 1567 he was allowed to resign and return to the south of England when he served again on the Privy Council.

He was interested in genealogy, a hobby he shared with his friend Cecil, and he caused the first pedigree of his family to be drawn up. It was full of errors and false assumptions, and it may be supposed that his purchase from the Crown of Kingston Russell about this time was made under the misapprehension that it was the ancestral home. He showed more concern for his vast and widespread holdings of land than the first Earl had done, but while he acknowledged his Dorset origins his interests lay further west. When he visited his estates in Devonshire he stayed in magnificent style at Bedford House in Exeter, where the townsfolk saw to it that his cellar was well provided with Gascon wine, and sugar loaves were offered to his wife.

With many houses to choose from, Chenies was his principal home; there were two houses in London belonging to him, one on either side of the Strand, and he must from time to time have lived at Woburn, which still maintained its monastic character, for his first wife, Margaret St John, died of smallpox in the Abbey in 1560, and it was there that he entertained Elizabeth in 1572 with such a prodigal show of hospitality that the Queen declared that he and the Earl of Derby by their liberality 'made all the beggars of the kingdom'. The expense of a royal progress fell heavily on the nobles who had to entertain the sovereign and her court as she moved about the country. Before this visit to Woburn, Bedford wrote nervously to Cecil stating his hope that the Queen would not stay too long.

I am now going to prepare for her Maties coming to Woburne, which shall be done in the best and most hartiest manner that I can. I trust yor L. will have in remembraunce to provide and helpe that her Mats.

tarieng be not above two nights and a daye; for, for so long tyme do I prepare. I pray God that Rowmes and Lodgings there may be to her Mats. contentacion for the tyme. If I could make them better upon suche a sodeyn, then wold I, be assured. They should be better than they be.

He was a practical man and dispensed his wealth judiciously, telling his son that he ought to be satisfied with the allowance he was given of £200 a year.

'My Lord and father being Privie Seal', wrote the Earl, 'and able everie waie to dyspend with more yerely than now I can do dyd allow me no more than such, alwyt I had then wyf and chyldren to care for. And therefore yf my sonne do complyne he dealeth hardlie with me, yet I hope to leave him as great revenues as my father left me or rather better, notwithstandinge that my charge everie waie hath byn great.'

Two years before her reception at Woburn Abbey the Queen had made use of Chenies in the Earl of Bedford's absence. In attempting to stave off that visitation he had belittled his simple home to Cecil.

I understand her Majesty is coming to Chenies, where, if the house was sweet and the lodgings commodious, I shall be glad thereof. But as to the soil and seat thereof, as no art nor diligence can amend Nature's doings, so I am sorry that it cannot now be amended, if ever it might be for a time, to ease so noble a guest, and so large a train . . .

There lay, doubtless, the root of his trouble – 'so large a train'. He anticipated the large disbursements necessary, the disturbance to his household and the annoyance that would surely be created for the people on his estate, who, within a circuit of three miles, could be called on by the officials of the Board of Green Cloth to supply provisions at a fixed price for the large retinue; but *Che Sara Sara* had been adopted as the family motto and he was resigned to what must be. Struck by the fatalistic philosophy of this maxim Christopher Marlowe thought fit to make a passing jest of it in Dr Faustus: 'What doctrine call you this, che sera sera? What will be, shall be?' Perhaps it was this doctrine of resignation to fate that governed the Earl of Bedford in the last months of his life.

An ailment in his foot became gangrenous, and although his physicians

('Western men of no great learning, who have, nevertheless, done some very great cures') declared that the foot must be cut off at once to save his life, it was not done, and the Earl died at his house in the Strand, aged fifty-eight, fortunately unaware that the elder of his surviving sons had been killed a few hours previously in a Border fray.

The portrait at Woburn shows the Earl to have been a plain and homely man. There is a clumsy look about him, but the expression of his face is kind and the eyes are clearly blue under the white eyebrows. If he looks uncomfortable it is because his garments do him less than justice; the shaggy fur trimming of his gown is unbecoming to his short, thick neck, and detracts from the dignity which the collar of the Garter with the pendant George, hung around his shoulders, aims to enhance. The Bishop of Aquila, describing the appearance of Queen Elizabeth's suitor, Charles of Austria, declared that his head was even bigger than the Earl of Bedford's. But the course of the second Earl of Bedford's life shows him to have had that large head well screwed on to his broad shoulders.

The procreative vigour absent in the first Earl became apparent in the second. Besides three daughters, Francis raised four sons who might have been expected to produce a numerous progeny; but the uncertainty of the human condition and the dangers of the times prescribed that only one of these outlived their father, and of the four only two bred one son apiece who survived infancy. It was the Earl's youngest son, William, who assured the continuance of the Russell line, and who sired the man who was to rebuild Woburn Abbey and make it a home for his large family.

Of Lord Bedford's eldest son, Edward, little is known; he died before his father, having married the daughter of his stepmother. There is however a picture of him at Woburn that has long posed a question. The young man grasps five serpents in his hand, two of which hold in their teeth a label with a Latin inscription comparing faith in men with fraud in serpents. Through a window at one side may be seen a garden like a circular labyrinth in which a man is walking. Beneath the window is written FATA. VIAM. INVENIENT. That is: Fate will find the way. Here indeed is an enigma. In the companion portrait of Edward's younger brother Francis, a window frames a view of a woman seated on the ground surrounded by wild beasts; through a window on the right a ship can be seen sailing on an unquiet sea. A tradition was current in the eighteenth century – Pennant propagated it, and Horace Walpole heard it from the

Duchess of Bedford herself – that the plot of Otway's *The Orphan* was founded on some tragic story in which these two brothers played a part. If Edward's narrow eyes and small tight mouth seemed to fit him to have acted the base part in such a tale, other claims have been made for the source of Otway's tragedy, and modern scholarship may have solved the conundrum. In Elizabethan times it was not unusual to insert some small allegorical scene or emblematic device into a portrait 'embodying the hopes and aspirations in general philosophical terms' of a particular person. There were collections of emblems that painters might study, and the device in the left-hand corner of Edward Russell's picture was taken from one which had been used by Bois Dofin de Laval: a labyrinth with a motto.

Of John Russell, who became Lord Russell on his elder brother's death, there is no portrait at Woburn. His features can be seen in Westminster Abbey, where he reclines in effigy on his elbow, arrayed in gaudily painted robes, his flaxen curls dressed neatly on his forehead. His tomb is inscribed with Greek and Latin verses composed by his widow, a bluestocking with a passion for epitaphs. As Lady Hoby she had buried her first husband in Bisham church, and had shown a gift for poetical funerary tributes. She was a daughter of Sir Anthony Cooke, who bred two other women of distinction: Mildred, who married William Cecil, Lord Burleigh, and Lady Bacon, who became the mother of the Lord Chancellor. With such a breeding, an intellect as acute as that of Robert Cecil and as formidable as that of Francis Bacon might have been born in a son of the Russell marriage, proving the equal of those two great minds. But at the foot of Lord Russell's tomb lies the object of such high hopes – a small bundle closely bonneted and laid straight, with rigid feet stretched out in thick black shoes. His name was Francis, and his term of life had been five years. Intellectual powers must be looked for elsewhere. A picture at Woburn in the style of Marc Gheerhaerdts shows Lord Russell's younger daughter Anne, wearing a scarlet dress with a white apron and holding a coral rattle with bells attached to it – a typical Flemish portrait of a child. Anne married Lord Worcester, and a little spark of genius flickered in their son, but never blazed. He undertook mechanical experiments and made suggestions in a book for the construction of an hydraulic machine 'for drawing up water by fire': but there is no evidence that he attempted to build such a steam pumping engine, and it must be assumed that he was without the practical energy necessary for such a task.

A monument to Lord Russell's elder daughter Elizabeth, a godchild of the Queen who died young, is near his in Westminster Abbey. She sits in a curious chair woven from osiers, and a legend attaches to the prominence given to the drooping forefinger of her left hand. When Addison wrote in the *Spectator* of his visit to the Abbey, he directed Sir Roger de Coverley's attention to 'that martyr of good housekeeping who died by the prick of a needle', and the worthy knight 'regarded her finger for some time'. Addison allowed Elizabeth a merit denied her by others, for there were those who believed she had been punished for sewing on a Sunday. More probably she died a martyr to consumption.

While the second Earl of Bedford governed Berwick his son, Francis, enlisted in the armies that were engaged upon the Border. His reckless bravery during many years of foray and defence in the North earned him a knighthood. While honouring the young man, the Queen charged his commander to pay particular regard to his safety, but the injunction was of no avail. In midsummer 1585, on a day of truce, a quarrel broke out between the English and the Scots. Sir Francis was wounded by a treacherous shot and died next day, a few hours before his father. A mound of stones – 'Lord Russell's Cairn' – on Windyghyll, high up in the round-headed Cheviots, is his monument; his body lies in Alnwick parish church.

Death had removed three of the Earl's sons before their father; there remained William, the youngest, later and best known as Lord Russell of Thornhaugh from the property in Northamptonshire that he inherited from his grandmother, the first Countess of Bedford. He, too, was a soldier by profession, but of greater fame than his brother Francis. As lieutenant-general of cavalry under Leicester in the Netherlands, he fought so hard at Zutphen the enemy reported him 'to be a devil not a man, for where he saw six or seven of the enemy together, thither would he, and so behaved himself with his curtle-axe, that he would separate their friendship'. He could not however save his friend Sir Philip Sidney, who, dying after that battle, bequeathed to him a suit of gilt armour used in jousts and tilting. Stepping into Sidney's shoes as Governor of Flushing he made himself popular with the Dutch churches by his piety and simplicity, until after a year he was transferred to Ireland.

As a young soldier he had made acquaintance with the unruly Irish, and he now undertook a frustrating period of service as Lord Deputy of Ireland. For three years he was to be embroiled with that slippery rebel the Earl of Tyrone – who outwitted him – and other Irish insurgents, who eluded him. The Queen's displeasure with Russell for believing the fair promises of Tyrone was great, and she added in her own hand a trenchant postscript to the angry letter she sent to him and the Council in Dublin, after Tyrone had been allowed to go free:

> Good Will – Let not others neglect of what they should make you for company do what is not fit; and above all things hold up the dignity of a king's rule, which more consists in awe than liberty, which honours more a prince than fears a traitor. God bless you, and send you mend what hath been amiss.

Pursuing the rebels through the wild glens he sometimes turned to hunting wolves instead, and he was known to like a day's fishing in the Wicklow Hills. He took great pains to prevent the excesses of his army, that the people might have no cause to complain of hardship imposed by the soldiery. Peace he could not bring to the unhappy country. Appealing for reinforcements from England to further his operations, Russell found that the policy of the general sent to help him was in conflict with his own. Sir John Norris, an experienced soldier, had previously shown hostility to Russell in the Netherlands. Annoyed now to find himself in a subordinate position, but endowed by the Queen with independent powers, he pursued a course of his own, favouring measures of conciliation, while Sir William Russell believed in a vigorous prosecution of the war. Russell saw his authority weakened and his rule imperilled. It was a government divided. He wrote to Sir Robert Cecil and to the Earl of Essex complaining that the official support he expected to receive had been transferred to the general. Taxed with jealousy, he pleaded to be relieved of his government; Cecil enjoined him to consider his position with a cool head.

Sir Robert Cecil to Sir William Russell

July 22, 1596

My good Lord – I know you will be troubled with this despatch when you see how much her majesty is displeased with the state of the kingdom. But out of my love, I must use freedom of speech to you, that you and others are guilty of much of your own troubles. For now that you and Sir John Norris are entered into taxation of each other, doubt ye not but advantages will be taken of it, yea, though it were in a country that yielded to the Queen no other sours. And where I find you desirous to be revoked . . . I do protest unto you, that I do think it cannot be done without infinite touch to your reputation, and prejudice to her majesty's service. For first, if you should be revoked at this time, it would never be conjectured but that it grew upon some note of weakness in you . . . Besides, if her majesty by your importunity should revoke you, I know not what man this day in England that should come raw to deal with Ireland but would find himself a little confused to succeed a man that now hath the experience and judgment gotten in three years . . . I beseech you to resort to your own wisdom, and do not *ponere rumores ante salutem*, but use that authority which her majesty hath given you, superior to all other in the kingdom . . . But if you will believe bruits, and think that others are graced with secret authorities and commissions, when you know the contrary . . . then I shall look for none but bad effects, whereof protest, even for your own private discontentment (whose heart I know doth joy when things should go well for her majesty's service) I shall be as sorry as if my brother were in your place . . . Sir John Norris is sharply written unto particularly . . . I will only conclude that I did not expect from two such as you are (that are no young ones in the world), so plain a course to prejudice yourselves to so little purpose, by contending for things wherein you might so easily satisfy: better expedite her majesty's service and rid yourself of much vexation . . .

A wise and excellent letter: one that through the centuries has been written in many forms to discontented servants of the Crown who have fancied themselves slighted.

Before he left Ireland Sir William tracked down and killed the outlaw, Fiagh McHugh, who had for so long evaded him, and he had the satisfaction of being acclaimed by the country people, who called down blessings on his head for having rid them of this scourge and tyrant.

His deputyship brought little change in the state of Ireland; and he left affairs there very much as he had found them – rife with treachery and revolt. His proposal to settle that turbulent and intransigent country by distributing the confiscated lands of the Church equally between the leading men of both religions was not listened to in London. He held that the acceptance of the spoils of their own Church would have attached the Catholics to the government that bestowed them. A naive credence, perhaps, but one that found favour in the eyes of his descendant, Queen Victoria's Prime Minister, Lord John Russell.

For a time William Russell returned to that part of England with which his father and grandfather had been closely associated. As Commander of the Forces in the West he was sent down to prepare against a Spanish invasion that never came. While he was frequently called to the Queen's councils to give his views on Irish matters, he steadily refused, though pressed, to assume again the chief command in Ireland. He entertained the old Queen at his house at Chiswick, and after her death, so Lady Anne Clifford tells us in her diary, 'my Uncle Russell' was one of the first to be honoured with a barony by James I.

There are two portraits of Lord Russell of Thornhaugh at Woburn. A magnificent full length shows him in the prime of life attired not as a soldier, but in a dress he might have worn at court. The black suit, slashed and padded, looks stiff enough to stand by itself without the support within it of his great frame. His stance, the legs well apart, is resolute but without swagger. Fourteen large round silver buttons trace the opening of his doublet; eighteen more on the sleeves outline the puffed white underdress. A ruff like a cartwheel sets off his slight pointed beard, and his gaze is direct and discerning. A dog at his feet is domestic rather than sporting, and of a breed that Shakespeare would have called a 'water-rug': an alert but small companion for so great a man.

Elizabeth Long of Shengay was his wife. Her portrait shows her with a stiff arrangement of her hair, which, swept back to frame her large and bony forehead, suggests a ram's horns. Her huge but delicate ruff, dividing under her chin, and circling behind her head, bears out the horned effect, and her prominent eyes and pallid features are mildly sheep-like. Her jewellery is quite remarkable, for imposed on her dress which is sewn with pearls there are brooches and pendants on her shoulders and in her hair, and on her cuff a small jewel is attached to her wrist by a black thread. She holds a fan of singular beauty composed of peacock's feathers mounted in silver filigree. The stoicism of Lord Russell of Thornhaugh's death – upright in his chair – was becoming to a General. 'He never lay a day from his first day's sickness to his last, nor wore so much as a nightcap.' Regrets for the oaths and quarrels, the too-high prizing of himself, the profanation of the Sabbath that had marred his younger days, troubled him at the end, but the words of Christian piety that issued from his lips would have been expected from him by his Calvinistic father.

When Algernon Swinburne indicted some of George Chapman's

poems as being 'as tough and tedious a task for the mind as oakum-picking or stone-breaking can be for the body', he excepted the mild verses Chapman contributed to the memory of this Elizabethan warrior, and the Victorian poet conceded that Lord Russell of Thornhaugh's 'romantic and homeric valour was worthy to have employed the pen of the translator of the Iliad'.

And for retreat a parsonage made his home;
Where near the church, he nearer God did come
Each week day doing his devotion
With some few beadsfolk, to whom still was shown
His secret Bedford's hand; nor would he stay
The needy asking; but prevent their way
And go to them, t'inquire how they would live,
And to avoid even thanks where he did give
He would their hardly-nourished lives supply
With shew of lending; yet that industry
Might not in them be lessen'd to relieve
Their states themselves, he would have someone give
His word for their repayment, which sweet lord
He never took, nor asked a thankful word.

4

Three Ladies

GEORGE CHAPMAN and his contemporaries, Spenser, Jonson, Daniel, Drayton and Donne, all celebrated in verse the virtues of some women, who, from their rank or qualities, were prominent at the courts of Queen Elizabeth and James I. Among those who received testimonies of respect and admiration from the poets who lived on the fringes of society, seeking the patronage of the rich and the powerful, were three ladies of the Russell family, the eldest and the youngest daughters of the second Earl of Bedford – Anne Countess of Warwick and Margaret Countess of Cumberland – and their niece by marriage, Lucy Countess of Bedford, wife of the third Earl. They were three women of outstanding character.

Lady Warwick had no children, and she held her position in the family as a beloved sister, aunt and honoured sister-in-law. Living close to the Queen, she was quietly influential. Visits to the palace by her niece, the young Anne Clifford, were prized, because on these occasions she was allowed 'to lie in my Aunt Warwick's chamber on a pallet, to whom I was much bound for her continual love and care of me'. Lady Warwick was reputed to have 'a nice discrimination' and her 'clear judgment' was, perhaps, more masculine than womanly; there were those who saw something of her father's shrewdness in her, and Lady Bacon, writing to her son Francis, urged him to caution:

I would earnestly counsel you to be wary and circumspect and not be too open in wishing to prolong speech with the Countess of Warwick. She, after her father's fashion, will search and sound and lay up with diligent marking *quae nec sentias antica perferre ad reginam, et patrissat in illa re nimis.*

(She is inclined to behave too much like her father, marking old matters of which you have no inkling, to convey to the queen). Her portrait shows her to have been plain, pleasant, serious and sedate, and dressed finely without pretension; the delicate painting of her transparent muslin sleeves which protect the embroidery beneath emphasizes her distinguished appearance more than any abundance of scattered jewels. She was given the wardship of her nephew Edward, who succeeded his grandfather as third Earl of Bedford, at the age of thirteen when his father was killed on the Border, but it may be doubted if subservience to a childless, strong-minded woman was the best upbringing for that orphan boy. Both his aunts, Warwick and Cumberland, were 'ladies who feared God and loved his word zealously': Bedford House was traditionally a puritan centre, where prayers were long and sermons must have seemed unending to a boy whose attendance was compulsory. Destined to be outshone by his brilliant wife, Lord Bedford's protest against female domination can be detected in the foolish and thoughtless way in which, making a show of independence, he joined the Earl of Essex on that fatal February day in 1601. It was a wild escapade for which Lord Essex lost his head, and Lord Bedford was heavily fined. The weak and shameful apology he submitted for his action might have been subscribed to by a lad of seventeen, rather than a married man of nearly thirty.

Edward, Earl of Bedford to the Lords of the Council:
from Alderman Holyday's House,
February 14, 1601

It was after ten o'clock, prayers and sermon begun, that the Lady Rich came to my house, and told me that the Earl of Essex desired to speak with me, upon which I went with her in her coach, none of the family following me out of the sermon-room, and I going unknown to my family. About eleven o'clock I came to Essex House, where, shortly after, the Earl of Essex with others of his company, drew themselves into secret conference, whereto I was not called, nor made acquainted with any thing, but only of some danger which the Earl of Essex said he was in, by the practice of some private enemies.

Howbeit I, doubting that that course tended to some ill, and the rather suspecting it for that I saw not my uncle Sir William Russell there, presently desired to convey myself away; and for that purpose withdrew myself so far, that I neither heard any thing of the Earl of Essex's consultation, nor yet of the speeches of the lords of the council. From that time I endeavoured to come from the Earl of Essex so far as

I might with safety; and to that end severed myself from him at a cross-street end; and taking water, before I heard any proclamation, came back to my house about one o'clock; where I made no delay, but with all convenient speed put myself and followers in readiness; and with the best strength I could then presently make, being about the number of twenty horse, I went toward the court for her majesty's service.

We can guess that it was dictated by his uncle William of Thornhaugh and penned under the surveillance of Anne Warwick, but it raises doubts about the stability and the strength of his character.

Margaret, the youngest of the second Earl of Bedford's daughters, deserves to be remembered as the wife of her father's ward 'that great, but unamiable man' George Clifford, Earl of Cumberland, renowned for his sea voyages and naval exploits, but she is better known as the mother of the redoubtable Lady Anne Clifford, successively Countess of Dorset and Countess of Pembroke, whose devotion to her 'blessed mother' is one of the principal themes of Lady Anne's reminiscences. Both ladies have left an account of their unhappy marriages, but Lady Cumberland comprised the story of much of her life into the space of a single letter addressed to her husband's chaplain before she was thirty-five, comparing her life to a dance that she called the Pilgrimage of Grief. She told of her early sorrows; the death of her mother at Woburn and the loss of her two elder brothers, her devotion to her father, and her fear of her stepmother. Married at seventeen, she was taken to live on the estates of the Cliffords in the predominantly Catholic north of England – 'separated from all I knew, in a country contrary to my religion'. She was a dutiful and loving wife – 'sweet Meg' to her husband – yet they were not well matched. 'Our minds met not but in contrarys and thoughts of discontentment.' She inherited her father's 'great sharp natural wit', and had his discerning spirit, and love of study, and she had been well grounded in his religious convictions. Simple in her tastes, with little love for riches, her sober temperament was too rigid for the high spirit of her adventurous and pleasure-loving husband. Restless, extravagant, and unfaithful, Lord Cumberland went his own way. Excelling at all sports, he spent his time in good company and near the Court, where he found favour with Elizabeth; as her champion, Nicholas Hilliard painted him in all his swaggering glory, wearing her glove in his cap.

Sick, sad and barren for close on six years, Lady Cumberland lived at

Skipton Castle, and then 'time took and brought many things of trouble away. My Lord's affections turned from a strange manner and carriage to much and very much love and kindness known to all and most comfortable to me.' But the Dance in which she saw herself taking part went both forwards and backwards. The two sons she bore died as children; grief followed grief. Her father's untimely death, and the treacherous murder of her favourite brother on the Scottish border, were sorrows which came hand-in-hand. When her daughter was born Lord Cumberland – with 'new thoughts of greater worlds' – had already embarked on that succession of voyages that earned him the King of Spain's appellation of 'Arch Pirate'. The most spectacular of his buccaneering enterprises was the capture of a Spanish treasure ship. When her cargo of precious stones, gold and silver, spices and silks, musk, civet and ambergris was unloaded on the quays of Dartmouth there was such confusion, such theft and plunder that, according to an eyewitness, 'the port looked like Bartholomew Fair'. For his share in this booty Lord Cumberland was awarded £36,000. Since his wife's spirit had more 'converse with heaven and heavenly contemplation than with terrene and earthly matters,' she was indifferent to this material success, and significantly Lord Cumberland's account of his twelfth and last voyage was addressed to his shrewd sister-in-law Lady Warwick, rather than to his wife.

'When my mother and he did meet', Lady Anne Clifford tells us, 'their countenance did show the dislike they had of one another.' After the birth of her daughter Lady Cumberland left Skipton for the south. Increasing discord with her husband ended in total separation, and henceforth she devoted herself to the education of her child, heiress to the vast Clifford estates. It was to her elder sister, who had mothered her in childhood, that she now attached herself, and while Lady Warwick lived these two ladies were seldom apart. The slow increase of the Russell family – the living descendants of John Russell, the Dorset gentleman, numbered less than ten at the turn of the sixteenth century – ensured that those few were well known to each other. The second Earl's widow and the Dowager Lady Russell were still to be seen about in their black garments. The latter, having composed learned epitaphs for the tombs of her Hoby and her Russell husbands, was now preparing her own, but still had spirit enough to entertain the old Queen with 'nectar'd flatteries' at Bisham Abbey. Lady Cumberland's daughter writes of the uncles and aunts and cousins who visited her mother at her house in Clerkenwell. They made excursions to the country together, they met at Bedford House, and they visited each other in sickness. This powerful family feeling may account for Lady Cumberland, who had buried her elder son at Skipton, interring her younger among her own people in the vault at Chenies, where her old home, the manor house, overlooked the churchyard. Many years later, in 1630, Lady Anne chose to be married to her second husband, Lord Pembroke, at Chenies, where in the chapel adjoining the church the monuments to her great-grandparents, her grandfather and her aunt Warwick had lately been set up.

Lady Cumberland entrusted the education of her daughter to the poet Samuel Daniel, whose stoical and Christian outlook on life approached her own. He, having observed her at close quarters, wrote that she was 'strong as beechwood in the blast'. He lamented that 'being constrained to bide with children' there was a hindrance to his literary work, but his pupil loved him and erected a tablet to his memory. In a compassionate *Epistle* that he addressed to Lady Cumberland, extolling the inward peace of a tranquil and unworldly spirit, he touches on her unhappy life.

This concorde, Madame, of a well-tun'd minde
Hath been so set, by that all-working hand
Of heaven, that though the world hath done his worst
To put it out, by discords most unkinde,
Yet it doth still in perfect union stand
With God and man, nor ever will be forc't
From that most sweet accord, but still agree
Equal in Fortune's inequalitie.

Being of her own age he may have felt more than compassion for her. If in his dedication to her of his *Letter from Octavia* he had in mind the analogous situation of his patroness and Antony's wife (Lord Cumberland having fallen to love 'a lady of quality'), the sonnet which precedes the poem is worded with a delicate discretion.

An older poet came, too, under her potent influence, and we may wonder if it was her sharp and witty appraisal of his early poems or the indomitable firmness of her character that induced Edmund Spenser to surrender to her puritanical judgement. Dedicating to her and Lady Warwick his two *Hymns to Love and Beauty* he confessed that in the 'greener times' of his youth he had imbued the earlier version of the poems with too much passion. 'I was moved by the one of you two most excellent ladies to call in the same, but being unable so to do by reason that many copies thereof were formerly scattered abroad, I resolved at least to amend.' The reformed poems of 1596 sang the praises of *heavenly* and *celestial* love.

The poetical effusions of one of the weaker of her own sex must have been less agreeable to Lady Cumberland than Spenser's recantation.

> Thou being rich, no riches dost respect,
> Nor dost thou care for any outward show,
> The proud that do fair virtue's rules neglect
> Desiring place, thou sittest them below.

– wrote Emilia Lanier with shrewd observation of the noble lady's firm character and lack of ostentation. In befriending the unfortunate, ambitious, dissatisfied and promiscuous wife of a court musician, the Countess had lent her countenance to a woman who had failed in her desire to achieve a place above her station and, conscious of her sins and errors, was repentant and regenerate. Dr A. L. Rowse has loftily identified Emilia Lanier as the Dark Lady of the Sonnets, and notes that her highly competent verse has sometimes a Shakespearean ring. At Cookham on the Thames, near Bisham where old Lady Russell ruled, Lady Cumberland had effected Emilia's conversion, and had directed her to express in poetry her new spiritual nature. To prove submission to her patroness, the reformed wanton duly set her hand to verse.

> And pardon (Madame) though I do not write
> Those praiseful lines of that delightful place,
> As you commanded me in that faire night,
> When shining Phoebe gave so great a grace,
> Presenting Paradise to your sweet sight,
> Unfolding all the beauty of her face
> With pleasant groves, hills, walks and stately trees,
> Which pleasures with retired minds agrees.

Exulting in her new virtue, Emilia addressed her poems in tones of mingled humility and adulation, and with an unseemly boldness, to several noble ladies at the Court with whom she was, and sometimes was not, acquainted. In many lines written for Lady Cumberland she sounded a note of greater intimacy, and alluding to that lady's unhappy life – well known to all – she improperly assumed for herself an equality in misfortune that put her on the same plane as that virtuous and superior woman.

More important to Lady Cumberland than the salvation of Emilia Lanier's soul must have been the repentance of her husband for his past unkindness. The letter that brought her to his death-bed he signed, perhaps with truth: 'Thine as wholly as ever man was woman's'.

Towards the end of her life, Lady Cumberland returned to the north, where at Brougham Castle she led the country life most dear to her. Dabbling in alchemy, compounding medicines for her dependents and caring for the poor, she passed her remaining years. Bound closely to her daughter – herself an unhappy wife – they rarely met, Westmorland and Kent being at opposite ends of the kingdom, but in the celebrated dispute over Lord Cumberland's will she gave her support to her daughter's claim to the Clifford estates. Lady Dorset made the long journey to visit her mother in the north in 1616. Beside the main road a little way from Brougham there still stands 'the Countess's Pillar', which the devoted daughter set up to mark the spot where 'with many tears and much sorrow' she bade farewell to her mother for the last time; Lady Cumberland returning to Brougham Castle to die a few weeks later, her daughter going forward on her journey south to Knole. Where sheep and rabbits once cropped close the turf round the base of this strange monument – emblazoned at the top with coloured armorial shields – weeds and long grass now prevail, waving and bending in the noxious draught from passing traffic. It remains a strangely moving memorial to filial love.

> That modest stone which pious Pembroke reared,
> Which still records beyond the pencil's power,
> The silent sorrows of a parting hour.

When Edward, the youthful third Earl of Bedford, married Lucy Harington, a girl of thirteen, in 1594, he was probably being guided by his aunt Warwick and his uncle Sir William Russell, for she came of an impeccably Protestant family. He had wished to marry Katherine Brydges, daughter of Giles, Lord Chandos of Sudely Castle, but this preference was ignored, and he later saw that young woman become the wife of his first cousin, Francis Russell, who one day was to succeed him as fourth Earl.

After his involvement in the Essex rebellion Lord Bedford was confined for five years to his estate at Moor Park, of which his great-grandfather had been Keeper, and which the second Earl had purchased from the

Crown. Unable to appear at Court while Queen Elizabeth was living, he looked after his estate and went his own quiet way, leaving it to his talented wife to shine in the next reign at a Court that was notable for the extravagance of its amusements.

There is no reason to suppose that the marriage of the Earl and Countess of Bedford was unhappy; their misfortune was an inability to make healthy children. 'The young Bedford is dead', wrote John Donne, after Lucy had given birth to a daughter in 1602, and ten years later Chamberlain reported that 'the Countess of Bedford miscarried of the child there was so much hope for'. Breeding in great ones did not unwatched go.

In the summer of 1603, after the death of the old Queen, an official deputation of courtiers arrived in Edinburgh to attend Anne of Denmark on her journey south when she followed James I to England. 'Other ladies', wrote Stow, 'have voluntarily gone thither.' Among those who travelled north were Lucy, Countess of Bedford and her mother Lady Harington, and they managed to reach Scotland before the royal party set out. Lady Warwick and Lady Cumberland, too, had shown their sense of what was due from two ladies who had been very close to the old Queen. Lady Warwick got away on her journey in good time, but her sister was delayed for lack of horses, and when these were supplied, Lady Cumberland travelled so fast to catch up with the party gone ahead that she 'killed three horses that day with the extremity of the heat'. While curiosity may have played no negligible part in a scramble that was barely a whit less unseemly than that which had preceded the arrival of James I in his new kingdom, self-interest must have sent many halfway up England to meet their new mistress, as others had gone before to meet the King. Sir William Russell had been among those who welcomed James at Theobalds, and the barony of Thornhaugh was conferred upon him. When further honours were distributed, Lucy's father was raised to be Lord Harington.

Whether dutiful, curious, or self-seeking, the youthful Countess of Bedford was seen to be, as the royal party progressed south, 'so great with the Queen as everybody much respected her'. Anne of Denmark had fallen in love with the Harington family. Lucy was chosen before others to be her Lady of the Privy Chamber, and became her principal favourite until death ended the friendship sixteen years later; while the upbringing of Princess Elizabeth, the King's daughter, was entrusted to the care of Lord Harington and his wife, a distinction that annoyed the Catholics, cost him a fortune, and probably hastened his end, for he died on his way home from Heidelberg, whither he had escorted the Princess after her marriage to the future King of Bohemia.

Fulsome praise and severe criticism of the character of Lucy Bedford has done less than justice to a woman who had great influence at the frivolous and corrupt court of James I. Her virtue and her piety have not been questioned, but she has been charged with vanity, extravagance, heartlessness, and a morbid interest in illness and death. Extravagant she was, but she was also affectionate, generous and compassionate. Denied motherhood, she found solace in bestowing her affection on the children of her friends, and to John Donne's daughter she gave her own name when she stood godmother to the poet's child. The all too frequent deaths of babies and the very young harrowed her, recalling her own losses. 'If God had continued me a mother,' is a cry of suffering.

Rich and talented, with abundant vitality, she took a prominent part in the extravagant masques devised by Samuel Daniel or Ben Jonson, and presented with ingenious effects by Inigo Jones at Whitehall; entertainments that squandered thousands of pounds consecrating, the King declared, the birth of the new great hall in his palace, which his predecessors had left him built of wood, but he had converted into stone. In these lavish displays of beauty and bizarre dress the Countess of Bedford was singled out for favour. She sat beside the Queen in a moving chariot, or great scallop shell, while dancers disposed themselves in the form of letters honouring the name of Prince Charles. She took part in the Masque of Blacknesse – a piece of folly which shocked one of the older courtiers who questioned the charm of seeing beautiful women wearing rich apparel – 'but too light and courtesan like for such great ones' – with their faces and their arms up to the elbow painted black. It was observed that the Spanish Ambassador was lucky not to have his lips blackened when he kissed the Queen's hand. One of the portraits of Lucy at Woburn shows her dressed for some such fanciful occasion: her red skirt is shortened for dancing, her cheeks are rouged. The pose is as stiff as the wired veil which extends in an arc behind her head.

The woman who was termed 'Musis delecta' – beloved of the Muses – had at a very early age been noticed for her 'rarest virtues' by Michael Drayton. He dedicated a poem to her before she was married, and soon after she became Countess of Bedford he addressed her again:

Rarest of ladies, all, of all I have
Anchor of my poor tempest-beaten state.

– an indication that she had opened her purse for him (as she did for Donne) and rained upon him her 'sweet golden showers'. Her rank and wealth drew needy poets to her like a magnet. Chapman's version of the *Iliad* bore her name in the dedication; Samuel Daniel wrote for her in *terza rima*, and called her 'learned lady'; Donne adored her; Ben Jonson sharpened his wit and employed his fancy in her honour, and in a captivating sonnet named her:

Lucy, you brightnesse of our sphere, who are
Light of the Muses's day, their morning starre,

Minor poets issued their works under her aegis. While men of letters were eager to publish under the patronage of a courtier, the discriminating nobility were gratified to accept homage from a poet.

In 1607 Lady Bedford acquired the lease of an estate bordering on the Thames, where her style of living invited comparison with the royal household of Princess Elizabeth recently established at Kew. In the rural surroundings of Twickenham, withdrawn from the Court, Lucy was the centre of a brilliant literary group. If we would seek the particular quality that bound those gifted men to her, other than the base enticement of her wealth and position, we must look to the most devoted member of her circle for the answer. John Donne expressed it in one line:

Your radiation can all clouds subdue.

He, of all the poets who paced her garden walks at Twickenham, was most in thrall to her life-enhancing qualities. They met at a time when his fortunes, health and spirits were at a low ebb. Her generous patronage, developing into friendship, rekindled his interest in his art. She, too, wrote verses, and sometimes diffidently showed them to him: 'Those your Ladyship did me the honour to read in Twickenham Garden, except you repent your making them and have mended your judgment'. The poems he addressed to her are passionate, and it would be pleasing to believe that he felt genuine love for her, but we may ask if the literary intercourse between them was more than that 'passion which moves the poet most constantly, the delight in making poetry'. She filled his thoughts, indeed, and in his troubled letters to his friend Goodyer he stressed his need to stand well in the opinion of that intelligent, learned and accessible woman. But no path was ever quite smooth for Donne – he was something too calculating – and so it is no surprise that after some years, when Lady Bedford's lavish generosity and uncontained extravagance had placed her in pecuniary straits, and she was unable to give more than modest aid to the suppliant Donne for the payment of his debts (he being about to enter the Church), he wrote peevishly to Goodyer of her meanness, suggesting that the author of an *Elegy* for her defunct and dearly loved brother deserved greater reward from her than a gift of thirty pounds. 'She was somewhat more startling than I looked for from her; she had more suspicion of my calling, a better memory of my past life, than I thought her nobility could have admitted. For her other way of expressing her favour to me, I must say it is not with that cheerfulnesse as heretofore she hath delivered herself towards me. I am almost sorry that an Elegy should have been able to move her to so much compassion heretofore as to offer to pay my debts.' One must like Donne the less for such querulous and venal egoism. Lucy Bedford has, alas, left no comment on this most interesting relationship; it is not touched upon in such correspondence of hers as has come down to us. The restless energy that compelled her to move from one to another of the half-dozen houses of which she was mistress, also drove her pen, but her breathless, affectionate letters to Lady Cornwallis are written to amuse a person settled in the country, who, having been a member of Lady Bedford's household, was acquainted with Court personages, but, perhaps, took scant notice of poets.

A dangerous illness when only thirty undermined Lucy's health and caused her withdrawal from the Court. Further misfortune kept her away for more than a year. The Earl of Bedford, while riding in his park, was thrown from his horse against a tree and suffered serious injury affecting his speech and causing some paralysis. Two portraits at Woburn show him with his arm in a bulky sling, and in one a muff covers his useless right hand. Looking a little nervous, as though daunted by the formality of his tall hat and fine embroidered gown, he faces the artist with a diffident but patient gaze.

When Lady Bedford showed herself at Whitehall again, her changed appearance was noticed; there was an unusual moderation in her attire and she had given up painting her face. This contempt for fashion and absence of fard was attributed to the influence of Dr Burgess, the nonconformist divine turned doctor, for he had been 'much about her in her sickness and did her more good with his spiritual counsel than with natural physic'. Forbidden by the King to practise within ten miles of London, Burgess had set up at Isleworth, which was but a stone's throw from Twickenham. Donne, who had been able to disregard the other poets in Lady Bedford's orbit – he never mentions one of them – was moved by jealousy to comment with bitterness that the doctor's ascendancy over the Countess was the cause of her new coldness to him.

If Lady Bedford's piety was quickened by her illness, her zest for life was not abated, nor was her extravagance curtailed. Perhaps she hoped to profit from a piece of folly conceived in the high spirits that must have endeared her to the Queen – a race from St Albans to Clerkenwell between one of her footmen and an Irishman in the service of a nobleman. The event drew great crowds to see the outcome, and the King was present, but when the race was won it was Lord Buckingham who raked in three thousand pounds from those who had backed the Irishman; Lady Bedford's gains are not recorded. She was responsible with Lord Pembroke for introducing George Villiers to the Court, hoping that the handsome young man would catch the eye of the King and undermine the influence of Robert Carr. 'To drive out one nail by another', as she put it bluntly, and their efforts were successful. With her debts standing according to the gossips at fifty thousand pounds, Twickenham Park was parted with in 1617, and hereafter Lady Bedford directed her restless energy to adapting Moor Park to her taste – 'that place I am so much in love with, as, if I were so fond of any man, I were in a hard case'. The garden she made, which Sir William Temple described as 'the perfectest garden I ever saw', had probably been already planned by her retiring and country-loving husband. He had too the idea of making a piazza in Covent Garden, but credit for any ability has been withheld from him; the garden at Moor Park has been ascribed to Lucy's genius, and the laying out of Covent Garden is remembered as the creation of the fourth Earl of Bedford.

Although the ties of her own marriage appear to have been weak and she and her husband lived much apart, Lady Bedford was eager to contrive marriages for others, but since her zeal for making matches among the high-born was not always governed by tact, her schemes sometimes went awry. Impelled by her restless energy to pursue many interests, she entered into competition with that great patron of the arts, Lord Arundel, for the acquisition of paintings, and in her eagerness to have the best she made an indiscreet proposition to the wife of Nathaniel Bacon:

I was told last night that your father-in-law was like to die, and that he

48

had some peeses of painting of Holben's, which I am shewr, as soon as Arundell hears he will try all means to gett: but I beseache you entreate Mr. Bacon, if they will be parted with to any, to lay hold of them afore hand for mee . . . for I am a very diligent gatherer of all I can gett of Holben's or any other excellent master's hand; I do not care at what rate I have them for price . . . Some of those I have, I found in obscure places, and gentlemen's houses, that, because they were old, made no reckoning of them . . . When Mr. Bacon comes to London, he shall see that though I be but a late beginner I have pretty store of choise peeses. Dear Madam . . . make them shewr eyther for me or nobody: and be not curious to thinke I maye paye too much, for I had rather have them than juels.

It is not known for certain which pictures now at Woburn may be accounted to her taste and enterprise, but perhaps the Armada portrait of Queen Elizabeth, and the picture of Lady Russell of Chippenham were acquired by her.

Anne of Denmark died in 1619, and the death of Lady Harington two years later turned Lady Bedford's thoughts towards the person who had been dear to them and to herself. Princess Elizabeth had been her friend since girlhood; the Haringtons had brought her up and had gone with her to Germany when she married the Prince Palatine – Lady Harington remaining with her as companion and lady-in-waiting. The rise and fall of fortune took the royal couple from Heidelberg to Prague, and after the defeat of the King of Bohemia by the Emperor, the Winter Queen had taken refuge in Holland. It was Lady Bedford who communicated to Elizabeth the changes and shades of political opinion in England, imploring her to be more circumspect in her freedom of speech. Bidden to visit the melancholy Queen at The Hague, Lucy was given leave to go, but it was stipulated that she was to take no companions but her own servants; it was not to be an occasion for revelry in the company of her friends. Declaring that 'though ther be little ods between the Theams and sea', she took the precaution of making her will before crossing the North Sea – 'as whatsoever becom of mee, evry one shall be shewr of ther owne'; showing her intention that those of her friends who had lent her money should be repaid.

The presence of this brilliant and learned woman at The Hague startled Elizabeth's little court, and the precedence accorded to her by the English ambassadress provoked ill-feeling among the Dutch ladies of rank.

But Lucy Bedford's brilliance was on the wane. She fell a victim to smallpox, which 'so seasoned her all over that they say she is more full and foul than could be expected in so lean and thin a body', and her sight was threatened by 'a pin or web in her eye'. She complained of rheumatism – that appanage of gardeners – of lameness and gout, and that she was weary of life, but she wrote courageously of following a course of physic proposed by Sir Theodor Mayerne.

Charles I had been a year on the throne when she wrote to a friend:

God, I trust, will give mee thankfulness to Him and patience till His appointed tyme of releasing mee from all misserie; of which wee are yett like to have in generall more and more, if this Parlement and the King part not upon better termes than yett they stand, the King having declared himselfe stiffe one way, and they growing stronger and stronger in their resolucions another.

Fifteen years were to pass before the Civil War began, but the quarrel between Crown and Parliament was already engaged. The third Earl of Bedford died in 1627, and she, who had been so little united to him in life, joined him in death twenty-three days later in her forty-sixth year, 'her strength and spirits being as they say farre spent'. She did not, however, join her husband in one tomb, for while he was placed among his fore-bears at Chenies, she chose to lie with the Haringtons at Exton.

A dark romantic picture at Woburn shows her seated in an attitude of serene tranquillity, thoughtful and attentive, her head resting on her hand. It is an image that denies the restlessness of her life, but so may she have sat when Donne was with her, her body resting and her ear tuned to his impassioned reading of a new poem.

Blasted with sighs, and surrounded with teares,
Hither I come to seek the spring,
And at mine eyes, and at mine eares,
Receive such balmes, as else cure every thing;
But, O, selfe traytor, I do bring
The spider love, which transubstantiates all,
And can convert Manna to gall,
And that this place may thoroughly be thought
True Paradise, I have the serpent brought.

Three Ladies

'Twere wholesomer for mee, that winter did
Benight the glory of this place,
And that a grave frost did forbid
These trees to laugh and mocke mee to my face;
But that I may not this disgrace
Indure, nor yet leave loving, Love let mee
Some sensless peece of this place bee;
Make me a mandrake, so I may groane here,
Or a stone fountaine weeping out my yeare.

Hither with christall vyals, lovers come,
And take my teares, which are loves wine,
And try your mistresse Teares at home,
For all are false, that tast not just like mine –
Alas, hearts do not in eyes shine,
Nor can you more judge woman's thoughts by teares,
Than by her shadow, what she weares,
O perverse sexe, where none is true but shee,
Who's therefore true, because her truth kills mee.

5

Puritan Earl

THE genius of Van Dyck was never more powerfully displayed than in his compassionate portrayal of middle-aged and careworn men. The features of those richly clad nobles, seemingly assured of all the material needs and pleasures of their position, lack peace of mind. Their troubled faces betray the harassment of doubt – the twinges of religious conscience, uneasy political allegiance, or the gnawing of ambition. The age of Charles I abounded in anxious men. Van Dyck's great portrait of the fourth Earl of Bedford depicts a man who appears careworn indeed, though not oppressed by uncertainties; rather one who, sustained by steady beliefs and strict principles, is strong in the knowledge that his life has not been wasted in idleness and frivolity. It is evident that he has no use for the gaudy trappings of nobility – plainness is all. Cast in the Protestant mould, he stands every inch a Puritan in sober black garments without so much as a border of lace to his deep white collar. His gaze is straight and as severe as his attire, and he ignores the affectionate spaniel who claims his attention with an uplifted paw. Clarendon said that he was a person of great civility and much good nature, yet from Lady Anne Clifford we learn that during the long dispute about her inheritance 'My Coz. Russell came to me . . . and chid me, and told me all my faults and errors in this business. He made me weep bitterly.' Contemplating the stern face, it is not hard to believe that there was an intention in this good man to inflict pain on the young woman, whose stubborn defence of her rights had involved the King himself in useless argument and failure to make her abandon her claim to the northern estates of her father. Severe with others, the Earl did not fail to discipline himself. In thirty existing folio volumes of notebooks he registered in his angular hand-writing his thoughts about religious doctrine and dogma, and recorded his stringent self-examinations. 'These writings', he declared, were set down 'more by prayers than with pains.'

In August 1625, having succeeded his father as Lord Russell of Thornhaugh, he begged for the loan of Woburn Abbey from Edward, Earl of Bedford; he wished to get his family away from Chiswick, where he had been living with his wife, Katherine Brydges, and their ten children. An outbreak of the plague in London had assumed an alarming aspect, and he himself had experienced some danger from it, for there was a story that 'My Lord Russell being to go to Parliament had his shoe-maker to pull on his boots, who fell down dead of the plague in his presence.' Since those who fled from the city were liable to carry the infection with them, Chiswick, which was easily accessible by water, no longer seemed a safe abode, while Woburn had all the charm of unpolluted air and remoteness from London. His request was granted, and during the autumn and winter months Francis and his large family occupied the old abbey buildings. We may imagine the children on their arrival, gleefully chasing the coneys, whose warren had been a valuable asset of the monastery; but his wife in the first days fretted over her pet bird, the seed for whose nourishment had been forgotten in the hasty flight: she bewailed, too, her exile from Chiswick, where she had been happy. She and her husband wrote affectionately to friends there, to urge them to make use of the gatehouse at Woburn as a refuge – 'since the sickness grows very grievous' – holding out hopes that they might all shortly return to Chiswick when the pestilence had abated. When it was known that there were sixteen cases of the plague in the town of Woburn, Lady Russell's fears for her children were painfully renewed, but no case of the disease occurred among them. Throughout these months her thoughtful husband was able to ponder on the sad neglect of the Abbey, the charm of its situation, and its potential for development. Early in the new year it was thought safe to return to their home by the Thames, and in February Lord and Lady Russell were present at the coronation of Charles I in Westminster Abbey. In the following year the third Earl of Bedford died and Francis entered into his great inheritance, and assumed all the cares attached to his position.

Endowed with a vigorous and practical mind, he was to allot much of his time and energy to three great constructive enterprises. He rebuilt Woburn Abbey and made it the principal home of the family; he carried out the improvement and development of the Covent Garden estate, tentatively begun by his predecessor; and he was the chief promoter of a scheme for draining the fens in the counties of Cambridge and Huntingdon; the reclaimed area, when the work was completed by his son, becoming known as the Bedford Level. In Parliament his reputation was that of a man of great integrity and moderate opinions, and as the leader of the popular party he was involved in the struggle between the King and Parliament for the life of Strafford.

It was the rebuilding of Woburn Abbey that first claimed the attention of Bedford after his succession to the earldom. If it was an idea that had entered his head when he lived as a tenant in the old monastery, he was now as the owner of the estate in a position to order the construction of a house as fine as any that other noblemen were putting up all over England. The old buildings were razed to the ground and the new mansion, which occupied exactly the same site, was built round a courtyard in the Jacobean style. In the north wing where the church had stood the family had their living apartments. Sunless they must have been – and are today – but sunlight then was eschewed rather than sought out. The windows of these rooms looked on to the area that had been the monks' burial ground, which was levelled and laid out as a garden. The site of the monastery church was commemorated in the name of a passage in the house on the north side of the court, still known today as Paternoster Row.

The rooms on the south side were allocated to offices and servants' quarters: state rooms occupied the first floor of the west wing as they do now, and included a great salon known as the Star Chamber from the golden astral decorations of its walls; but there may, perhaps, have been in this freedom-loving household some wry and humorous allusion to the King's suspect Court of Star Chamber.

At the south-west corner the Earl had his library, and when he raised his eyes from his book, in the margin of which he had a habit of scribbling comments on what he had read, he had a fine view of his orchards and deer park. At the opposite corner of this wing was the state bedroom, which Charles I occupied on three occasions. A long gallery at the back of these rooms had eight windows looking into the court, and here was hung the Earl's inherited collection of pictures to which he made additions with portraits of his own family.

Because of Lord Bedford's association with Inigo Jones in the Covent Garden undertaking, it was formerly supposed that it was Jones who made the designs for the rebuilding of Woburn, but there are no plans existing to show that he did so, although he may have advised the Earl on his project. It was probably Isaac de Caux, a man closely connected with Inigo Jones, who was engaged to build a grotto in the north wing, between the living-rooms on the ground floor. De Caux had constructed

The third Earl of Bedford by
Gheerhaerts

Lucy Harington, Countess of
Bedford by Honthorst

The fourth Earl of Bedford by Van Dyck

such a room under the Banqueting House in Whitehall, but nothing of that now remains. The grotto at Woburn, the finest existing in England, was built to serve as a place for sitting out in the air, where the most delicate complexion need fear no hideous darkening by the rays of the sun. Fitted up originally with gilded wooden chairs, it was a charming retreat for conversation and repose on the hottest days of summer. By the eighteenth century the cold draughts that must have circulated in that shady area open to the northern breezes were no longer acceptable to ladies less robust; glass doors were installed so that in effect it became another room – but a room of the most bizarre appearance. The stonework, corrugated to resemble stalactites or seaweed, is inlaid with ormer shells, whose native shore is the Channel Islands, their nacreous lustre serving to decorate the roof in arching bands, while more homely cockles and black mussel shells complete the broad patterns and, densely packed, fill in the space between. Above an alcove where once was heard the tinkle of water falling from a fountain into a rocky basin, a head, part human part marine, sprouts tentacles that threaten to entrap one of the sailing nymphs or dolphin-riding boys, who play among the starfish and the coral. The chairs and stools that furnish this marvellous cavern today are of the kind that were fashionable in the eighteenth century; carved in wood and silvered to look like mother-of-pearl, they have forms appropriate to their setting. Chair backs and seats simulate scallop or oyster shells, and dolphins upended twist their tails to serve as legs. Hard, and even spiny, they were not made for the prolonged repose of loungers, but rather to act as perches for those who came in out of the sun to check a pulse quickened by walking in the heat of the day, and to lose the heightened colour that was superfluous to a well-rouged cheek.

The Earl of Bedford's third great concern was the draining of the fens. It was a scheme that had already been put in hand by his father, who, while serving in the Low Countries as Governor of Flushing, had seen how the Dutch had reclaimed tracts from the sea to become fertile agricultural land, and in 1590 he had petitioned the Privy Council for leave to import Dutchmen, 'certain persons of good ability and skill in draining marsh grounds', to work on his lands at Thorney in the Isle of Ely. A company was formed, headed by the fourth Earl, to promote the draining of the Great Level, with a Dutchman, Cornelius Vermuyden, as chief engineer. Bedford had been promised 43,000 acres of the reclaimed land and the King was to have 12,000. Six years later the Earl and his partners had spent £100,000 without completing the work, and having encountered much opposition from the inhabitants of that swampy area, fishermen and fowlers, who resented the destruction of their livelihood. The King then intervened and took over the whole enterprise, but since in a few years he had need of his resources to save his crown rather than the fenlands, the completion of the project remained in abeyance for another decade.

When a contemporary wrote of Bedford as being 'so noble, so religious, and so favoured by his Majesty', it was at a moment when the drainage operations were in full swing and the King was anticipating a fine profit from his share in the reclaimed land; he had not always regarded that noble lord with favour. Early in the reign Bedford had been sent down into Devonshire – of which county he was Lord Lieutenant – and detained there until the end of the session as a mark of the King's disapproval of his subscription to the Petition of Right. At the time of the unpopular Scots War, when Charles marched north and the peers of England were called on to join him with troops levied and maintained at their own charge, or to compound for a sum of money, the Earl of Bedford, among others, purged his attendance on the King at York with a fine of £1,000. He was one of the most stern opponents of the increasing power of the Crown, and a strong upholder of the rule of Parliament. Pym's declaration that 'the parliament is that to the commonwealth which the soul is to the body', found none more ready to endorse it than Lord Bedford. The member for Tavistock had risen to prominence under his patronage, and the determined line Pym took in the Commons to preserve constitutional principles was upheld by Bedford, with equal firmness but less passion, in the Upper House. Although Pym was the enemy of bishops and attacked the Church, Bedford had no wish to see any alteration in the government of it, and was on friendly visiting terms with Archbishop Laud. When Strafford was impeached the King turned to Bedford as a man able and wise, in whose hands negotiations might safely be placed. The Earl recognized that it would be possible to win concessions from the King in exchange for Strafford's life. It was rumoured that the parliamentary leaders were to be admitted to the King's Council, and that Bedford was to be Lord Treasurer, with Pym as Chancellor of the Exchequer. Clarendon tells how he was present when Bedford and his friends met at 'a place called Piccadilly' during the crucial days before the Bill of Attainder came before the House of Lords; how Bedford, who was against the death penalty for Strafford, sought to moderate the violent opinions of some of his fellow peers, the Earl of

Essex being heard to declare vehemently: 'stone dead hath no fellow'. A few days later it was learned that Lord Bedford had taken to his bed with an illness that soon disclosed itself as smallpox.

'From how little accidents and small circumstances', wrote Clarendon, 'the greatest matters flow towards confusion.' Deprived of the Earl's wise guidance, the King made one mistake after another, believing that he could still save the life of his devoted servant. On a spring day, while Londoners surged in the streets clamouring for Strafford's head, Bedford died at his house in the Strand.

Laud, who reckoned him one of the main plotters of Strafford's death, thought it served him right for having raised his hand against the King's General. 'But God', he wrote, 'would not let him live to take joy therein, but cut him off in the morning, whereas the Bill for the Earl of Strafford's death was not signed till night.'

Clarendon wrote that there were those who thought that Bedford died at the right time: 'he would have proposed and advised moderate courses, but was not incapable, for want of resolution, of being carried into violent ones, if his advice were not submitted to, and therefore many who knew him well, thought his death not unseasonable, as well to his fame as his fortune, and that it rescued him as well from some possible guilt, as from those visible misfortunes, which men of all conditions have since undergone'.

The fourth Earl of Bedford's marriage with Katherine Brydges enriched the collection of pictures at Woburn with portraits of her own family and forebears. Outstanding in quality and interest, each one demands a leisured study. Katherine was a granddaughter of that Earl of Lincoln who married as his second wife Elizabeth Fitzgerald, celebrated in the verses of Lord Surrey as 'Fair Geraldine'. 'Bright is her hue', he claimed, and in her picture here in the style of Clouet, her neat bright auburn hair is contained by a jewelled cap, and gems are sewn to her bodice; her sidelong glance is searching but prim. Without children herself, she saw her stepdaughter married to Giles, Lord Chandos, the father of Katherine Brydges, and his portrait by the little known artist Jerome Custodis is one of the most engaging of the Elizabethan portraits at Woburn; the rounded buttons of his doublet find their counterpart in his bulbous nose and are a witty comment on his kind and healthy face. A superb jewel secures to his high domed hat a tuft of heron's feathers – precious trophy for a sportsman – formed from the short plumes taken from the head of the great bird when it lies grounded by the huntsman's falcon. It is not unusual to see such clusters decorating a hat or cap in pictures of this period. The black dress worn by Lady Chandos in a companion portrait is worked with gold thread in an intriguing pattern of butterflies and pagan altars, and her jewels are delicate figures and emblems derived from myth and legend. She may be counted as a well-loved parent, for she ended her days at Woburn and was buried at Chenies among the Russells.

We may compare the pictures of this couple's handsome daughters – Elizabeth and Katherine. Both were painted in fancy dress, perhaps as performers in the masque presented to Queen Elizabeth at Sudeley Castle by their father. The stiffly wired lace head-dress of each girl, the velvet robe bordered with gold braid worn over an embroidered bodice, represent the extravagance demanded by a special occasion. Katherine's face has a sweetness of expression not seen in that of her elder sister. As a maid of honour to Queen Elizabeth, Elizabeth Brydges had dared to attract the attention of the Earl of Essex; she had been well cuffed by the old Queen, and was briefly banished from the court. Her marriage to Sir John Kennedy, a gentleman who attended James I out of Scotland, was as unhappy as any that a headstrong and extravagant young woman and a violent and dishonest man could between them contrive. We see again in the portrait of Sir John one of those inset pictorial puzzles, such as figured in two Woburn pictures of an earlier date. The partially curtained figure of a woman appears behind him, indicating, it has been supposed, his concealment of a previous marriage – his wife being living at the time of his contract with Elizabeth Brydges.

With four sons and four daughters to settle in life, the fourth Earl of Bedford could hardly escape being plagued by some incidental worries. The passionate attachment at an early age of his eldest son, William, to Lady Anne Carr, the daughter of James I's disgraced favourite, Robert Carr, Earl of Somerset, was principal among them. By having Sir Thomas Overbury poisoned, Frances, Countess of Essex, removed a hostile witness in the suit she brought for divorce from her husband, and successfully obtained, in order to marry Somerset. The King had countenanced the divorce and the subsequent marriage of his favourite to Lady Essex, but when scandalous rumours spread he had them both imprisoned in the Tower. At her trial Lady Somerset confessed her guilt; her husband was sentenced to death for being an accessory to the murder, but was reprieved, and for six years he and his wife were confined within the Tower, where their daughter had been born. Lord Bedford had sat at the trial of this base couple and had been dismayed at the revelation of corruption; he enjoined his son never to think of uniting himself to Anne Carr – he must choose anywhere but there. But the young people were 'all aflame with love' and the young man would have no other. The Earl was firm, but William Russell's determination matched his father's obstinacy. Two years later, since their passion was unabated, Lord Bedford agreed to let them marry if Somerset would give his daughter a dowry of £12,000. Perhaps he hoped that Somerset, whose resources had been crippled after his trial, neither would nor could comply, but that lord protested that since one or other of them must be undone he would that it were he should suffer, rather than his innocent daughter. The wedding was in St Benet's church, Paul's Wharf, in July 1637, and the Earl of Bedford's fears were allayed, for the marriage proved most happy.

Anne Carr was brought up in ignorance of her mother's crime, and only in the last year of her life, nearly seventy years later, finding by chance at Woburn a pamphlet setting forth the story, did she learn of it. The shock was so great that she fell senseless on the floor and was found with the paper in her hand.

The fourth Earl of Bedford's daughters were suitably affianced when they reached the age of fourteen. All were painted in early girlhood by Johan Priwitzer, an obscure Hungarian, whose only documented portraits are those at Woburn. Noble in feature and richly attired, the strong resemblance each sister bears to the others can be traced from adolescence to the mature and spirited young women they had become when they were painted again by Theodore Russel, assistant to Van Dyck. The single pear-shaped pearls that hang from the grave children's ears are in the later pictures doubled in size and number; fitter ornaments for such poised and sophisticated beauties.

Katherine, the eldest, was already a young widow when she was painted for the second time by Russel, and her covered head and demure dress have an air of puritan restraint, unlike her sister's ringlets and satin gowns. She was perhaps her father's favourite daughter, and she was with him when he sickened and died of the smallpox. Her husband, Lord Brooke, was a parliamentarian general, killed in an attack on Lichfield early in the Civil War. He had written a serious book on the nature of Truth, and although it inspired one of his friends to declare that 'Brooke was a fool in print', Milton held him in great honour and praised him for his meekness and piety.

Anne, the next daughter, was united to George Digby, Earl of Bristol, a brilliant, impetuous and inconsistent man, who won the respect and affection of his father-in-law, and joined him in opposing the Bill of Attainder against Strafford. In the heavy business of securing a wife for John Russell, the third son of Lord Bedford, Digby was entrusted with the negotiations, and from the witty letters that passed between Sherborne Castle and Woburn Abbey it is apparent that the Earl and his son-in-law were on the best of terms and derived a good deal of amusement from their correspondence. The lady in question – the widowed Countess of Bath – was being courted by the successor to her late husband's title. While her parents favoured his suit, the young woman herself fancied Lord Bedford's second son, Francis, rather than his brother John.

George Digby to the Earl of Bedford

My most honoured Lord – My unsuccessfulness in the way of your service would much afflict me, but that I can raise comforts to myself both from your wisdom and your goodness. . . . Let me at once relate to you how unlucky I have been, and how industrious.

On my arrival at Tawstock I was much surprised to find my Lord of Bath there, who I thought would have been at the assizes, but he had altered his resolution between the time of my intelligence and my coming. I surprised them all as much, filling the countess with blushes, her parents with confusion, and the count with jealousy. She covered hers well with hearty welcomes; they sought to disguise theirs with civilities; and his lordship (I had never seen the Colossus before), you will easily believe looked big. . . . We were all easily parted the first night, to go to bed. The next day there was much less farouchness between his Lordship and me; we grew to reconnoitre one another, by conversation in the learned way; the countess was full of serenity; her mother very accostive; and Sir Robert somewhat costive. . . .

Next after this I address myself to my Lady Bath: press her in behalf of my brother John; reason with her against the sacrificing herself again to an antique partner, having by the former penance purchased to herself all accommodations she could wish in point of fortune. She made not nice to tell me she could affect neither; whereupon I fell to sounding about Frank, alleging many expressions of her own that leant that way; wherein, after great debate with her modesty, she became a very clear interpreter of what she had written to your Lordship. . . . Here ends the first Act. Does it not look like a comedy? but what follows is tragical.

He describes Sir Robert Lovett's vexation and ill-temper when he discovers Digby's endeavours to queer the pitch for the candidate he has chosen for his daughter's hand.

> . . . he flew into such a passion, that he swore he would work for my Lord of Bath. . . . I was glad I had proof out of his own mouth . . . that his late protestations of neutrality were as false as his former to your lordship of powerful assistance; and upon this he went his way . . . leaving me to make this conclusion of him, that I had never known so fit an officer for Satan, if he had but wit correspondent to his falsehood.
>
> Upon this the Earl of Bath sets so close to the countess and her mother, applies the father's authority – such threats – (a new way of dagger courtship), such proffers! . . . but I took my leave, and went away to a cousin's thereby. . . . I am deceived if you have her not shortly in your power. . . .
>
> My humble service to my Lady Bedford; she will excuse my not writing, for here is trouble enough for both of you.

A week later Digby wrote of his renewed hopes of capturing the Countess for a Russell.

> . . . If you continue to think the Countess of Bath worthy of your son Francis, I dare to say, that if she be not his the fault will be yours. Be pleased only to impose upon yourself in this business a strict secrecy for a while.
>
> It seems my Spanish treating hath been like some chymic medicines, which have at first no relish in the mouth, but digested, prove of most violent operation; or else I have had the same fortune a-wooing which hath often happened to me a-hunting – to shoot, think I have missed, and afterwards to find the deer wounded in the brake. *Haeret lateri laethalis arundo*: apply it to the Countess. . . .
>
> In the meantime, I beseech you to believe that no child of your own is fuller of duty and love to you than
>
> Your Lordship's most affectionate and humble servant
>
> George Digby   Sherborne, this 21st of August 1637

To this the Earl of Bedford replied:

> Son Digby, it is a country business observation, that you must not

put warm eggs under a sick hen; so, in the incubation of business, the warmth of industry discloses the bird. You may proceed, conditionally that the earl shall fully go off before we come on; and I wish, that if it might be coming on the earl's part, that peace might be the *cor de fiore* between my lady and him, for I will not marry my son Frank to a demurring, though I would have ventured my third son to have argued it. . . . Your presence here I shall not need for this business, for I dare trust your judgement in a woman's love; – and see the coast is clear before you put for the port.

I am &.&.

F. Bedford

'The subject being thus but languidly enforced, came to a void but courteous conclusion' was Jeremiah Wiffen's comment on this episode. Frank married elsewhere and no wife was ever found for John Russell. During the Civil War he fought with courage and distinction for Charles I, but growing disillusioned with the Royalist cause, he threw up his commission in disgust. In a picture painted by Dobson, we may see Prince Rupert and Colonel Murray urging him over a bottle of wine to resume it. At the Restoration he became colonel of the First Regiment of Foot Guards, afterwards to be known as the Grenadier Guards.

Grammont tells us that 'le vieux Russell' was his unsuccessful rival for the hand of 'la belle Hamilton'. Unacceptable as a husband, or perhaps with no great taste for the fetters of wedlock, John Russell found peculiar joy in the strains and rhythms of music; he was one of the best dancers in England, and from his collection of two or three hundred printed country dances he was able to undertake the most intricate measures at sight. Grammont mocked him for his old-fashioned clothes, which like his style of dancing had been out of date for twenty years. Perhaps Addison had some knowledge of this casual Cavalier, taking him as a model for Sir Roger de Coverly, who 'wore a coat and doublet of the same cut that were in fashion at the time of his repulse', which 'had been in and out twelve times since he first wore it'.

6

A Family Home

WHEN the Civil War broke out the fourth Earl's sons and sons-in-law were divided in their loyalties; some taking the side of Parliament, and some attaching themselves to the King's party. The eldest son William, who succeeded his father as fifth Earl, received his commission as General of the Horse for Parliament in August 1642, and in October that year he fought at Edgehill, when the captain of his 67th troop of horse was Oliver Cromwell. Less than a year later, disliking the course that parliamentary politics were taking, he made his way with two other lords to Oxford to offer his services to the King. They had but a cold reception from the indignant Queen in the absence of Charles, and were kept waiting for their pardon until his return. At the battle of Newbury Bedford charged bravely in the King's own regiment of horse. For this change of party he was taken into custody for a short time and fined eight hundred pounds, and the parliamentary commissioners saw that the payment was made good by removing from Bedford House a quantity of his fine furniture. His estates were sequestrated. Lady Anne Clifford remarked with penetration that the trouble with the Russells was that at one and the same time they disapproved of the character of the Stuarts and the politics of Cromwell. It is therefore no surprise that, uncertain in his mind, William, Lord Bedford, disliking his treatment at Court, after four months again joined the side of Parliament, but becoming disillusioned with both parties he withdrew wholly from politics in 1643, and applied himself to the management of his estates.

Shortly after the death of his father the young Earl had settled his family at Woburn Abbey. He and his wife Anne and their two small sons were joined by his widowed mother and his sister Diana, as yet unmarried. The Dowager Countess had been left the house at Chiswick for her lifetime, but she turned her back on the scenes of her early married years, preferring to make her home with her son at Woburn, where rooms in one wing were allotted to her and Diana. This girl, the youngest, and from her picture the most bright-eyed of the Earl's sisters, was soon wedded to Francis, Lord Newport, an ardent Royalist. When three years later he was captured by parliamentary troops, and his wife found herself besieged in their home, her distressed mother sent an urgent message to her from Woburn.

> Never was there a sadder heart of mother than I have for you, and know not which way to give you comfort . . . All I can devise to do is to beg this favour of Sir Sam. Luke . . . Certainly they did not give you good advice to tarry there. For God's sake come away and have a care of your little boy, and little love, which I fear you will lose.

Some knowledge of her daughter's strong, perhaps obstinate character infused her letter to Sir Samuel Luke, a Parliamentarian – the supposed model for Butler's 'Hudibras', and a neighbour in Bedfordshire:

> 'Give comfort to this poor afflicted heart of mine,' she wrote, 'and that is about my poor daughter Newport, who I hear is besieged . . . I write to her to charge her to come away; I do beg of you to write to Sir William Bretherton that he will be pleased to let her out with some favour, if she be not wilful and will not come out . . .'

Lying as it did so near one of the main roads from London, Woburn was often disturbed by the passage of armies during the Civil War, and there were clashes between opposing forces in the little market town. Twice in these years the King came to lie in the state bedroom in the south-west corner of the Abbey. He had been there before in 1636, and Henrietta Maria had been with him. At that time it had been thought that his influence would induce Lord Bedford to yield to his son's determination to marry Anne Carr, but despite the King's known wish for the union, it had been another year before the Earl gave way. In 1645 Charles spent two nights under the roof of the young Earl and Countess, and was witness of a domestic happiness now denied to him; for the Queen had taken refuge in France with her youngest child, the future Duchess of Orleans. Henrietta Maria had given birth to this daughter at Bedford House in Exeter, which had been put at her disposal by the Earl of Bedford when it was thought wise to remove her from Oxford, further to the west of England. Two years later the King came again to the Abbey and stayed more than a week; he was the prisoner of the parliamentary army, whose headquarters were at Bedford. A short time before he had been allowed to see those three of his children still remaining in England. Cromwell had been present at that meeting, and spoke of it afterwards with tears in his eyes; now he came to confront the King under the Earl of Bedford's roof:

'In this mournful plight', wrote John Ashburnam, 'I found his Majesty at Woobourne, in treaty with Mr. Cromwell and Mr. Ireton, and some other officers of the Army.' Another pen bore witness to the great courtesy with which everyone had been received, 'in the great house his Majesty was honourably and affectionately welcomed, the Commissioners and attendants entertained with high civility, as were also the army officers'. The delegates from the army had come to submit to Charles the Heads of the Proposals as a basis for their negotiations with him; but the obstinate and unhappy King rejected them against the advice of his more moderate counsellors.

During the period of the Commonwealth Lord Bedford took no part in public affairs. He lived quietly at Woburn consolidating his resources. When in 1641 his mother had handed him the keys of the great Flemish money chest that served as the family bank (a similar one may be seen at Woburn) it contained £1557 14s. 1d. Two hundred and fifty-five pounds had been taken out to pay for his father's funeral. The mourning provided for the family and household, and for the black hangings of the house, came to another five hundred pounds. There was every need to economize until his affairs were regulated. After the execution of the King, Bedford continued the fourth Earl's enterprise of draining the fens. It called for heavy outlay, but one that eventually brought in a fine profit.

At the Restoration the Earl rode in the procession that welcomed Charles II at his entry into London, and having received a Letter Patent of Pardon, absolving him from anything he might have done contrary to His Majesty during His Majesty's absence from the kingdom, he was deputed to carry St Edward's Sceptre at the Coronation.

A delightful book[1] based on a mass of surviving household bills covering every aspect of the fifth Earl of Bedford's expenditure during a period of nearly sixty years, gives a remarkable picture of the management of a nobleman's household in the second half of the seventeenth century; carried on at first with simplicity and economy but expanding in due

[1]*Life in a Noble Household*, G. Scott Thomson, 1937

course to a grandeur that, however, remained unpretentious and domestic, and was rooted in the belief that the first business of an aristocrat was to be a country gentleman living on his estates.

At the centre of this large, well-organized household is the figure of the Earl himself, father of six sons and three daughters: very much in command of what went on, and demanding a precise account from his receiver general of how the money that came in from his large and scattered properties was disbursed in each branch of his establishment, indoors and out of doors. From the accounts of his privy purse, and the ordering of his kitchen and wine cellar, his stables and gardens, the homely comfort of his daily life may be imagined. The direction and conduct of all departments of the great house was in the hands of men – even the buying of the children's clothes; trifles such as ribbons and combs were always bought for them from pedlars who came to the door. Seven or eight women only were employed in the house, none in the kitchen. If Lord Bedford had chosen – as some great men did – to have his servants' likenesses taken as well as those of his family, we should not now be ignorant of the features of Betty Buskin and Alice-about-the-House; we might smile at the raw appearance of the snotty scullions who plucked the swans, the ruffs and the reeves, the little knots and dotterels, that were snared in the damp, low-lying lands at Thorney and brought to Woburn for the Earl and Countess's table; and we could with confidence assert that Mrs Abigail, for whom 'anti-scorbutic juices' were prescribed with depressing frequency, looked scurvily or had an air of hypochondria.

Beside the dominant figure of the Earl, the character of his lovely wife is shadowy; her personality is unclear, her voice not heard among the many in that family. We only know her as Van Dyck saw her, clad in white silk with a blue bow on her breast and rosebuds tucked into her waistband – gentle of countenance, loving and lovable. If the thought is present, and cannot be entirely banished, that in that ravishing little head there was, perhaps, scant room for brains, the radiance of her presence must have been more pleasing to those around her than wit or erudition.

It is recorded in the accounts that she had smallpox at Woburn soon after that disease had carried off her father-in-law, and that a fee of twenty pounds was paid to Dr John Clarke, an eminent physician, who was summoned from London to attend her; the hackney coachman, who brought him down, receiving two pounds and four shillings. After her illness the Abbey was thoroughly fumigated with pitch and frankincense, while the family went away to London. Bills show that she sometimes joined her daughters in dancing lessons, and that she had instruction in playing the guitar, but we would like to know much more about her. On the paved west terrace of the house she would have moved among myrtle and orange trees grown in pots – sweet-smelling ornaments on which care was lavished, and formal flower beds surrounded the house on three sides. If the long lists of flower seeds sent to the nurserymen were compiled at her request, they show her love for gillyflowers and candytuft, marigolds and Amaranthus, Humble Plant and Marvel of Peru.

In the 1660s a man well known in the horticultural world from his connection with the laying out of the nursery gardens at Brompton Park – an enterprise much commended by John Evelyn – became gardener at Woburn. He captured the affection of the Russell children, to whom he was always 'very dear John Field'. He was surely one of those good-natured men whose company is like a magnet to the young, who will follow him about, and stand by him while he works, ready to catch the stream of information, anecdote, conundrum, and humorous comment laced with wisdom, that is spellbinding to children, and flows from his lips as freely as the sweat from his brow. John Field, with the help of male and female labour, extended and improved the garden and money was spent liberally on new plants and fruit trees. Did the large orders despatched to the nursery men near London reflect the wishes of the Countess? Was a study made of her preference for a Bona Magnum plum, a Purperry peach, or a Berri de Roi pear? Were the Red Coralina gooseberries (greedily devoured by Celia Fiennes, who paused at Woburn on her ride through England in 1697) planted by her choice? Was her approval sought in the laying out of the new kitchen garden, where purslane, cardus, and rouncival peas were sown with a lavish hand, and a visitor might stumble on melons? These are idle questions, and we may well believe that gentle Anne Carr was wholly subservient to her husband and his wishes.

Almost as important as the Earl himself was the man he chose to educate his children – a man who shared his Protestant opinions. A portrait of the Rev. John Thornton, a lifelong Nonconformist, shows him to have been strictly evangelical in his dress, and although there is a humorous glint in his eyes, this promise of wit is not borne out by the extreme dullness of his letters to his pupils when they were away from home. The girls received their education in his schoolroom as well as the boys; loved and respected by his charges, his influence was profound and lasting. The two youngest sons were eventually sent to Westminster, thus beginning for the Russell family a long connection with that school. It was perhaps unfortunate that George, the youngest of the six brothers, was removed from the stern moral guidance of Mr Thornton, for his career was in no way a credit to his family or school. His habit of incurring debts led to his despatch to a North American colony in the unfulfilled hope that his problem might be settled far from home; but in spite of receiving a generous allowance, bills of exchange given by him in Boston or New York were liable to arrive in London to be settled by his father. A picture of this erring son, aged ten, in a suit of coarse grey material, is the earliest portrait known to exist of a Westminster schoolboy. Mr Thornton spent his long life between Woburn Abbey and Bedford House, acting as tutor, chaplain, and librarian. As a self-appointed medical adviser, his confident recommendation of remedies for the Earl's disorders – toothache, colic, and rheumatism – appears to have been the only cause of friction between the two men, and if 'a powder made of three acorns and two peach stones . . . as much as will lie on a shilling' was considered a preventive of pleurisy, the Earl's refusal to take such medicine showed a wisdom ahead of his times, and he was undoubtedly better without it.

The physical disability of the eldest son, Francis Russell, was a source of lasting anxiety. Weak from childhood, he was sent after a course at Cambridge to travel abroad with his next brother William, and a French tutor. They were away for six years. Increasing lassitude and melancholy he was unable to overcome made Francis unfit for normal life and he spent his allotted term of forty years travelling in search of health, sampling the waters of European spas, ultimately having recourse to those of Bath itself.

A more instant sorrow troubled the Earl and Countess. Their seven-year-old daughter Anne, while playing with her sister in the park, picked unwholesome berries, ate them and died. The grievous error that destroyed her can be easily conjectured: the poisonous scarlet and green fruits of the wild arum – 'Lords and Ladies' – pushing through the grass in some dark corner of a coppice and looking like comfits, must have been quickly seized and swallowed unobserved; or the crimson berries of bryony, climbing in showy brilliance over the hedgerow, proved irresistible to a child who could not perceive the difference between them and the red currants that, crystallized in sugar, were laid on platters in the

Abbey still-room. That the little girl was fond of fruit appears in the house-hold accounts, which show a special purchase made for her in 1655:

For six sweet oranges and cherries for my lady Anne 1s. 4d.

Lely, painting her and her sister before this tragedy, chose a characteristic pose for the two children, in which Anne is helping herself to her favourite cherries from the apron that Diana Russell holds up with both hands.

There is another picture of this child who was to die young, and it has an interest beyond the record of her merry face, for her arm encompasses a white cockatoo with a sulphur crest – a bird found only in Australia, at that time a continent unknown to Europeans. As a vagrant it may have reached some distant island to be bought or captured by the sailors of a vessel trading in the East, and carried to the Port of London found a buyer: a rare object, fit to take the fancy of a rich man's child.

A more dreadful event than the death of this child lay as yet many years ahead. William, the second son (known after his brother's death as Lord Russell), has passed into history as 'the Patriot', and a martyr to the Whig cause. In early manhood he entered Parliament as the member for Tavistock, where he sat for twelve years without speaking. Burnet relates that 'he was a slow man, and of little discourse, but he had a fine judgment when he considered things at his own leisure.' Lely and Riley have represented him in this solid and sluggish character, dull-eyed and heavy of jaw. While these portraits deny his latent energy and the qualities that made him an adored husband, there is a miniature that suggests his firm character and undoubted good looks. Lacking great talents but subject to high principles inculcated by his father and tutor, William Russell's judgement ripened slowly. Returning as a very young man from abroad he was attracted by the gaiety and manners of the fashionable people who surrounded Charles II after the Restoration, but the growing threat of popery, the fear of France, and the perfidy of the dissolute Court, drove him into opposition. Once sure of his right course he followed it with vigour and sometimes with imprudence, since his opinions were not those likely to be popular with the King, and still less with the King's brother, for Lord Russell was among the foremost of those who strove to exclude the Duke of York – an avowed Catholic – from the councils of the King, and from the succession to the throne. He was in close touch with the Prince of Orange many years before the Glorious Revolution, which he did not live to see. If his mistrust of the Stuarts was inherited, it was matched by Mary of Modena's relentless dislike of his own family; at a moment of crisis in James II's fortunes she was heard to declare that she could not sleep until she had voiced her hatred of all the Russells. William Russell once remarked to his domestic chaplain that he was sure he would fall a victim, since arbitrary government could never be set up in England while he lived to oppose it with the last drop of his blood. His wife detected in his character an imprudent element, for one day, learning he was to speak in the House, she sent in a note begging him on that particular occasion to hold his tongue.

His marriage to Rachel, the widow of Lord Vaughan, and the daughter of Thomas Wriothesley, fourth Earl of Southampton, took place when he was nearly thirty; she was three years older. It was a union of the most perfect trust and happiness and her steadfast and honest character matched his own. Her French mother, Rachel de Ruvigny, was known as 'la belle et vertueuse Huguenotte'. The worldly appearance in Van Dyck's rich portrait of this beautiful woman, already past her first youth, seems to belie that part of her title suggesting moral excellence, were it not that her daughter was a mirror of her good qualities. A considerable heiress, Rachel Wriothesley brought to the Russells as part of her inheritance the Bloomsbury estate that has contributed so much to the fortune of the family. On this property stood Southampton House, which became the William Russells' home; later the name was changed to Bedford House when the old mansion in the Strand was pulled down. Between London and Stratton, Rachel's country estate in Hampshire, they led the happiest of domestic existences, and since ties of affection made Woburn a centre for all the family they were often there and saw their children become favourites with the Earl and with their grandmother. Mr Thornton too could see that the precepts he had instilled in his pupil were being carried on into another generation.

At those times when the William Russells were apart – he perhaps at Woburn, supervising affairs that would eventually concern himself (for after 1678, when his elder brother died, he became the heir to the earldom and the estates), she with her three children at Stratton – Rachel's letters to her husband overflow with confident and happy love. He was her 'best life', her 'dearest heart', and she claimed to be 'as passionate a lover as ever a woman was'. That he was not backward in returning her affection is certain: 'You', she wrote, 'that know so well how to love and to oblige, make my felicity entire.' Her fluent pen ran on to tell him of her rural occupations; her care for his hawks and his dogs, pears laid up for him in

Katherine Russell, as a child by Priwitzer

Diana Russell, Lady Newport by Theodore Russel

Prince Rupert, Colonel Murray and Colonel John Russell by William Dobson

The fifth Earl of Bedford and his wife Lady Anne Carr by Van Dyck

paper and linen, a red deer pie eaten, and the comic antics of their children. The elder little girl – another Rachel – prattled of Woburn: 'She says papa has sent for her to Wobee, and then she gallops and says she has been there'; and the baby son Wriothesley: 'winking at me, and striking with his drumstick whatever comes within his reach'. At the end of the day she wrote: 'boy is asleep, girls singing a-bed', and she expressed her own eager anticipation of her husband's approaching return. It was, she declared in her widowhood, a life of 'full and sweet content'. But the tenderness of a loving family, domestic pleasures, wealth, and all such contentments, were the support of any man, and not things deserving and sufficient in themselves to occupy solely one who cared passionately for the welfare of his country. The goal of William Russell's ambition, and the object of his pursuit, was the safety of England and the preservation of the Protestant religion. Imprudence carried him into doubtful company and dangerous by-ways; indiscreet rather than culpable, he was involved in the Rye House plot of 1683 – a conspiracy to assassinate the King and the Duke of York on their way back to London from Newmarket races. Lord Russell was arrested and taken to the Tower. He denied that he had conspired against the King's life, and it had not perhaps been made known to him that the plot was to end in assassination. 'Strong in his own righteousness, he was satisfied that where his own conscience approved his actions, the world must accept them also', but his unwary conduct, misrepresented at his trial, ensured his destruction. During the proceedings in Westminster Hall, he asked that he might have someone to take notes for him; he was told roughly that he might have a servant to do so. 'My wife', he said, 'is here, my Lord, to do it', and each day Rachel sat with pen and ink and paper, to perform this service for him. The news that Lord Essex, another person implicated, had cut his throat in the Tower on the morning of the day the trial began did much to influence the jury. They found Russell guilty of high treason and he was condemned to death. Many petitions were sent up to save his life, and it is possible that the King might have yielded had it not been for his relentless brother; the Duke of York would have had the beheading take place in front of Southampton House, but this Charles would not allow, and the scaffold was set up in Lincoln's Inn Fields.

It is impossible to read without emotion Burnet's account of William Russell's last days in Newgate. The Bishop remained with him to the end and was a witness of what passed, and of Russell's calm acceptance of his fate. The three children were brought by Rachel to take leave of their father; the broken-hearted old Earl came, and Mr Thornton visited his beloved pupil. On the last evening Russell said farewell to his wife. 'He kissed her three or four times, and she kept her sorrow so within herself that she gave him no disturbance by their parting. After she was gone he said: "Now the bitterness of death is past." '

7

A Dukedom and the youthful Heir

RACHEL lived on for forty years a disconsolate widow. Corresponding with several eminent divines, she confided to them her sacred memories of her husband; her past happiness and present misery. Lamenting her own general unworthiness she wrote: 'I had made him my idol though I did not know it, and neglected my God.' Sunk, as it seemed she would be, in perpetual woe – keeping the anniversaries of Lord Russell's arrest, sentence, and execution as days of total retirement and private prayer – her religious faith and her strength of character enabled her in time to surmount her grief, although her letters remained tinged with melancholy. After the death of the Countess of Bedford, who, long ailing, could not survive the death of her son, she lived much at Woburn, and the trust and tenderness that grew up between herself and the Earl was balm to them both.

In 1688, when William of Orange was expected to land on the coast of England, Lady Russell wrote from Woburn that 'Lord Bedford is preparing to move from this place if the Prince lands northwards, to Chenies.' The Earl had no love for James, he had not attended his coronation, and his private feelings made him naturally averse to the court, but he was a loyal subject and took no part against the King. Tradition has recorded his mild and dignified reply to James's plea for help when faced with disaster. 'My Lord,' the King exclaimed, 'you are an honest man, of great credit in the country, and can do me now essential service.' The Earl's gentle rebuke: 'Sire, I am old, but I had once a son who could have served your Majesty', must indeed have discomfited the King.

And so it fell to a younger and more passionate member of the Russell family to welcome the Prince of Orange when he landed in Torbay. Edward Russell, later Earl of Orford, was Lord Bedford's nephew, and he had entered the Navy. Professing the greatest respect and deep personal affection for William Russell (to whose integrity, simplicity and good nature his own violent character stood in strong contrast) he was, after his cousin's execution, chosen by the opposition party to go between England and Holland, acting as liaison with the Dutch and the Prince of Orange, and he privately advised the Prince to make his appearance in England. He was one of the seven signatories to the invitation that was sent in cipher to William at The Hague, and he sailed with the Dutch fleet from Holland to Torbay and accompanied the Prince to London. But such a favourable outcome to many years of scheming failed to satisfy this arrogant and ambitious man; he quarrelled, he fostered grievances, and holding himself to be neglected by the King, he wrote intemperate letters to William, boasting, reproaching, and sneering. When Queen Mary held her Cabinet councils in the absence of her husband, Russell's presence made her uncomfortable, and the letters he addressed to her, uneasy. He seemed dissatisfied, she wrote to William, and did nothing but talk of retiring. Skilful and successful as a naval commander, his wayward nature and uncertain loyalty made him venture secret dealings with the Jacobite court at St Germains, even while beating the French at sea. To James's agent he said: 'Do not think I will let the French triumph over us in our own sea . . . if I meet them I fight them, ay, though His Majesty should be on board.'

Before the victorious battle of La Hogue in 1692, when he was in command, his exhortation to his seamen was characteristic of his temper and blunt speech.

'If your commanders play false,' he urged, 'overboard with them and with me first.' Something of his divided sympathies was apparent also in James II himself, who, watching from the French coast the great sea-fight, a combat of much importance to his own personal fortunes, could not forbear to exclaim: '*Voilà mes Anglais! Comme ils se battent bien!*' He had indeed been instrumental in their training.

Admiral Russell was the only living Englishman to have won a great victory, and for a time he was the most popular man in the country; his treasonable overtures to the exiled court being unknown until long after his death. His accumulation of a great fortune, and his difficult temper, made him as time went on less well liked. He married his uncle's daughter, Lady Margaret Russell, when she was already middle-aged, and remaining childless they devoted themselves to gardening on an estate he had bought at Chippenham in Cambridgeshire.

If in appearance he somewhat resembled his cousin William Lord Russell, he had many qualities that are generally alien to the Russell character, and two of these – violence and acrimony – mark his features in the portrait that hangs at Woburn.

One of the first Acts of King William's reign reversed the attainder of William Russell, and Lord Bedford, relieved of his anxiety for the honour and future prosperity of the family, was able to fix his hopes on his grandson Wriothesley. That the boy should have the most proper education was the joint concern of his mother and the Earl; Mr Thornton, invited to supervise, once more got out his precious globes and school books.

A practical worldliness was combined with the profound piety of Rachel's nature, and she contrived early and advantageous marriages for all three of her children. While Lord Russell had been confined in Newgate his devoted friend Lord Cavendish had offered to change clothes with him so that he might make his escape. The offer was refused, Russell telling Burnet 'he was very glad he had not fled, for he could not have lived from his wife and friends'. The amity between the two families was sealed when his elder daughter Rachel, barely fourteen years old, became the wife of William Cavendish, son of that same generous friend. Five years later Katherine, the younger girl, was married at Woburn Abbey to the heir of the Earl of Rutland, while a union with a girl who lacked aristocratic birth but was heiress to a great fortune was arranged for Wriothesley, now enjoying the title of Marquess of Tavistock, for in 1694 the earldom of Bedford was promoted to a dukedom, the Letters Patent proclaiming that this advance in the peerage was by reason of the Earl being 'father to the Lord Russell, the ornament of his age, whose great merit it was not enough to transmit by history to posterity'. Elizabeth Howland was descended from City drapers and clothiers. Sole heiress of her father John Howland's wealth, she inherited his estates of Streatham and Tooting Bec and Rotherhithe. Her mother, the daughter of Sir Josiah Child, powerful in the East India Company and creator of Wanstead Park, had a fortune of her own, which her only child might look forward to receiving. Elizabeth was thirteen when the wedding took place; Wriothesley was a year older. He drove with his grandfather from London to Streatham in a coach and six, attended by 'several persons of quality', and Bishop Burnet made the two children man and wife in the private chapel of the manor house. The solemn occasion ended with merriment and some dismay, for after the wedding banquet it was noticed that the young couple were no longer present; bored with the company of their elders they had slipped away to play. What games they had indeed!

When a search was made the girl, with her bridal point lace ripped and torn, was found hiding in a barn, while the bridegroom, cool and complacent, strolled casually back to the company.

Because of their youth, and following the usual custom, the two were kept apart for the next four years. Elizabeth returned to her mother and went on with her lessons, irksome though these may have seemed to a young wife.

'I am sorry', wrote Lady Russell to Mrs Howland, in her firm and sensible way, 'that dear Lady Tavistock has any employment that she does not take pleasure in . . . it is my opinion that if they teach her much grammar it increases her trouble to little purpose, for French is oftener and as well learned by ear.'

Wriothesley had less constraint and more pleasure in acquiring a knowledge of Italian. A year at Oxford had shown him there was little enjoyment to be had in the study of logic, in which science, however, his tutor affirmed 'he goes forward very well'. His mother wished him to travel and see Italy. The Duke, now eighty-four years old, would have restricted the journey to France and Holland, fearing that he might not see his beloved grandson again if there were a longer absence. 'I must confess it is a very great trial for me to part with one so dear to me as he is,' he wrote to Rachel. To Germany and Italy the young man went with a tutor companion, and if the Duke's worst fears were not realized and he lived to see Wriothesley return, enough disquieting news was received at Woburn from time to time to make him doubt the wisdom of sending a boy, whose character and stability were as yet not proved, to that vortex of temptation and popery, Rome. Liberated from the restraints imposed by his elders and escaping from the perennial air of mourning that pervaded Southampton House, Wriothesley responded with delight to the brilliant climate, the gaiety of the Italians, and all the distractions of Rome. Idling in the bookshops he indulged an early taste for collecting; buying prints and musical scores and fine books. In the warm summer nights he drove about the streets in an open calèche, listening, he told his mother, to serenades in the best possible company. Roman society received him with fêtes and flattering verses; cardinals courted and petted him – it was rumoured that he had made his submission to the Pope. The attentions he received from the princes of the church were perhaps fostered by the knowledge that the rich young nobleman had a strong Protestant background. Thirty years earlier Mr Thornton had from Woburn cast a kindly surveillance over this young man's uncles as they wandered about

Europe, and he did not fail now to keep in touch with the youthful heir who, from his exalted position, was likely to be subject to greater temptations than the previous generation. It may have been due to the old tutor's influence that a chaplain was despatched to strengthen the defence against popery, and to check the emancipated exuberance of splendid living embarked on by Wriothesley. Ultimately it was the gaming tables that ensnared him and not the Roman Church. His mother, who had early observed in him a love of gambling, must have learnt without surprise from her contrite son that he had incurred gambling debts that he could not pay. Dismayed, but confident in the trust existing between herself and the Duke, she humbly imparted to the old man the disagreeable news of his grandson's predicament, proposing at the same time practical suggestions for how the debt might be paid; stating her belief (in which she was later confirmed) that it was the folly of a very young man and would never be repeated.

But the business now is how to pay the money, and to do it so secretly, that the inquisitive town shall not make it their talk and scorn, and he be exposed as he calls it, as an easy gentleman, that can be cheated of his money.

But the Duke had his reasons for not releasing capital, and the interest on the debt was scrupulously paid for many years until the principal was redeemed after Wriothesley's death, when his son and heir, who had already embarked on a gambling course that made his father's loss of three thousand pounds appear a trifle, came of age.

In his last years little was seen of the old Duke in public. A weakness in his legs (for which Mr Thornton could find no remedy) kept him at home. As he moved haltingly through the handsome well-proportioned rooms at Woburn and shuffled along the picture gallery leaning on his stick, the old nobleman may have seen them peopled by the ghosts of those who once had been domesticated there and whom he had so long survived – the portraits on the walls acting as aids to his memory. His stern, darkly clad father; his mother, mistress of the new house, wearing a muslin apron, with a posy of flowers in her hands; the gentle and dignified King, who here had stubbornly resisted the proposals of the Heads of the Army; his own lovely and dearly-loved wife, whose delicate hand had lain in his own when in their youth they sat together in front of Van Dyck for their joint portrait; the merry undiscerning child who liked fruit; the

erring George, who had come back from North America and died; his
feeble eldest son, and that martyred one on whom all his pride and hope
had rested. Pausing by one of the westward-facing windows he might
have seen above the trees of his cherry orchards the flourishing great oak
that stood on a slight eminence – the tree, tradition said, from which one
hundred and seventy years before Abbot Hobbes had been strung up
until he died because he would not accept the new forms of religion
favoured by King Henry. If the Duke recollected the story and viewed that
area of the park without feeling compassion for the priest who had swung
there in the wind, his thoughts may have turned towards the more
honourable death suffered by one who had striven to prevent the old
forms rooting themselves again in England.

At the end of his life the company in which he took, and always had
taken, most pleasure was that of his children. When they came to visit
him at Woburn they paid down a sum on their arrival for the board and
lodging of themselves, their attendants and their horses, the receipt of
these monies being noted in the account book of the Duke's receiver-
general, as it always had been. The old man had no wish to welcome new
faces at his table nor company that was ignorant of his energetic youth,
when he had testimonies enough of love and respect to warm his heart
from his surviving children, and their sons and daughters too. In Mrs
Howland, his grandson's mother-in-law, he found a kindred spirit. She
often visited him at Woburn, and she too paid for the board of herself
and her servants with strict exactitude. He approved of her evangelical
turn of mind and her clear mastery of accounts, for, with admirable
precision, she kept neat household books and records of expenditure. As
the daughter of Josiah Child, she had much of her fortune invested in the
East India Company and its ships. Under her persuasion the Duke took
shares in these vessels that brought profitable cargoes from the Orient,
entering into the new venture with the zest of a younger man. In association with Mrs Howland he planned and carried out the construction of a
dry dock and a wet dock on the Howland property at Rotherhithe. Two
vessels were built there during the Duke's lifetime and were named the
Tavistock and the *Streatham*, in compliment to the two families concerned
in their origin. They sailed in the service of the East India Company, and
among the merchandise carried from the East in their holds were pieces
of the highly esteemed oriental porcelain that was coming into fashion,
and bowls and dishes of great quality appeared in due course in the rooms
at Woburn when the Duke took his choice of the goods. Half a century

later, when his great-grandson held most of the shares in her, the *Streatham* set sail on a voyage to India carrying a young man whose eminent future lay in that country. It was recorded in the log book on 5 April 1755: 'Saluted Captain Clive and his lady on their coming on Board.'

In 1700 a news letter announced: 'The old Duke of Bedford is gone to sleep with his fathers. He fell asleep with two poached eggs in his mouth. God send we make the same exit at his age.' He died at Bedford House in the Strand and he was eighty-seven years old. His daughter, Lady Orford, had perhaps been right when she cautioned Mr Thornton to see that her father did not over-eat himself. She wrote now to the old tutor: 'He wants us no more, though all that knew him must always miss him.'

The Duke's lack of conviviality, and his preference for the austere religion now going somewhat out of fashion, were commented on censoriously by his neighbour at Ampthill Park, Thomas Bruce, Lord Ailesbury:

'A graceful old nobleman', he noted, 'and his outside was all. He always had lived to himself, and his company in the summers were only his relations from London and elsewhere and sometimes some Lords and gentlemen, lovers of bowling and cards for about a week but few or none of the country gentlemen ever went thither. He kept a good house for eating among themselves, but no hospitality.'

'He went', added Lord Ailesbury, with a deprecating sneer, 'to the Parish Church on Sunday morning, but had a Presbyterian chaplain, and no common prayer in his chapel.'

When Wriothesley succeeded his grandfather as second Duke of Bedford he was not twenty-one, but he had only eleven years to live. Surrounded by doting, strong-minded and critical relatives, it might be wondered if in his short life this good, cultivated and domestic young man would ever be wholly free from the supervision of his elders. His ageing but active mother, so anxious for his good name and well-being, advised and cautioned; where her cherished son was concerned her heart was always in her mouth. She apprehended danger from every quarter, whether it were a fall from his horse or from bricks coming down the chimney of the room in which he lay with his wife during a great storm, or from the more real perils of infection and illness. There was watching him, too, his cousin, the Admiral. Lord Orford was eager to appraise the young man's conduct of affairs at Woburn, and he gave his observations and approbation in a pompous but kindly letter to Wriothesley's mother:

If I thought the account I am going to give your Ladyship of Woburn and the master of it, would be disagreeable to you, I should ease you of the trouble of this letter. I am newly come from thence, where I stayed a whole week, and upon my word, I never was better pleased to see the Duke and Duchess of Bedford both extreme easy in their house, and living with the greatest order and decorum that it is possible, so discreet, keeping a very good table, and everything in the house as regular and in good order as I have seen in any family that pretends the most to economy. Your son busies himself with improving his park and grounds, and has got the reputation of a great husbandman . . . He has a very good understanding . . . He shows himself a fond husband and kind father, two very good things.

At Streatham Mrs Elizabeth Howland was near enough to view the young couple's happiness with satisfaction, and could congratulate herself that the pains she had taken with her daughter's training ensured that her son-in-law's establishments would be run with a proper regard for economy while admitting no hint of parsimony. Elizabeth Bedford was, indeed, to leave behind her household accounts that rivalled in efficiency those kept by her capable mother.

Wriothesley was reputed to be the richest peer in England: the gossips put his income at £20,000 a year. The management of the estates by the late Duke had been well-conducted and enterprising, and there was no lack of money coming in from the widely spread properties. Wriothesley had character and good sense and he saw that the land on which Bedford House stood in the Strand was ripe for development. He already had a residence in Southampton House, and he was in possession of Woburn; in the future he might look forward to inheriting Stratton Park from his mother and the manor house at Streatham through his wife. He felt no sentiment about the old house that went back to the days of the first Earl, and which his grandfather had loved and would by no means consent to have pulled down. But the Strand was no longer the favourite residential street it had been since commerce had invaded it, and the gentry were moving to new quarters of the town.

About the time Bedford House was pulled down, the old tutor, Mr Thornton, died. He had moved from Woburn to take up his abode with Lady Russell in Southampton House, where he lived surrounded by his books and the portraits of the young people he had taught, most of whom had predeceased him.

The old Duke had been a Knight of the Garter; Kneller painted him in all the splendour of his robes, with velvet and lace and feathered hat, the Garter clasping his knee, the George hung round his shoulders. When he died in 1700 Rachel addressed a letter to King William asking what he wished her to do with her father-in-law's George. She knew full well that it was the rule to return it to the sovereign but, always working for the worldly welfare of her children, she allowed herself to suggest tentatively that as her son was now Duke of Bedford it might be his Majesty's wish that it should remain in the family. The King, who was in Holland, did not give her a straight answer, but he wrote a charming letter in his own hand.

A Loo, ce 23 Septembre 1700

J'ai été très mari d'apprendre la mort du Duc de Bedford, ayant eu autant d'estime que j'ai eu pour un homme de son mérite – Et puis que vous souhaitez, Madame, de savoir que quis vous faites avec son ordre, vous la pouvez la gardez jusques à mon retour en Angleterre. Et vous pouvez être assuré que j'aurai beaucoup de consideration pour le Duc, votre fils, et que je serai très aise de lui donner des marques de mon estime; et à toute la famille; et pour tout à vous, dont les belles et bonnes qualités me sont cognu ce qui me fait souhaiter d'avoir des occasions à vous donner des preuves de mon amitié.

William R.

When William died eighteen months later, no Garter had been bestowed on Rachel's son, but the King had not set her letter on one side and forgotten his obligations to the Russell family; he had duly made provision for the future. Six days after his death and before the obsequies had taken place, Queen Anne announced that the young Duke of Bedford was to be created Knight of the Garter.

Rachel Russell had indeed been latterly in King William's mind, for a letter from her was found in his pocket when he died. It expressed her deep gratitude for all his goodness to her family. She had heard, she wrote, that as one more instance of the King's favour, Lord Rutland was to be created a duke.

Thus she was assured that while one of her daughters was Duchess of Devonshire, the other would one day be Duchess of Rutland. At times an unsubdued worldliness took possession of this excellent and pious woman, who readily ignored consideration of heavenly rewards when the earthly prosperity of her children was in question: in a subordinate line she reminded the King of the virtues and deserts of her son. Although the second Duke in his short life never cut a figure in public affairs, he was no cipher, but a man of character, civilized and with opinions of his own, delighting in the privileges of his position and the opportunities afforded by his wealth. Becoming his own master at an early age, he was well able to gratify the light-hearted blossoming of his taste, which, in one direction at least, pursued a course unusual for a Russell. Sir Godfrey Kneller painted him three times. While still in the nursery he was depicted in a fancy Roman military costume to please his grandfather. Mrs Howland commissioned the same painter to portray the Tavistocks at the time of their marriage. He caught very well Wriothesley's air of alert intelligence and his aristocratic bearing. The stiffly posed girl at his side, whose hand is joined to his under a bunch of starry flowers, is notably still a child, flat of face and form, lacking even adolescent roundness. When Wriothesley sat for Kneller again he had matured; a few years of marriage had given him weight and authority. The setting of the picture is rural, and his unpowdered hair and plain velvet coat suggest the country gentleman, rather than the fine lord or courtier, though he combined all three characters in his modest person. As a countryman he practised a wide husbandry at Woburn. Being proud of his flower gardens and wishing to lure Hans Sloane to visit him, he wrote telling him that he had received a large consignment of *ranunculi* from Candia, such a one as he believed was never before seen in England. His liking for these showy turban flowers, cousins of the buttercup, was a taste that was to reappear in his great grandson, the sixth Duke, who, a hundred and twenty years later, wrote begging his son, then employed as envoy to Portugal, to send him a quantity of these plants to Woburn.

As the fine lord the Duke raced his horses at Newmarket, or went forth from the newly decorated rooms allotted to him in Southampton House, to drive about the town in a glass-fronted coach lined with white cloth, wearing a coat of flowered silk, his Duchess seated beside him with her hands concealed in a feather muff. His rank demanded that he should hold a post or two at Court, but preferring private life to the pursuit of power, he took no part in politics. When Dr Sacheverell was attempting to scare the country into believing that the Dissenters were dangerously in league with the Pope, and was tried for sedition, the Duke of Bedford acknowledged his allegiance to the Whigs and cast his vote against the fiery High Church cleric.

A disposition to like music has never been prominent in the Russell family; as individuals they have largely been tone deaf. The first Duke could recognize a tune known as the 'Woburn tune', which related to 'Four and twenty fiddlers all in a row, four and twenty trumpeters with a tan tara ra ra', and no doubt he could hum it and drum the rhythm with his fingers. Church bells rang for him when he entered a local town, but they rang to coax guineas from his pocket and not because it was known that the clangour would be musically pleasing to his ear. It was a convention that musicians played before him at New Year, and an entry in the accounts for the summer of 1689 records the payment of thirty shillings 'for musicians and trumpeters at the Abbey'. They came perhaps to celebrate with a fanfare a special occasion – the visit of a daughter or a son – or to pipe and fiddle for a dance, but there is no indication here that the Duke had that love of music that became apparent in his grandson. Wriothesley's musical taste was doubtless born during his sojourn in Rome, where he acquired a liking for all things Italian, and began to make his first purchases of music scores. Soon after his succession he took an unusual step, one that makes him unlike other Russells: he attached two musicians to his household – Nicola Cosimi and Nicola Francesco Haym. They were paid one hundred guineas a year each for their services, and were known to the Duke's servants simply as the 'Eytalians'. Their prime function was to be at hand to make music for the young nobleman, though they undertook various other duties; and he was so dependent on the pleasure he had from their performance that when he travelled they went where he did. A reluctant servant would take charge of the helpless foreigners on these journeys, pay their bills at the inns where a halt was made, and see that they reached their destination with the minimum of expense, whether it were Bath, Badminton, or Belvoir Castle. Haym, who played the violoncello, was the more interesting of the two Italians. He became known as a composer of some merit, and he did his best to make Italian opera popular in England. As an industrious adapter of the music of others he put his name to many compositions, not all of which were his own. Handel was indebted to him for the libretti of half a dozen of his operas.

The Duke, with Haym's help, amassed a collection of prints and engravings, and the musician was once sent to Rome in search of music scores. It was due to Wriothesley's taste and discernment that many fine illustrated books relating to the history of art and architecture, typical of the current fashion, took their place on the Woburn shelves. The political pamphlets and religious publications that were also acquired were of a Whiggish and a Protestant bias, and represent a dutiful recognition of the proper character to be maintained in the library of a Duke of Bedford. Among the very fine books bought by the second Duke is a copy of the *Thesaurus numismatum Romanorum*, which had appeared in 1605. The calf binding is emblazoned, not with the arms of the Duke of Bedford, but with those of Henry, Prince of Wales, the elder brother of Charles I, and it may well have been once in the library of Prince Henry. It seems legitimate to detect the influence of Nicola Haym in the acquisition of this royal volume describing Roman coins, for he was an authority on medals and later published a book about them. A clever, versatile man, he became at the end of his life a collector of pictures. In the Duke of Bedford's service he had opportunities to cultivate his taste and enlarge his knowledge of the art of painting.

Although his preference was for the new, fashionable Italian music, the second Duke did not entirely neglect the compositions of his own countrymen; he extended his patronage to John Weldon, a scholar of Eton College, who had been Purcell's pupil. *The Judgement of Paris*, Weldon's prize-winning opera, was given a special performance for the Duke in Lincoln's Inn Theatre.

There was another Englishman with musical pretensions – Dr James Sherard – who came to the notice of the Duke. Better known as a botanist and horticulturalist than as a musician, he was called in to make alterations to the park and gardens at Woburn. It is tempting to think of the two men – the Duke and the Doctor – viewing together the area of proposed improvement, and passing in conversation from the consideration of felled trees and new gravelled walks to discussion of music, the grave gardener confessing to the passion of his leisure hours. There is still at Woburn, in the original leather binding, the parts for a sonata for three instruments, composed by Sherard. Since Wriothesley was dead by the time this work was finished, the doctor dedicated it to his patron's infant son, the third Duke.

There can only be speculation as to what the second Duke might have achieved had his life been prolonged; what further enrichment of the collections he contemplated, and in what directions his patronage would have been extended. Handel arrived in England in 1710, and produced *Rinaldo* in February 1711. What more likely than the presence of the Duke and Duchess at the theatre in the Haymarket for the first performance? How glorious for the Russells had Handel enjoyed the patronage of Bedford rather than of Burlington!

The village of Streatham had always been peculiarly susceptible to outbreaks of smallpox; reason enough for Rachel Russell to view with apprehension the frequent visits paid by her son and his growing family to Mrs Howland at the manor house, but the young Duchess was fond of her old home: some of her children had been born there, and it was conveniently near London. Lady Russell, quoting Dr Hans Sloane (a tenant in Great Russell Street), who had warned her of the danger of incurring infection at Streatham, cautioned in vain. In the spring of 1711 Wriothesley, accompanied by his family and numerous servants, went to stay with his mother-in-law. He was as strict in the business of payment for board as Mrs Howland had been herself when visiting the old Duke at Woburn. For a visit lasting thirteen weeks in the previous year Wriothesley had paid her £250 10s. 0d. 'diet and washing for his Grace, his Duchess, three children and 22 servants'. There was included the stabling and food for eleven horses.

A few weeks after their arrival Wriothesley fell ill with symptoms of the dreaded smallpox. Dr Sloane and another doctor were appealed to and came down from London, but their remedies were of no avail, they could not save the Duke.

Once again Rachel's heart was nearly broken. Her old friend Bishop Burnet, who had comforted her when she was widowed, and had recognized then the depth of her despair, now endeavoured to sustain her with wise, affectionate words. 'For God's sake', he wrote from Salisbury, 'do not abandon yourself once more into a deep inconsolable melancholy: rouse up the spirit God has given you.' She had need to rouse up her spirit, for her cup of sorrow was not yet full. Before the end of the year the Duchess of Rutland died in childbed while Rachel held her in her arms. Having seen that daughter laid in her coffin, the stricken but valiant woman went on to visit the other, also presently awaiting the birth of a child and in no condition to be alarmed. Assuming a cheerful air and trying to be truthful, she reassured the Duchess of Devonshire, saying 'I have seen your sister out of bed today.'

Rachel Russell was not released from a life she would gladly have relinquished forty years earlier until her eighty-seventh year. Charles I was on the throne when she was born, and the House of Hanover had reigned for ten years when she died.

8

❧❧❧❧❧

Dicing and Drinking

THERE is at Woburn a very large picture painted in 1712 by Charles Jervas, of Elizabeth, Duchess of Bedford and her four orphaned children; an oval portrait of the late Duke may be seen hanging on the wall above the grouped figures. The widow wears a black, shrouding garb that is identical in style with the habit that had clothed her mother-in-law Rachel for so long. Her dejected pose – head resting on her hand – is one that was to be adopted by Queen Victoria, when photographed in similar circumstances. The mourning worn by the two daughters Rachel and Elizabeth, and the boys, Wriothesley and John, is less profound – their grey or white dresses being merely banded or striped with black. Wriothesley, the infant third Duke, stands at his mother's knee, her hand clasped in his. Although he was five years old, his dress is exaggeratedly feminine – more than was usual for a male child, even at a time when the breeching of boys was late. Could it be that he was wearing his sister's outgrown clothes? Long skirts fashioned with a bustle trail on the ground, and his pretty face is framed in light curls – an early promise of good looks that later was not to be confirmed. When he grew up he could lay no claim to being handsome; his prominent eyes were noticeably dissimilar – a personal misfortune that may have accounted for his reluctance to have his portrait painted. Isaac Whood caught him unawares and sketched him in profile in his dressing-gown while he was reading a book, which he held close to his face in the manner of those who suffer from poor sight. Subject to some constitutional weakness which forbade expectation of a long life, he suffered from an instability of character that nullified his innate good sense, and prevented his rational enjoyment of those advantages that he had been born with – rank and wealth. Tied in boyhood to a powerful, capable and possessive mother, her death from smallpox after thirteen years of widowhood left him without a rudder at the age of sixteen. Since both grandmothers, Lady Russell and Mrs Howland, were

86

William, Lord Russell by Riley

Rachel, Lady Russell by Lely

Rev John Thornton by an
unknown painter

Wriothesley, second Duke of
Bedford and his wife Elizabeth
Howland by Kneller

by this time dead, trustees put Wriothesley and his brother, and his un-married sister, in the care of a French tutor to live in the house at Streatham where they had been brought up. The eldest girl was already married to Scroop, Duke of Bridgewater, a boorish widower with an only daughter, Lady Anne Egerton. Anne's mother had been a daughter of the great Duke of Marlborough and his formidable wife Sarah.

In the winter of 1717 the widowed Duchess of Bedford had put forward to the Duchess of Marlborough a proposal for the marriage of one of her daughters with the heir presumptive to the Marlborough dukedom – Sarah's grandson. The two ladies met in London and talked it over; the Duchess of Marlborough then retired to consult her husband and to con-coct her reply. On February 20, she wrote:

Madam,

Since I had the honour of seeing your Grace in town I have as I promised, consulted the Duke of Marlborough, as far as the state of his health would give leave, upon the affair which was the subject of our late conversation, and I must now acquaint your Grace, that he thinks he cannot in prudence consent to what is proposed, considering all the circumstances which ought to be considered. My Lord Ryalton shews of himself no inclination at present towards marriage; he is very sober, very well disposed, and as likely to continue so as any young man in the world, so that it is not judged necessary to hasten such an affair, or to engage him to think of what he does not think of . . . Madam, believe me there is no family in this island whose alliance I, for my part, would more seek after, by inclination, and particular respect, than your Grace's, and I cannot but hope that a time may come, when there may be a more favourable concurrence of circumstances to the satisfaction of both familys at once, without trusting to future uncertainties. My Lord Ryalton's age will not be too disproportionable to the younger of your two ladies, and when it shall be proper to think of such a pro-posal I can not but hope that it may be not improper nor imprudent, for another affair to be settled at the same time, to the mutual satisfaction of both familys . . .

The Duchess of Bedford's letter accepting the postponement of her hopes for a splendid match and agreeing that the Marlboroughs must know best, lay for many years in the muniment room at Blenheim endorsed by

Sarah: 'I said that I would endeavour to compass it upon condition that they liked one another and that she should engage to make the settlement so as that the Duke of Bedford should marry one of my grandchildren without a portion as the Duke of Marlborough would take her daughter or oblige him to pay forty or fifty thousand.'

In an age when marriages were too often contracted without regard for the wishes of the persons principally involved, and young people were used like pawns in a complex struggle for aggrandizement of family or fortune, it is pleasing to find the Duchess of Marlborough – herself the subject of a passionate love match – decreeing that the young people must have some liking for each other before any engagement could take place. Lord Ryalton did not in the event take one of the Russell girls for his wife, and his grandmother's complacent estimate of his character was sadly mistaken, for when he grew up and became Marquess of Blandford he was rarely sober, and his disposition was such that it procured him in his family the title of 'Lord Worthless'. He died when he was no more than thirty, having married the daughter of a Dutch burgomaster. When Sarah heard of his death, she said: 'I hope the devil is picking that man's bones that taught him to drink.'

Although nothing came of the Duchess of Bedford's scheme for marrying her daughter to the Marlborough heir, in due course the Duchess of Marlborough found herself in a position to dictate to two successive Duchesses of Bedford – she being grandmother to both.

Anne Egerton, after the death of her mother, went to live with the Duchess of Marlborough, and was brought up by her with care and affection. The grandmother designed to marry her to the Duke of Chandos, but her plan was overthrown by the Duke of Bridgewater, who abducted his daughter from Marlborough House with the intention of marrying her to his second wife's brother, the Duke of Bedford, who was not yet seventeen. That the young man liked Anne and wished to be married there can be no doubt, and he made it clear in his letters to his betrothed's grandmother that he liked her as well. Too young still to be his own master, he regarded her (now reconciled to her defeat by Bridgewater) as an ally against his grasping, disagreeable future father-in-law. Sarah, for her part, was prepared to see nothing but good in the youth who confided in her with such charming freedom before his marriage. He wrote to her from Streatham on April 12, 1725:

The sincere Respect and esteem I have for your Grace would not have permitted me to have been so long near town without waiting upon you, had not my living with ye Duke of Bridgwater unfortunately prevented it. His Grace's treatment of me as well as of his daughter convinces me more and more that it is impossible to live with him with any tolerable degree of Satisfaction to either of us. Your Grace who are so well acquainted with his temper may easily imagine Abundance of Reasons which make us desirous to be away from him as soon as we can. We are therefore determined the first minute after we are married to go away to Wouburn, but to keep it from his Grace till we are gone, by Reason the violence of his passion, if he should come to know it, would not let Lady Anne have a moment's Ease.

They were married a week later, and before the month was out the Duchess of Marlborough, kind and full of good intentions, but overpoweringly curious, paid a visit to Woburn. Her arrival may have been untimely, and her reception have fallen short of what she considered her due – she was not one to check her irritation or contain her remarks when displeased – for the Duke found it necessary to apologize for the shortcomings she had noticed in his house and begged her to 'excuse all faults you met with at Woburn considering nothing is yet settled there as it ought to have been for your Grace'. Nevertheless he felt himself to be in favour with her and, confident that she liked to receive his letters, their correspondence proceeded amicably. When Sarah enclosed verses in a letter, he sent her some on the same theme, knowing that she would enjoy any jibe at the expense of Sir Robert Walpole:

Quoth King Robin the Ribbons I see are too few,
There's St Andrew ye Green and St George of the Blew,
I must find out a Red one, a Colour more gay,
Which will tye up my subjects with Pride to obey.
Th'Exchequer may suffer by prodigal Donors
The King ne'r exhausted that Fountain of Honours,
Men of more Wit than Money our Pensions will fit,
But these will bribe those of more money than Wit,
Who with Faith most implicit obey my commands,
Tho' as empty as Y . . . . g and as saucy as S . . . .ds.[1]
Who will soonest leap over a stick for the King
Shall be qualified best for a Dog on a String.

[1]Young and Sandys

The Duchess was as anxious to hear of his quarrels with Bridgwater as he was to recount them. There was a typical dispute about jewels – a common source of conflict, when they were regarded as so much capital, rather than mere ornaments – the Duke of Bridgewater ordering his daughter to return hers to him, 'though she has as much right to ye jewels as I have to ye pen I am writing with', declared the indignant husband. 'The jewels he sent for were ye same that were made of buckles, which were ye late Countess of Bridgwaters, your Grace's daughter. Their value under £200 which makes his Grace's action rather ye meaner.' In a letter of seventeen quarto pages the Duchess of Marlborough congratulated him on having 'very good sense and principles', and informed him that 'nobody on earth ever govern'd me, nor ever shall . . . I believe your dear Grace is of the same temper and I like you much better for it.' It was all very flattering for the young man, and, encouraged by her esteem and outraged by the rough behaviour of his father-in-law, he wrote again: 'His Grace's conduct to me is amazingly rude and shocking. I have received ye rudest letter from his Grace that I believe ever was writ to ye civilest I could possibly invent . . . His Grace was pleased to add that your Grace ordered me to be rude to him, as if I did as I was bid.' He begged her 'not to make so many excuses for ye length of your letters, I assure your Grace the longer they are the greater pleasure they afford me.' Perhaps he meant it, he was in need of distractions.

The Duchess of Marlborough had a great admiration for Southampton House, which had been unused for some years. It was her wish to see the young couple living there, and although she found they were more interested in Woburn, she undertook to renovate the house in Bloomsbury for them; she enjoyed exercising her own practical good taste. They dutifully thanked her, helpless before the hurricane of her decisions. They listened to her discoursing on the beauty of the mansion, agreed with her choice of paint and furnishings, and attended to her requests for the measurements of this and that. The Duke was a little nervous at the scope of her arrangements, and wrote tentatively of 'a doubt whether the plain black and silver Cabinet at Streatham belongs to me or my brother. I desire you will enquire whether it is mention'd in my mother's Will before you order it to be remov'd to Southampton House.'

At the end of May the young Duchess submissively sent her grandmother the 'measures of the Bed which is 7 feet 2 inches long and five feet 8 inches wide, it stands fourteen feet high'. The Duchess of Marlborough was interested in beds and had opinions on how large they should be to accommodate a husband and wife; she wished now to refurbish the matrimonial one in a suitably magnificent style. Were her eyes still closed to the predicament of the grandchild she had lovingly brought up? Did she allow herself to detect a note of boredom in Wriothesley's letter from Woburn Abbey in June, telling of the visit of some country neighbours? 'They went to bowls after dinner and then drunk their bottle till they thought proper to go away . . . I do not doubt that the news from London is more diverting.'

By August it was becoming known that the marriage of the Duke and Duchess of Bedford was no marriage at all. Lady Mary Wortley Montagu, writing to a friend, spread the news:

I am in hopes your King of France behaves better than our Duke of Bedford; who by the care of a pious mother, certainly preserved his virginity to his marriage-bed, where he was so much disappointed in his fair bride, who, (though his own inclination) could not bestow on him those expressless raptures he had figured to himself, that he already pukes at the very name of her, and determines to let his estate go to his brother rather than go through the filthy drudgery of getting an heir to it . . . This comes of living till sixteen without a competent knowledge either of practical or speculative anatomy, and literally thinking fine ladies composed of lilies and roses.

It was a tragic situation. The dissatisfied and bored youth looked about for distractions. At Toddington, not far from the Abbey, lived the Earl of Strafford, a man Wriothesley liked and respected, and who might, he hoped, relieve him of his ennui. He took up his pen and wrote to him on 20 July, 1725:

I am now at Woburn where I shall be proud of ye honour of your Lordship's company as soon as it suits you with your conveniency. I beg you will bring Mr Pope with you, or in case he should have left you by this time that you would be so kind as to desire him to meet you here. For I have an earnest desire to be personally acquainted with that gentleman whose works I have so long admired.

Unhappily Alexander Pope had been detained at Twickenham by urgent personal affairs, and was not at the moment in Bedfordshire. He was working himself into a passion over a proposed alteration in the parish church, where Lady Kneller wished to remove the tablet put up by Pope to the memory of his parents, in order to replace it with a monument to herself and her late husband Sir Godfrey. 'That pious widow', fulminated the poet, addressing Lord Strafford, who, well endowed with estates, was Pope's neighbour in Middlesex,

> desires their leave to pull down ye tablet I set up at ye head of your Lordship's pew, to fix there a large one to Sir G. and herself with both their figures. If your Lordship should really chance to take no great pleasure in beholding my name full before your eyes (which I should not wonder at) yet at least (dangerous as that name is, and dreadful to all Protestant ears) it cannot incommode you so much as a vast three hundred pound pile projecting out upon you, overshadowing my Lady Strafford with ye immense draperies and stone petticoats of Lady Kneller, and perhaps crushing to pieces your Lordships posterity.

The Duke of Bedford was disappointed to have no meeting with the poet.

> I am sorry ye circumstances of Mr Pope's affairs will not permit him to come to see me this summer. Your Lordship will be so kind as to assure him that whenever he does me that favour nobody shall be more welcome . . . I do not know anything he has published that I have not got. I am a subscriber already for his translation of Homer's Odyssey. If there be anything else that he is going to publish I shall be very glad to be a subscriber to it.

Pope's translation of the *Odyssey* with handsome title page and end pieces designed by William Kent is on the shelves at Woburn today.

Deprived of the literary company he so longed to receive and felt himself equipped to entertain, Wriothesley sought other diversions – more exciting and more perilous. In two letters to Sarah Marlborough he wrote of 'ye Tranquility of ye Mind', but he was alluding philosophically to a serenity that neither, at that moment, can have been enjoying, for he had announced his intention of going to 'ye Bath', and Sarah, alerted to the dangers inherent in his discontented mood, had voiced her disapproval. 'My journey there shall be very short,' he promised, 'because I see your Grace dislikes it. I am sorry I am engag'd for the present, but will be never more so without asking your leave.'

He had, he told her, engaged himself to meet several of his friends there, 'who are by no means what your Grace calls swordsmen', and he assured her that he did not mean to gamble at the Spa. 'As to ye others if I lose money to them either there or anywhere else, I will venture to forfeit all the esteem and kindness your Grace has ever had for me. I take very kindly whatever you say upon the subject, tho' I am sure your Grace is much mistaken if ever you think I shall hurt myself by gaming which I have ye utmost aversion and detestation to.' From Bath, he wrote in October: 'I have kept my resolution that I have neither won nor lost anything considerable and that I am determined not to venture the loss of so much here as will make me in any degree uneasy. There is mighty deep play here.' He had, alas, already fallen into evil company; his addiction to gaming was firmly established and his losses were to become notorious. In an attempt to improve the Duke's relations with his wife, the Duchess of Marlborough called on Lord Strafford to approach the young man, and he wrote hopefully the following spring:

I have just now seen the Duke of Bedford who designs himself the honour of waiting on you at seven this evening. I hope your Grace will remember not to press him to expostulations, which is what I doubt would be very disagreeable to him. I hope this will produce a thorough reconciliation which will be a great satisfaction to me as your Grace has been pleased to make me the instrument.

But Wriothesley's assurances were unreliable, and while seeming to comply he was obstinate. It is impossible to know the state of his mind at this time, but there can be no doubt of the misery and confusion of his wife's. In 1726 Anne took a desperate step and left him, but unsure of herself and of the wisdom of such a reckless move, she was persuaded by her grandmother and her friends to return to Woburn. From Cassiobury, the home of Wriothesley's sister Lady Essex, she wrote a few contrite lines to the Duchess of Marlborough announcing her decision to go back to her husband, and in return got a characteristically trenchant reply.

Nov. 8, 1726

I have received your letter of yesterday, in which you say it was your misfortune to have had some Difference with me, tho' much against your inclinations. That is an Expression which I can't in the least comprehend: For you know, that for many years I us'd you with as much kindness & tenderness, as if you had been my own Child: And what you call Differences so much against your Inclinations, was only my giving you good advice, for saving you from such Misfortunes, which anybody might see would happen to you. That I labour'd to prevent . . . And when no Reason nor kind Expressions could prevail in anything, I said I fear'd you wouldn't care to come to see me, because I must tell you every thing that I heard that could hurt you: Upon which you answer'd that you didn't know if you would come to see me or not, and since that time, I have never seen you or heard from you. Most people if they had not follow'd advice would at least have taken it kindly, and have been civil. And I could say a great deal more upon this head: But at this time I will not add to your Trouble by repeating things past. Nor should I say so much, but in my own Vindication: Because you say the Differences you had with me were against your Inclinations. But when you reflect you must know that what I write is the Truth & that I have always been a very kind Parent. The Duke of Devonshire, who is the most reasonable & worthy man that I now know in the World & to whom you are infinitely obliged for the Trouble he has taken, has told me all that has happen'd in this Affair, which I was very sorry to hear: And I was as much surpriz'd to find that you had so great a Difficulty in acknowledging that you had been in the wrong, which every body must think you, to go to any place that the Duke of Bedford desir'd you not to: And I think tho' it were not to a Husband, when one has made any Mistakes, it is a Satisfaction to one's self to own them: And to have the least Scruple to say to him what he desir'd, in order to save yourself from Ruin, is to me an incomprehensible thing. I will acknowledge it to you now, tho' I never did before, that I have thought him extremely in the wrong. But you know I have told you, without entering into Particulars, that few people were at one time so happy in all things, as I wish'd you: That the Duke of Bedford was very young, & had a great foundation of Sense, & that time would mend every thing, if you took care not to displease him. And I still think that if you can't make yourself easy at home, you can never have any great happiness abroad. I hope the Duke of Devonshire's endeavours to make you happy, will not be fruitless: But if they should you have nothing in the world to do, to save you from utter Ruin, but to throw yourself at your Father's Feet, who, no doubt, will be mov'd to give you his Protection; since you never disobliged him in anything till he dispos'd of you. But to live well with the Duke of Bedford is the best thing that any body can advise, & in any way that he shall insist on. You can't do too much to compass that, for your future Quiet. I do assure you that you may end your Life as happily, as I did when I was very fond of you, & thought I had a great deal of reason to be

Your affectionate Grand-mother

S. Marlborough

Five years were to elapse before Anne was released from the bonds of marriage, but during these years she was not without compassion for her husband as his character and health deteriorated. While the estranged couple lived principally at Woburn – and it may have been first choice because it was easier to live apart in that great house – Wriothesley was interested for a year or two in another property that hitherto had not been greatly regarded but as a source of supply for the kitchens at Woburn. From Thorney in the fens, fish and marsh fowl, cattle and corn had been sent across country by waterways and wagon since the days of the fifth Earl, who had built a house there in 1660 on the site of the ancient abbey, to serve his agent and bailiff. In this house Wriothesley spent many weeks at a time. His fancy for Thorney is inscrutable, but there is some evidence that he thought of making it his chief residence. Furniture was put into the house, the gardens were planted with fruit trees, and he gave lavish entertainments for his tenants. Bills survive to show that in the summer of 1728 twelve gallons of arrack and six gallons of brandy were ordered to be delivered there. Perhaps this place, remote from Woburn and London, served as a refuge from the temptations he was not strong enough to resist, and allowed him to forget the practical affairs that should have had his attention elsewhere. Woburn Abbey was showing signs of dilapidation and cracks had appeared in the fabric. Advised to rebuild, the young man lacked the directing force for such an operation, and he gave his opinion that the building would last his lifetime. He preferred to avert his eyes from the decay, and to contemplate from a small and well built house the strange landscape of the fens, where his eyes could wander over marsh and dyke and corn land, and travel to the horizon without the distraction of any change in the level. Seated in the pleasure boat he had ordered for his use, he could pass along the waterways trailing his hand among the floating weeds, or helping to pull in the light fishing-nets. Here for a time he was able to forget the unsatisfactory course of his life.

While he was living at Woburn with his wife, visitors helped to ease an awkward situation, and Anne wrote to her brother-in-law, Lord John Russell, who was in Paris with his tutor, that she welcomed them even if they sometimes fell asleep at backgammon before it was time to go to bed. 'All wish you was here to put new life into us.' The future fourth Duke was already well liked for his merry good-humour.

When Wriothesley could no longer keep away from the gaming houses of London, or it was deemed necessary to appear at Court, the mansion in Bloomsbury was made use of; an evening at St James's Palace – the Queen's Birthday – was well described by Mrs Delany: 'as the clock struck twelve . . . every man took the woman he liked best to dance country dances. The Prince set the example by choosing the Duchess of Bedford, who is the Queen of his fancy just now.' Such an evening at the Palace could be dismissed cynically by Lord Hervey as 'Dice, Dancing, crowding, sweating, stinking in abundance', but the Duchess and her young admirer must have made a handsome pair, for the Prince of Wales was dressed in 'mouse-coloured velvet turned up with scarlet and richly embroidered with silver'.

It was observed by another contemporary that 'The Duchess of Bedford is to put herself at the head of the Jacobite party, as one of the conditions of living with her Lord'; an indication that the third Duke lacked the Whiggish convictions of his family, perhaps due to his friendship for Lord Strafford – a Jacobite – or simply because he wanted to be different to his forebears. When Pope wrote the line:

And mighty Dukes pack cards for half a crown

Wriothesley's obsession with gambling had become the talk of the town. Endowed with a fund of good sense, his weakness and self-indulgence blinded him to the character of the men with whom he played all night. A member of his household expressed the fears of those nearest to him: 'I cannot say but I am always in expectation of some terrible blow, for he is now engaged with the Groom porters where all the sharpers in town meet, and he never suspects he is cheated by any body.' His fortune was being dissipated by his enormous losses, and his estates were in jeopardy when money had to be raised to pay his debts.

For the time being the Duchess of Marlborough ceased giving advice and washed her hands of so unsatisfactory a pair. Her thoughts were turned in another and more promising direction. Of all her grand-daughters the one nearest her heart was Diana Spencer, the daughter of Anne Churchill and the Earl of Sunderland. Like Anne Egerton, Diana had lost her mother while she was a child, and she had been brought up by the Duchess of Marlborough. Younger and more tractable than Anne, Diana was the object of her grandmother's passionate affection. When she was old enough to be married the Duchess sought a suitable husband for the precious girl, and she aimed high. Horace Walpole recounts maliciously that she offered Diana with a fortune of a hundred thousand pounds to Frederick, Prince of Wales – that he accepted the proposal and a day was fixed for them to be secretly married, but Sir Robert Walpole hearing of the plot prevented it, 'and the secret was buried in silence'. The Duchess had, perforce, to look elsewhere. It was conspicuous that Anne Bedford had been married for six years and had not borne a child; Wriothesley's heir presumptive was his brother Lord John Russell, and since the Duke was rapidly ruining his health by drinking, and keeping late hours in close rooms, it was more than likely that his brother would, before long, succeed to the dukedom. Sarah Marlborough's choice fell on this young man, who had not yet returned to England from the Grand Tour he had been enjoying with his tutor. He was, she thought, 'much the greatest match in England', and she said so to the Duke of Bedford. He was perhaps a little nettled by her frankness, detecting her doubt of his own prolonged life, for while he thanked her for the great honour she did his brother, and agreed that 'Lady Dye' was possessed of every good quality, he slipped in an astute comment on a salient feature of his brother's character – obstinacy. 'I am sorry to say there is a certain suspiciousness in his temper that makes it difficult for his best friends to persuade him to what is most to his advantage.' Lord John had already shown a liking for Lady Fanny Shirley, a girl much older than himself, but the Duchess brushed aside such foolish calf-love and, to her infinite satisfaction, John Russell and Diana Spencer were married in October 1731. Henceforward she was to pour out in letters to Diana a vivid account of her own activities, her thoughts, her quarrels, and her tender concern for the well-being of the beloved grandchild – a solicitude that was not unmixed with criticism, jealousy, self-pity, vindication of her own behaviour, and lavish abuse of her numerous other grandchildren – letters that reveal the lively mind and passionately egotistical character of a woman who was her own worst enemy.

Living happily at Cheam in a house bequeathed to Lord John by the late Rector of St Paul's, Covent Garden, Diana described to her grand-mother the charm of her new home, where there was a large room full of books but 'scarce any furniture but beds'. They were employed, she wrote, in putting the books in order and making a catalogue of them, and for air and exercise they walked and drove on Banstead Downs. Far removed from this happy domestic scene, the card-sharpers were speedily destroying the Duke of Bedford. During a visit to Woburn soon after her marriage, Diana wrote with shocked concern of Wriothesley's latest gambling excesses, describing a scene that might well have been depicted by Hogarth.

We came here to dinner and found the Duke of Bedford in much better humour than I expected, for I suppose you have heard of his Loss, which till you have it confirm'd I fancy you will scarce give credit to it, but it is most certain that he has lost thirty thousand pounds at Newmarket at one sitting, from ten o'clock on Saturday night till eight on Sunday night; there was only Janssen and Bladen that play'd with him, and as there might be no time lost Mr Menill kept the scores on both sides, so you will rather wonder I believe that he did not lose his whole estate. He was quite drunk when they first began, and one would think he continu'd so for the whole two and twenty hours, for 'tis incredible that a man in his senses would suffer such a villain as Menill is known to be to keep the Account of so vast a sum of money without once asking any questions about it, till he rose from the table. These four were locked up in a room together and had candles and the Shutters shut all Sunday, because they were afraid (being very scrupulous people) of giving offence by being seen to play on Sunday. The Duke of Bedford has not once named it to anybody here and seems afraid to hear so much as the name of Newmarket.

The sequel to these events was the principal matter in her subsequent letters.

The Duke does not even imagine that he did lose it unfairly but says he believes them to be all very honest and Sir Humphrey Moneux trys all he can to keep his Grace in that opinion which makes me suspect that he is a sort of under officer to that gang of villains. He said one thing that provok'd me vastly, that he thought it extremely good natur'd in Menill to sit up two and twenty hours only to take the trouble of scoring when he had no share in the gains . . . all that Sir H. says the Duke takes for gospel, at least he pretends to do so for there is no knowing what he really thinks.

What others thought of his gaming associates is clear. The Duchess of Marlborough, long afterwards, wrote of Sir Humphrey Moneux as a Jacobite and a scandalous man 'who picked the late Duke of Bedford's pocket and was a confederate in all the mischief that happen'd to him'. Twenty years later Horace Walpole knew of Janssen as a 'celebrated gamester who cheated the late Duke of Bedford of an immense sum'. Alexander Pope, too, had known where the Duke was to be found most days when he wrote the line

Or when a Duke to Jansen punts at Whites.

An attempt was made to keep Wriothesley away from London and the temptations of White's Chocolate House – an establishment of such ill-repute that a certain Lord, according to Swift, never passed the building 'without bestowing a curse upon that infamous academy, the bane of half the English nobility'. But the Duchess of Bedford wrote sadly from Woburn in the winter to tell her grandmother of the small success she had had in managing her husband.

I am afraid our reason for staying here will not turn to much account; for tho' here there is no Hazard, he will always have people to play at Whist, who will win enough, I am afraid too much, before he will leave off, but there is no remedy for this for he has used himself so long to it that he now knows no other way to divert himself, what is a melancholy thing to think of, when one considers how little use his good sense is to him, 'tis pity he can't give some of his sense to so many who want it, since he won't make use of it himself.

In the eighteenth century a voyage to Portugal was a prescribed cure for shattered health, and many an English man or woman tried the desperate remedy, but unable to support the rough sea passage and the damp, debilitating climate, left their bones in the Protestant cemetery at Lisbon. Such a journey was now proposed to the Duke of Bedford as a means of regaining his health. He himself regarded the scheme as a way to save money, but the Duchess of Marlborough judged that if he allowed himself, as he estimated, twelve thousand pounds for his expenses, it would hardly be an economy. Tormenting his wife with his tyrannical vagaries and irresponsible behaviour (she complained of being left without horses, and of her coach having broken glasses which let in the rain) his decision to take her to Lisbon with him roused the family in determined opposition to his plan when it was realized that the prospect of the sea voyage terrified the wretched girl, who was having trembling fits and whose constitution was 'extremely worn'. Letters flew between the two cousins and their grandmother; Anne begging to be allowed to live with the Duchess of Marlborough if she were not forced out of England by her husband; Diana writing indignantly of the Duke's barbarous behaviour. Their grandmother showed unusual kindness and consideration.

> I have always persuaded her to submit to everything in the world, and to live in any manner that her Lord would have her in his own house ... She has taken my advice, and I know of no instance of any woman who has so much gentleness in their nature, as to submit to everything, as she has done under such terrible usage ... And as the Duke has always lived with her he can't possibly have any pleasure in taking her with him.
>
> The Duke made me a visit since he came to town and told me what he designed. To which I made no reply ... and am very clear in my own opinion that she should not hazard her life to go with so great a brute.

A great portrait of Sarah Marlborough by Kneller, that once hung in Southampton House and now hangs at Woburn, shows her in a regal and commanding pose. Although equitable dealings with her friends and relations were never among the most conspicuous of her actions she seems in this painting to personify some graceful but severe figure of Justice, about to dispense from her elevated seat impartial praise or censure. In her awkward interview with the Duke of Bedford, when she for once held her tongue, we may speculate whether, in the presence of this great and intimidating woman, he was disconcerted by the silence which met his formal statement, or if his latent good sense allowed him to acknowledge and accept the reproof; while the Duchess herself, during that brief meeting, may have been moved to pity by the emaciated condition of the ailing young man, and have been prompted to remember the good relations that had once existed between them, for a few weeks later, when Wriothesley had consented to let his wife remain in England, she paused on her way to Scarborough and dined with him at Woburn Abbey. The account given to Diana of this visit shows that the Duchess of Marlborough, at least, enjoyed the occasion:

> . . . 'tis not possible for any man to behave better than the Duke of Bedford did in all respects. He spoke on every subject that offer'd with perfect good sense, was as civil as anybody can be without being troublesome and in the most obliging manner . . . If I had time and spirits I could tell you a thousand pretty things he said and there is nothing so amazing to me as to see a man that seems to have so much good sense and yet to have made a havoc of his constitution and of his estate. For I am told when he was last in town, he lost a great deal of money and added £6000 more to Mr Johnson's [Janssen's] debt . . .

His family, she added, thought him very ill, and so did she think he was worse, but he would not own that it was so.

> Yet I observ'd when we went into the gallery to see the pictures, he sat down very often, which I conclude proceeded from weakness. I made him as easy as I could in everything, for I find he cannot endure to be thought ill, and therefore did not take any notice that I saw it, but contriv'd to sit down very often as we talked over the pictures.

There is a rare gentleness in her consideration for the young man who, at some cost to himself, attended her patiently and listened to her comments on his pictures. A martyr to rheumatism and gout, the old lady was carried round the house in a chair with short poles, but she may have chosen to make use of her crutches in the gallery. She dismissed briefly the portraits as 'only valuable as they belong to the family and in antique dress', though she greatly admired Van Dyck's portrait of the Countess of Bedford: 'I mean her that the father forbid his son to marry. I really fear if I had been a man I should have disobeyed my father in such a case, for she was both beautiful and good.' Mindful that in all probability Diana, before very long, would be mistress at Woburn, she filled her letter with appraisal of the house, admiring the beauty of some ceilings, relating what she would do if Woburn were hers: 'I am sure I would never pull it down, but I would alter several things in it by degrees and make it a better house than any architect can build now.' Her contempt for all of that profession moved her to add: 'knowing of none that are not mad or ridiculous.'

She gave it as her opinion that if the Duke of Bedford escaped being sick at sea he would reach Lisbon alive, but he did not get so far. On 23 October 1732, he died on board his ship while it was in the harbour at Corunna. He was twenty-four years old.

From some letters that Anne Bedford wrote to her grandmother a few months after her husband's death, it appears that she had been in love with her cousin, John Spencer, during the Duke's lifetime, and now, released from her marriage bonds, proposed to marry him. The Duchess of Marlborough's fury that her favourite grandson should entangle himself with the young woman, upon whom she had wasted so much good advice, can only be imagined from the frantic tone of penitence in which the poor girl wrote seeking to excuse herself. That marriage did not take place, and eight months to the day after Wriothesley's death, Anne married the Earl of Jersey. She bore him children and he, it seems was devoted to her. A lady who called on the happy pair remarked that 'Lord Jersey sat the whole visit upon the arm of Lady Jersey's chair, and kissed her and hugged her all the time before the company'. The Duchess of Marlborough stated candidly that she was convinced he had a sincere passion for his wife's jointure; she was more sceptical about their happy future. 'My Lord Jersey . . . thinks himself a fine man for ladies and consequently will soon be very tired of her' – but Anne had never been a favourite grandchild.

Before the news of Wriothesley's death reached England, Diana had given birth to a son who lived one day. Lord Hervey heard a story that there was such concern to prevent her knowing that her child was dead 'that after grand consultation when old Aetna[1] was speaker, it was determined a Child should be brought to replace the Defunct, till she was strong enough to hear the truth and be told it was only a pretender'.

A miscarriage followed a few months after the loss of her son. Increasingly delicate of constitution, Diana was reproached for not taking more care of herself, when an heir was so much desired. Her grandmother urged her not to drive a chaise: 'because I know the reaching out of your arm to whip the horse is a very improper motion at this time'; she had

[1]The Duchess of Marlborough

Elizabeth Howland, widow of the second Duke of Bedford and her children by C. Jervas

Anne Egerton, Duchess of Bedford by C. Jervas

herself, she said, miscarried of a son: 'from follies I committed when I was very young'. In the summer of 1735 Diana believed herself to be again with child, but her symptoms were ominous rather than auspicious, and instead of waxing big she got thinner and her strength waned; several doctors prescribed remedies, and her grandmother sent her the Duke of Marlborough's 'Turkish Tent', to be put up in the garden at Woburn so that she might lie in the air. It was the tent the great Duke had used upon his campaigns, and there were furnishings to go with it. 'There is a carpet with it to put upon a table and a great carpet to lie on the ground. . . . Some of the chairs the rats have made holes in, and as I remember are whimsical odd things; but you will put in what you like.' The Duchess of Marlborough at this time found a new pet name for her granddaughter and used it tenderly – Cordelia, 'which I think is the name of King Lear's good child and therefore a proper title for you, who have always been good to me'. Her apprehension that she was going to lose the person that she loved best in the world must have lain like a stone on her heart. While unable to suppress her anxiety for Diana's condition she tried to be comforting and reassuring, and from wherever she was she wrote all that passed through her head, recounting with her usual verbal felicity the gossip of the day, and the wounding slights she had received from her grandsons. In August her uneasiness mastered her discretion and she begged that Diana might be brought to London from Woburn. When this was done it was recognized that the Duchess of Bedford's illness, hitherto thought to be a natural one, was a galloping consumption, and a month later she died at Bedford House aged twenty-six.

It would have been surprising if the Duchess of Marlborough, in her profound distress, had shown self-control or compassion for anyone but herself. Plaguing the unfortunate widower with her demands, she created a situation of ill-feeling and family dissension. The news reached as far as Swift in Dublin that the Duke of Bedford had offered to supply the Duke of Marlborough with ten thousand pounds a year 'if he would go to law and torment the old dowager', who had managed to put herself on bad terms with both of the young men.

Eighteen months after Diana's death the Duchess of Marlborough wrote the Duke of Bedford a letter of finely calculated abuse; it revealed a long-pent-up store of resentment and dislike – probably founded on jealousy – of the man who had been her 'dear Angel's' husband. She wished to quarrel and her complaints were various, and one grievance was that after his wife's death he had delayed returning the Turkish tent to her; that he had kept her portrait by Kneller, and that he had been slow sending back the jewels she had given Diana on her marriage, contriving to withhold as well an object of small value that was a legacy from her granddaughter. Throwing out a few contemptuous remarks at him ('that he was certain never to use the tent as a soldier') she also aired an ancient grudge: that he had some years before thwarted her plans in the matter of an election in Bedfordshire. Her bitter reference to what may have been a terrible and poignant scene between them in Bedford House when Diana was dying gave her, no doubt, as much pain as that which she wished to inflict on the young man. Having discharged this volley composed in the powerful language over which she had such command, we hear of her no more at Woburn or Bedford House, though she lived another ten years. Her onslaught was perhaps prompted by hearing a rumour that the Duke of Bedford was about to marry again.

9

A Happy Marriage

W HEN John, fourth Duke of Bedford, married Gertrude Leveson Gower in 1737, he entered on a period of great and lasting personal happiness. She was the eldest daughter of the first Earl Gower – a Jacobite turned Whig – whom Dr Johnson would have named in his *Dictionary* as the definition of a renegade: 'one who deserts to the enemy, a revolter; *sometimes we say a Gower*' had not his printer discreetly struck it out. Her mother was a daughter of the Duke of Kingston, and sister to Lady Mary Wortley Montagu, some of whose asperity Gertrude seems to have shared.

Bound to each other by strong affection and an unswerving mutual admiration, the Duke and Duchess were well matched in intelligence and outlook, exhibiting a unity of purpose and behaviour to a critical and often cynical world, apt to view with reserve the display of such straightforward marital respect, fondness, and content – a happiness founded on virtue, wealth, rank, and a natural sense of duty. Their devotion to each other was never clouded; there was no dissembling when she addressed him in her letters as 'my dear Love', and when he subscribed himself to her as 'ever unalterably yours', it was the statement of a plain truth. He had a warm heart and a simple boyish gaiety (to Horace Walpole he was 'our merry little Duke'); she had a cool one and high spirits. Humility was conspicuous by its absence from the character of the Duchess, and the Duke's self-confidence was sometimes attributed to vanity.

Without abilities of the first order, he had a good intellect and a capacity, if not an enthusiasm, for hard work when engaged on public business – he ruefully called himself indolent – but to the management and improvement of his estates he gave unstinted attention, working closely with his advisers and the men in his employ. He was independent and courageous in his views, though often wrong-headed, and steadfast in his opinions. He was loyal to his friends, he tried to be just, and he was always humane, but he never endeared himself to the public – indeed he was possibly subjected to more physical assault by mobs than any other of his fellow peers. Like many persons of small stature, he tended to create a bustle round himself, perhaps to swell his own importance, and this commotion, which no doubt he was not aware of, coupled with his warmth of temper, often laid him open to ridicule. Neither of the sovereigns he served faithfully had much liking for him; George II was civil to him, respecting so great and powerful a subject, but found him negligent and idle. George III had a particular aversion to his high-handed manner and pronounced him to be 'all passion and absurdity'. Loved and respected by his wife and two children for his goodness and his affectionate nature, it was in the heart of his own family that he passed his happiest days.

The rank and riches that gave the Duke of Bedford confidence and his counsels weight, made the Duchess haughty. The evidence of her contemporaries shows all too clearly that she was arrogant and insolent, and not at all popular in society where her bad manners and lofty airs were resented and ridiculed. She had for her home one of the finest houses in London – Bedford House was coveted by the Prince of Wales, but the Duke from his position as one of the richest men in England ignored the hints that Frederick let fall; mistress also of Woburn Abbey, her good fortune, or perhaps a desire to show the worth of her husband, made her proud and overbearing. Pushing for precedence in doorways, snubbing persons of inferior status, she gave offence to many by her rudeness. Horace Walpole, who found her good company, laughed at her and called her the Duchess of Bloomsbury, and told many malicious stories about her. Passionately fond of playing cards, she was sometimes excluded from the whist and loo parties she would have liked to join, because of her ill-humour. An invitation was once sent to her accompanied by lines from a well-known nursery rhyme:

Come with a whistle and come with a call
Come with a goodwill or not at all,

but she was adept at overlooking the slights offered by the enmity of other aristocratic ladies. It was less easy to ignore the hostility of the common people who flung dirt and cabbage stalks at her while she was crossing the Abbey Green at Bath on a summer day in 1743. Can her arrogance have been so rudely conspicuous? her dress too opulent? Or was it on that visit to the waters that the Duke of Bedford insisted on those around him being inoculated, and the people of Bath thought that he would give them smallpox instead of preventing them having it? As near relatives of Lady Mary Wortley Montagu the Duke and Duchess believed firmly in the practice of inoculation, though admitting the greatest anxiety when it was carried out on their own children.

The Duchess was able to afford fine clothes and her dresses were magnificent. The richness of the materials used and the wealth of embroidery displayed on one of her gowns was described by Mrs Delany to a friend less well placed than herself to observe such splendour.

'The Duchess of Bedford's petticoat was green paduasoy embroidered very richly with gold and silver and a few colours; the pattern was festoons of shells, coral, cornflowers and seaweeds' – a design that was suggested, perhaps, by the ornamentation of the Woburn grotto; it was no more fantastic than that of a dress worn by another duchess, which was a veritable lesson in botany: 'the petticoat was embroidered with *brown hills* covered with all sorts of weeds, and *every breadth* had an old *stump of a tree* . . . round which twined nasturtiums, ivy, honeysuckles, periwinkles, convolvuluses.' When confronted by so much finery, Mary Delany was pleased to lessen her own envy by adding sharply that, despite her grandeur, the Duchess of Bedford looked as 'yellow as a Kite's foot'; she had no liking for her Grace's *de haut en bas* manners and she never missed an opportunity of saying so, and crying her down. The jaundiced pigmentation of Gertrude's skin was noticed by another unfriendly female eye at the coronation of George III, when a peer waiting in an antechamber 'put rouge upon his wife and on the Duchess of Bedford', but the effect of this delicate attention was only to make the latter look 'like an orange-peach, half red and half yellow'.

Gertrude was painted several times by the best artists. No bizarre colouring was recorded by Gavin Hamilton in a very large canvas portraying the Duchess as a young and beautiful woman, presenting her daughter Caroline to Minerva. The poise of the mother's head verges on the sentimental, a mood impossible to associate with the Duchess, so alien does it seem to what we know of her. Thomas Hudson painted her in fancy dress, holding a mask, and he remarked an expression in her face that is more typical. The bright eyes with a sidelong questioning glance do not distract the observer from noticing the extreme firmness of the mouth, that indicates a strong and unyielding character. Reynolds caught the same dry, humorous look when he painted her sitting at ease in an armchair, in her early middle age, smothered in lace and blue silk bows, holding what must be a French novel – a yellow paperback. Gainsborough was to depict an older woman, stiff and proud, with less humour and a clear knowledge of her own worth. A conviction of her own and her husband's pre-eminence was not conducive to being widely cared for, and there can be little doubt that her virtues were chiefly apparent in the home. They had two children: a son, Francis, Marquess of Tavistock, and a daughter Caroline. The happiness she spread within her family circle shows her to have been an excellent home-maker and a careful and sensible mother to her children. 'It is one of the best bonds both of chastity and obedience in the wife if she thinks her husband wise,' observed Francis Bacon, and in the Duchess of Bedford's eyes the Duke could do no wrong. She always praised the wisdom of his actions and, while deferring to his wishes, it can be guessed that she had a comfortable assurance of her power over him – an ascendancy the King and his ministers never doubted. The strength in her character was conspicuous as obstinacy in his. It was a quality already noticed by his brother and commented on by the Duchess of Marlborough, when she told him that he had 'such a talent for, and strength in argument that in all combats of that nature you support your opinion and never yielded to any body'. She had liked him the less for it, but it was an aptitude that served him well when he came to negotiate the Peace of Paris.

Proud of the history of his family, the Duke was very much aware of the part taken by his grandfather, William Lord Russell, in the cause of liberty, and the harsh punishment he had suffered for his opposition to the Crown. In the House of Lords, as a young man, the Duke spoke against a proposal to extend the penalties for high treason to the posterity of persons convicted of corresponding with the sons of the Pretender, and he remarked with feeling how narrowly he himself had escaped 'the blast of an attainder'.

Entering early into politics as the most natural occupation for one in his position, and who bore the name of Russell, he attached himself to the tails of two big fish, Pulteney and Carteret, and with a young man's zest joined them in the clamour against Sir Robert Walpole. For this Horace Walpole was not able to forgive him, though he went to the Duchess's parties at Bedford House, and stayed at Woburn, and even spoke with near affection of the Duke's 'little round person'; he had a low opinion of his talents, but always maintained that he was perfectly honest, with a great love for his country.

While the Duchess of Bedford was ruled by no one, the Duke was susceptible to the influence of his wife, and the flattery of the friends and political adherents who attached themselves to him from affection, or from self-interest and hope of advancement. This small group of men came to be known as the Bedford House Whigs, or the Bloomsbury Gang, and when a government was to be formed, the Duke of Bedford and his friends had to be accommodated. Faction confused eighteenth-century politics; Whigs contested with other Whigs for place and power, and government was an 'ever changing labyrinth' of alliances. Political combinations broke up, and like grains of quicksilver that join and integrate with other particles hitherto separate but not distinct, new groups coalesced to form a ministry. Pride and jealousy precluded able men from taking office together, personal ambition strained their relations with the King and vanity made them stubborn.

Among the men who influenced the Duke and upon whom he relied for support in his political attitudes, two or three stand out. His brother-in-law, Lord Gower, acted closely with him. A genial companion and a kindly, capable man, he held posts in government and rose to be Marquess of Stafford; fathering by his third wife that handsome trifler with women's hearts, Lord Granville Leveson Gower. The Earl of Sandwich, a hard-working hedonist lacking moral principles, was the Duke's intimate friend. They shared political views and a love of country life. The influence of Sandwich over the Duke was generally thought to be as great as that exercised by the Duchess. Both men were able administrators, but they were guilty sometimes of allowing the affairs of their estates and the lure of country sports to distract them from their official work. The Duke of Bedford's neglect of public business, in order to take part in cricket matches and theatricals at Woburn, earned him the reproaches of his fellow ministers, and many years later Lord Sandwich was to shock David Hume by being discovered with his rod in his hand on the banks of a trout stream sixty miles from London, when his attention should more properly have been fixed on North American affairs. The Duke may be forgiven his preference for games played in the open air, with tents set up for the festivities upon his lawns, and Garrick's help invoked for his play-acting, to the company of uneasy ministers outside the door of the Closet at St James's, and the sour looks and guttural accents of George II within it.

A short-term favourite was Henry Legge, a successful politician 'who aspired to the lion's place by the manoeuvre of the mole', but a sycophant and faithless friend, who acted an unworthy part towards the Duke, deserting him after some years of close attendance and careful flattery. It was, however, for the confidence placed in Richard Rigby that the fourth Duke of Bedford has been most severely censured, incurring the opprobrium of having chosen his friends badly. A well-to-do member of Parliament and an associate of the Prince of Wales, Rigby forsook Leicester House for Bedford House and the delights of Woburn Abbey when he could no longer afford to lose large sums of money to Frederick at the gaming table, with no conspicuous return for that obliging service. He became the Duke's firm friend, and later his secretary. A bachelor who made himself agreeable to women, he was pushing and boisterous, overbearing and insolent, and his unabashed place-seeking was notable. An addiction to claret and brandy had suffused his face with a '*lumen purpureum*'; a feature that allowed Junius to allude ironically to Rigby's 'blushing merit'. He showed little concern for upright principles of conduct, nor appeared to believe that others possessed them, yet his immutable devotion to the Duke of Bedford, and his affection for the Duke's wife and children, can be reckoned as at least equal to his hope of gain from such close intimacy, and reflects the better side of his nature; he could be counted on for every kind of service to the family – domestic and political. His lively, affectionate letters must have been a source of pleasure and amusement to the Duke, who, when staying alone at Bath, as he often did, depended on receiving news of political intrigues from the Duchess and Rigby.

The Duke was touchily susceptible to marks of neglect, but while often professing he had himself no wish for office, he obstinately demanded places for his friends. During the years when he took an active part in politics he had to contend with the jealousy of Newcastle, the enmity of Egremont, the duplicity of Bute, and the reproaches of Pitt. In political controversies he had the unfailing support of his wife, who, when he was uneasy or thwarted, counselled him in brisk, uncompromising words to treat with contempt 'Ministers and such trash'. It can be no surprise that one of those ministers reported that the Duke of Bedford 'hates his colleagues and despises the Cabinet'.

The Duke held high office for the first time in 1744, and serving as First Lord of the Admiralty in Pelham's administration he carried out efficiently many reforms in the Navy, and brought forward the men who were to make their names as commanders in the wars with France and Spain – Anson, Hawke, Rodney and Keppel. It was at this time that a resolution was taken that commissioned officers should wear a uniform dress. The King was consulted about the colour, and having lately seen the Duchess of Bedford riding in the Park wearing a habit of dark blue with white facings, he determined that the uniform of the Royal Navy should be similar. The adoption of it was notified in an order dated 13 April 1748.

When the Pretender landed in Scotland in 1745, the Duke raised his own regiment, in which Lord Sandwich enlisted as a captain. Twenty-one men were drafted from Woburn to the Grenadiers, and the little Duke noted in his pocket book that the tallest of these measured 6 feet ¼ inch, and the smallest 5 feet 6½ inches; a respectable height for those days. Attacked by gout, a complaint that plagued him cruelly all his life, the Duke was left behind when his regiment marched north, a circumstance that may have compelled him unwillingly to recall the Duchess of Marlborough's jibe at his non-military character, for when he rejoined his regiment the battle of Culloden had been fought and Charles Stuart was in full flight.

In 1748 he became Secretary of State for the Southern Department, while the Duke of Newcastle held the seals for the Northern Department. The two men's tempers were incompatible, but they had to rub along together for the next three years; Newcastle, with his 'shrill cockpit voice', could at least make a show of amity. Horace Walpole witnessed a meeting between the two, when Newcastle 'smothered the Duke with embraces . . . and has never born to be in the same room with him since'.

In 1751, when Newcastle, and eventually the King, wished to get rid of the Duke of Bedford – for his idleness was provoking; 'he is always riding post to Woburn' – a ruse had to be devised to do so, because Bedford, though confessing he had grievances, showed no intention of retiring. Lord Sandwich, who had succeeded Bedford at the Admiralty, was summarily dismissed from office, and the Duke instantly resigned, so staunch was his loyalty to his friend and ally. Although the King offered him the post of President of the Council, he declined and for the next five years he had no employment in the ministry.

Amid the distractions of public business, estate management, horticultural improvement, sport, and private entertainment, the Duke had been turning over in his mind a great project – the rebuilding of Woburn – but it was fifteen years after he took possession that he was in a position to fulfil his ambition. Soon after his succession as fourth Duke he had contemplated various improvements at the Abbey. In 1733 John Sanderson, a man of whom little is known, but who had done work for the Duke in Bloomsbury, and was to rebuild Stratton in Hampshire for him, prepared some drawings for restoring the Abbey. Charles Bridgeman was summoned to advise on alterations to the grounds; and the Duke engaged himself to pay Philip Miller, the director of the Apothecaries Garden at Chelsea, £20 a year 'for inspecting my garden, hot houses, pruning the trees etc., and to come to Woburn at least twice a year, oftener if wanted'. Miller provided plants and rare shrubs, and took an interest in the garden for many years, and when he wrote to the Duke on these matters it was as one experienced gardener and botanist to another.

As the Duke of Bedford rode about his woods and fields he noted in a pocket almanach his ideas for essential work to be done on the estate; they were the thoughts of a practical farmer, and his observation was acute: 'One of the plows Rd Grace plows with is too light for that strong ground.' 'Speak to Paisy to mend up all the Barrs by ye road side and Brown to make the Banks so steep that no horses can get up them. All the Barrs to be kept shut while I am away.' 'With what horses the mares shall be covered.' 'That part of the warren which was Oats last summer and Turnips this, to be fed of the next with deer and then immediately to have it plowed and mucked with the best mold from Drakelow pond, and by constant harrowing to be laid down as smooth as possible and then pretty early in the season to be laid down with Barley (and hayseeds with some trefoil) and natural Grass seeds. N.B., a small quantity of pigeon's dung to be sowed with the Barley and if there should be any holes that can't be laid Level . . . Brown to help it with the Spade.' All his life he carried a memorandum book in his capacious pocket, and an intention carried out was marked 'Done' or 'have spoke'.

An anecdote is told of his obstinacy when his directions were opposed. At the birth of his daughter in 1743 a large area between the town and the Abbey was planted with non-deciduous trees, and named the Evergreens; when the time came to thin the plantation the Duke and his gardener disagreed on the method, and the latter protested that his professional reputation would suffer if the Duke's orders were carried out. 'Do as I tell you and I will take care of your reputation,' said the Duke. When the thinning was completed, he set up a board facing the road on which was inscribed: 'This plantation was thinned by John, Duke of Bedford contrary to the advice and opinion of his gardener.'

By the death of Diana in 1735 he had been deprived of £100,000 which had been promised to her by the Duchess of Marlborough; Wriothesley's excesses had threatened the future prosperity of the family, and Gertrude was no great heiress. The fourth Duke, therefore, though by no means a poor man, had to husband his resources before he was able to follow the example of other noblemen, who were altering or pulling down and rebuilding their great houses. Work at Welbeck had been completed and the Duke of Devonshire was engaged on the reconstruction of Chatsworth. There was a general move in England among the wealthy landowners to have a finer and more comfortable home; many of the gentry, too, were building a new mansion or adding a wing in the modern style to their manor houses.

Lacking the funds to rebuild Woburn, the young couple, rearing two tenderly loved children, infused, instead, new life into the dilapidated and heavily buttressed house. Cheerful amusements entertained their friends and relations, while small changes and improvements were undertaken. A fresh bowling-green was laid down, and a new garden was made for the Duchess, which by the Duke's direction was to be kept planted with a succession of sweet-smelling flowers. Racing or cricket might pass the daylight hours, while theatricals and cards filled the time at night. There was much lighthearted betting; a cricket match merited a wager of £500, and smaller bets were laid on lesser matters: one guinea on the chances of the King speaking to Lord Sandwich at Court; fifty guineas on a probable marriage; and £5 was staked on the capture of a French town. French defeats at sea were celebrated in the park: 'Lord Tavistock's bonfire is just out', wrote the first Lord of the Admiralty of his eight-year-old son's proceedings, to Anson, the victorious admiral. The little boy had his own garden 'between the brewhouse and the back door'; a good location, for it must have allowed him to waylay persons going in and out and detain them to discuss the prospects of his nasturtiums and his radishes.

The Duchess was seldom without the company of some member of her family – a brother or an unmarried sister, and a seat in the grounds named 'Lord Gower's bench' was, perhaps, the goal of her father's favourite perambulation.

'A plentiful discharge of nonsense' from Henry Legge was currently amusing, although his humour must have seemed at times a little strained. When autumn came men's minds were wholly occupied with 'pointers and partridges'; until market gardening reduced their numbers, Bedfordshire, with its light sandy soil, was celebrated for these birds. 'I am sorry', wrote Legge, 'the partridges have the insolence to breed in the very garden and under the parlour windows; this is such a nuisance that the parties behaving in so indecent a manner ought certainly to be treated as vermin.' The joke ran on into the shooting season: 'It is well done of the partridges to hold such riotous assemblies when they know I can't come to disperse them, I have often observed that at this time of year, when they begin to grow a little old, they are apt to hold drums, where they play at whist and quadrille, especially the hens'; and the subject turned up again the following year: 'It may not be amiss to condole with you upon the havoc which the present rains must unavoidably occasion amongst the race of partridges . . . I recommend to your Grace the sending out a powerful squadron of umbrellas into the park and adjacent fields of Woburn, which if properly stationed, will not only prevent the addling of many unborn partridges, but save the life also of those who have already seen the face of daylight.'

There were startling and disagreeable events that disturbed the tenor of pleasant country life, and inevitably it is from Horace Walpole that we hear of one gruesome occurrence. Lord Carteret's son, of whose sanity there were grave doubts, had been staying at Woburn: 'At 5 o'clock in the morning he waked the Duke and Duchess all bloody, and with the lappet of his coat held up full of ears – he had been in the stables and cropped all the horses.' The stables at Woburn were then located on the east side of the building, in what had been the crypt of the monastery church, and access to them from the house must have been easy. Today the report of so savage an act would be accompanied by musings on the deeply hidden causes that prompted it, but Walpole's account is brief and bald: 'he is shut up', he concludes, and no doubt the poor lunatic was whipped and ill-treated to help him regain his wits. That year saw other troubles. A drama within the family caused greater consternation but was not so bruited abroad. On 1 January 1744 the Duke of Bedford had been compelled to write to the Duke of Dorset, the father of Lord John Sackville, informing him of what had just passed at Woburn Abbey.

The Duke of Bedford to the Duke of Dorset

. . . last Fryday, the 30th of last month my wife was called out of her own room just as she was going to bed, to that of her sister Fanny's, whom she then found just delivered of a son, then in the bed with her, and not taken from her. The next day upon talking with her I found to my great concern that she was not married to Lord John Sackville, but had upon the most solemn promises and importunities consented to his Will. This, Lord John Sackville has this day confirmed to me, and has in the most handsome way upon entreaties consented to give her the only satisfaction he had now in his power by marrying her in true form, in presence of my wife, Mr Baptist Leveson, myself, and her maid, who are almost the only Persons in the House, who do not think they were married some time ago. The reason of my troubling your Grace with this, is to satisfie you and your family with Regard to the Birth of this Child, and at the same time to disculpate myself and the Dutchess of Bedford from any knowledge of this affair, and to assure your Grace upon the Faith of an honest man, and a Christian that I was absolutely ignorant of this affair, and that as much as one Person can possibly answer for others my wife and all her family were too.

We do not know what the Duke of Dorset thought of this affair; he was much troubled by the misbehaviour of all his three sons, but the erring Fanny's father, on hearing the news, thundered out his heartless reply by return of post.

Lord Gower to the Duke of Bedford

The shocking account your letter brought has so confounded me I hardly know what to say or do. It has fully confirmed my opinion, I have long had of Lord John and his Lady and the suspicions I entertain'd of her illness here three years ago and has I hope open'd your eyes so as to put you upon your guard and prevent your harbouring such snakes in your bosom for the future, but it is too late to look backwards now, we can only look forwards and endeavour to wipe the stain from our Family, and prevent its ruining her two poor innocent sisters that are not yet dispos'd of. Your Grace has already done all that any man of the highest honour and nicest punctilio can do, you have procur'd in the most expeditious manner all the reparation for our injur'd honour that the circumstances of the case would admit of, and have, I think, inflicted an heavy punishment on both the Offenders. He, I am persuaded, must think it so who has defer'd doing her justice to the last moment in the hopes that her death or Bedford Assizes would deliver him from the Yoke. . . . and she I am satisfied will find it so when she has starved a few years with a man of his temper who never lov'd her but only lusted after her. . . .

John Sackville and Frances Leveson Gower were made man and wife at Woburn before their child was forty-eight hours old. The boy was christened Philip a month later, and then the disgraced couple were packed off to the Duke of Bedford's house at Cheam, from whence Lord John's contrite protestations soon turned to assertive and ungrateful complaints, to which the Duke responded with firm and grave civility. Poor Fanny had to put up with her scallywag of a husband until he went off his head and died some twenty years later. Her 'poor innocent sisters', Elizabeth and Evelyn, were soon most successfully disposed of to Earl Waldegrave and the Earl of Upper Ossory.

❧❧❧❧❧❧

10

Rebuilding Woburn

ALTHOUGH for fifteen years funds to rebuild Woburn were lacking, the Duke was not poor, and he had a sound business acumen; when he could he bought land. The Woburn property had changed little in size since the days of the fourth Earl; there had been a few purchases in the early years of the eighteenth century, but it was the fourth Duke who was to extend the property. The Ampthill estate was acquired in 1738; Houghton and Oakley about the same time; farms and small areas of land were bought when the opportunity occurred; but besides the acquisition of land the Duke had other profitable interests. Not for nothing was he the grandson of the capable Mrs Howland, who, in her meticulously kept account books, had registered the profit and loss she experienced from the voyages of the East India Company's vessels in which she invested part of her fortune. The fourth Duke, too, had shares in ships sailing to the Orient, and also in some which went to Greenland in search of whales. The ships which brought their cargoes from the sultry East or from Eternal Frost tied up side by side in the dock at Rotherhithe that had been constructed by the first Duke of Bedford. The capture of a whale brought cash; a ship from the Indies might carry as well as a cargo of pepper and snuff, a bonus in the form of silks and muslins, or porcelain from the Far East, enabling the shareholders in a vessel to enrich their homes with the first choice of beautiful things from distant places. Mr Butcher, the Duke's agent-in-chief, would attend directly at the wharf-side to secure for his employer the best of what had been unloaded.

Like his Dorset ancestors, the merchants of Weymouth who sent goods abroad in their own vessels, the Duke of Bedford had an interest in exports as well as imports. From Tavistock, an important centre of the western cloth trade, bales of grey serge were sent up to London to be temporarily housed in the offices of Bedford House, until they could be put on board the ships going to Spain and beyond, the Duke taking a profit from what was handled. It was the echo of a tradition reaching back to the fifteenth century, when William Russell, the great-uncle of the first Earl of Bedford, held a licence to export broadcloths to Cadiz – but now the goods went even further afield.

A rise in the value of land, higher rents, the granting of new leases, particularly on the London properties, all contributed to the Duke's increasing wealth. When he decided that at last he could safely embark on the great work of rebuilding Woburn the plans prepared by Sanderson were discarded, and the Duke turned to his own surveyor, Thomas Moore – perhaps a descendant of Sir Jonas Moore, surveyor of fen drainage in the mid-seventeenth century, notable for having 'boyld his buttock to cure his sciatica', so Aubrey tells us, a complaint that must have been engendered by loitering on marshy ground. The fifth Earl of Bedford had employed Sir Jonas to make a survey in 1661 of the Abbey and its surroundings, and now Thomas Moore was called on to do the same. He prepared some plans for the rebuilding, but the Duke was not satisfied and in 1747 Henry Flitcroft was invited to visit Woburn.

Flitcroft came by the name of 'Burlington Harry' from his association with Lord Burlington. While working as a young journeyman carpenter at Burlington House, he fell off a scaffolding and broke his leg, thus coming to the notice of the Earl, who humanely 'put him under care' and, observing his talent for drawing, promoted him to be his draughtsman and architectural assistant. When twenty-five years later Flitcroft was summoned to Woburn, he had become Master Carpenter at the Board of Works. Sarah Marlborough had been in her grave some years, but it was she who had emphatically stated her belief to her granddaughter Diana that the decaying house should not be pulled completely down, but rather that several things should be altered by degrees, that would 'make it a better house than any architect can build now'. Her opinion was in direct conflict with Horace Walpole's view that a clean sweep must be made if a house with any architectural pretensions was to replace the old. The Duke took his opinions from no one, but he had no intention of making a clean sweep; he directed that the north side of the house, with its range of well-proportioned, moderately sized rooms, was to be saved in its entirety. His decision has an engaging inscrutability, but it may be conjectured that it was dictated by sentiment, for in those cold and sunless apartments he and his family and forebears had always lived, and not until his grandson made his own improvements to Woburn nearly fifty years

The fourth Duke of Bedford
by Gainsborough

Gertrude Leveson Gower,
Duchess of Bedford by
Reynolds

Thé à l'anglaise chez le Prince de Conti by B. M. Ollivier (Mme de Boufflers right centre in hat)

later were the north rooms abandoned for new ones on the sunny side of the house. Thanks to this conservative trait in the Duke's character it is possible to see today part of the house as it was built by the fourth Earl in the early years of the seventeenth century.

It has been pointed out that Flitcroft was committed to adopting a fifteen-year-old design fitted to a seventeenth-century plan, which itself emanated from that of a monastery. He proved willing to adapt himself to these somewhat cramping conditions and, being apparently without that jealousy that architects may be expected to exhibit to the work of rivals, he approved the sketches and plans that had been prepared by Moore. 'He has found no fault at all,' wrote Moore with satisfaction, and the two men were to work amicably together to carry out the Duke's wishes: Flitcroft as the professional architect, Moore as his aide, having a substantial knowledge of the house and site.

While Flitcroft was preparing his own drawings, which took two years, the great work of assembling essential materials for the building was put under way. Stone was brought from quarries in the neighbourhood – Tottenhoe and Oakley – and from further afield, from Ketton in Rutland, from Portland, and from the Isle of Purbeck. The local stone which had been used for the Caroline house weathered badly, and although a lot was used in the new building it was largely faced with a better wearing stone. The cost of transport was high, and at one time a plan was considered as a measure of economy to bring granite from the Orkneys, where the Hudson Bay ships called to take up stone as ballast, but it is uncertain if the scheme was ever carried out. Stone from Dorset went by sea to Lynn, where it was put in the charge of watermen, who brought it by barge along canals and rivers to the harbourside at Bedford; from thence carriers transported it in their strong slow-moving carts to Woburn. The Duke's own teams and broad-wheeled wagons were used to carry materials, but rarely heavy stone. Westmorland provided slate, bricks were made in the park, and lime was burnt in kilns on the nearby chalky hills. Earmarked for fire beams, timber was imported from the Baltic; some oak was procured locally, and more was purchased from landowners, including the Duke of Marlborough at Blenheim. The ships which brought wood from Riga travelled up the Nen to Wansford in Northamptonshire; here the timber was unloaded into barges and proceeded by waterways to Bedford, where it was consigned to the carters and their wagons for the last stage of the journey.

When the work was at last begun the Duke of Bedford was serving as

Secretary of State. There can be little surprise that he was censured at Court for neglecting affairs and for always being on the road between London and Woburn. Impatient to see how matters were proceeding, he could not tolerate being absent for long. Remaining in the north rooms, the family put up with the inconvenience of dust and noise while the east and south sides of the house were remodelled and improved to serve as domestic offices and servants' rooms. Flitcroft rebuilt the central part of the west front, keeping on the first floor the same number of rooms of exactly the same dimensions, and, accepting the Duke's demand that the two corner pavilions of the Caroline house were to be retained – in one was the state bedroom, in the other the library – he removed the gables from the corners and, replacing the casements with Venetian windows, incorporated the two pavilions in the new Palladian front; a central pediment contained the ducal arms. Structural decay necessitated underpinning the corner blocks, and the surveyor Moore expressed his relief that this hazardous operation had been successfully completed when he wrote to the agent-in-chief on 9 July 1752: 'This Day I Finnisht the Underpining the Libery at Wooburn Abbey and I Bless God Without Any Misfortens though one of the most Rottenest walls I Ever saw.'

Flitcroft has been charged with a lack of creative ability and a disregard for external ornament. A visitor to Woburn may form his own opinion of the noble west front of the Abbey.

New drains were laid, and pipes brought water to a cold bath and a hot bath in adjoining basement rooms. The cold bath was sunk in the floor like a small swimming-pool, and surviving for over two hundred years was, indeed, used as such when regular bathrooms were installed upstairs. There is no evidence of how the water for the hot bath was heated. An addition to the plumbing system, conducive to the personal comfort of the Duke, superior even to the hot bath, was a water-closet with piped water, which was put up in the north garden specifically for the use of his Grace; it was embellished with brass fittings and Dutch tiles. Welbeck Abbey had seen the introduction of two water-closets between 1743 and 1744; that at Woburn dated from five years later, and by 1760 three more had been installed, and one of these at least was within the house. All these improvements put a heavy strain on the water supply, which had never been satisfactory, but it was not till 1761 that Sanderson was recalled to Woburn to supervise the construction of two reservoirs, that were to be fed from a pond which lay in what had been the monastic hop garden, at some considerable distance from the house. They were lined with lead and the pipes which brought the water were of the same material, and not of wood.

Building and decorating went on all through the 1750s, and the Duke's pocket-books make clear how closely he was in touch with the men at work, giving his attention to detail and economy; materials were to be saved from the old building to be re-used in the new.

'To enquire of Mr Moore whether there is sufficient timber to finish the whole building (there is).' He himself rode about his park marking oaks for flooring boards. 'The team to be set to carrying Brick and Stone for underpinning the old wall of the Chappell.' 'About laying up the timber that came out of the old house for the stables that are to be built.' The stables were a matter in which the Duke appears to have changed his mind, and he now set economy aside.

'As your Grace has determined to have two buildings,' wrote Flitcroft as late as 1757, 'they can in my humble opinion be more considered as objects than when there was one.' Freed suddenly from the Duke's restrictions, he applied himself with vigour and imagination to design two extremely handsome stable blocks; these magnificent stone quadrangles were an adequate reason for the increased importance of the east side of the house and its architectural development in the time of the fifth Duke.

Horace Walpole stayed at Woburn in 1751, before the west front of the old house had been demolished, and he was in time to see unchanged the passage behind the state rooms, that served as the picture gallery. He was charmed, as Defoe had been some years before, by the little gold stars that powdered the panelled walls, and the 'millions of portraits'. 'There are', he wrote to George Montagu, 'all the successions of the Earls and Countesses of Bedford and all their progenies. One Countess is a whole length drawing in the drollest dress you ever saw; and another picture of the same woman leaning on her hand.' This was Lucy Bedford, the patron of poets, in the 'fantastick habit' of a Court masque.

The following year the Duke of Bedford made an excursion into East Anglia and visited several newly built great houses there. He was, perhaps, moved by a desire to see the architectural ventures on which other noblemen had been engaged. He stayed at Houghton, the palace built by Colen Campbell for Horace Walpole's father, Sir Robert. Curious and conscientious, he went 'thro all the rooms in the Basement and Attick stories', and he inspected the stable block. From Houghton he visited Holkham, the new and splendid mansion of Thomas Coke, Earl of Leicester, joint conception and achievement of the Earl himself, Kent, and Lord Burlington; and since Rainham, the property of Turnip Townshend, was not far distant he went there too, and on his way back to Woburn he looked in on the Duke of Grafton's new house, Euston Hall. His comments on these buildings have not, alas, descended to us, but it is not unlikely that the line of his mouth tightened with distaste as he viewed the yellow brick with which Holkham was built – a personal whim of Lord Leicester s – and he may have pondered with satisfaction on the fine stone being used at Woburn, as delicate in colour as the young deer in his park. And since it is every man's pleasure to censure the taste of others, he was, perhaps, tempted while contemplating the ostentatious splendour of Houghton, to make a criticism similar to Lord Oxford's unfavourable comment on that house twenty years earlier: 'there is very great expense without judgement or taste'.

As a son of that magnificent house and an admirer of its particular splendour, Horace Walpole was privileged to call Woburn 'plain like a College' when he came there again after 1759. His prejudices would not allow him to approve of what had been done; it was spoiled, he thought, by the Duke's obstinate retention of the grotto and 'some old parts at the angles'. 'There is little done in good taste, though no part very bad . . . the back of the house is Gothick.'

If the outside of the Duke of Bedford's great house was unostentatious, there was gilded mangificence within. As the building was gradually completed the decorators got to work. They were lavish in the use of gold, the upholsterers prodigal with Damask, Festoons, Silk Braid, Boot Tape, Cord and Buckram. The Duke's teams and wagons brought down from the London workshop of John Devall superb marble chimney-pieces; the fashionable firm of Norman and Whittle supplied carved and gilded pier-glasses of great beauty and superlative quality. The sober exterior of the house gave no hint of the riches inside, and the Duke's friends entering at the west front – then, as now, the principal entrance – were not instantly assailed by a display of noble grandeur. In the wide but low hall, divided by four pairs of Ionic columns, and with windows looking west and into the inner court, they could in winter have warmed themselves at one or other of two great fires, with fine carved stone chimney-pieces; a relief by Rysbrack surmounting each. Yet no magnificent marble flight of stairs was visible, as at Holkham, to arouse their admiration and lead them to the upper floor. The steep and substantial, but unspectacular staircase was placed in the north-west angle of a passage on the left of the hall, at its junction with the northern wing. Flitcroft had debated an alternative ascent: 'whether to ascend to the Saloon by two flights of steps or to enter by a basement hall', and it was characteristic of the Duke to choose the less imposing and, perhaps, more economical way up to the drawing-rooms and the great Saloon, where the coffered and vaulted ceiling rose two floors, the walls were hung with blue damask, and the chimney-pieces were carved by Rysbrack.

A great deal of money was spent on the state bedchamber, where the ceiling was enriched with an elaborate and dazzling design in gold copied from Robert Wood's 'Ruins of Palmyra'. The grand state bed was re-trimmed with 150 yards of 'the best blue Belladine silk crape fringe'; new curtains were put up and 'a fine needlework carpet' was tacked and glued down.

The decorators introduced columns into the re-modelled long gallery, dividing its great length in three sections. Above the two chimney-pieces panels were set in the overmantel displaying the Russell arms 'mosaicked with enrichments from a drawing of Her Grace's design'. This pattern devised by the Duchess was a little later sent out to China – probably in one of the Duke's East India ships – to be reproduced with a version of the arms on the large vases which today stand on either side of the chimney-pieces. No doubt the Duke was pleased to consult the artistic wishes of his wife when it was a question of furnishings and interior decoration, but he had to make a note in his pocket book to remind himself to do so.

In 1753 an agent of the Duke's at Rotterdam, when sending him a smoked salmon, let him know of a bargain to be had:

> I know of a Parcel of very fine China paper amongst which there are several sheets of the finest sorts and such as Lady Holderness has a screen of. Perhaps my lady Dutchess would like to have it. I think I can get it at a very reasonable price.

The Duchess was agreeable and the north room where the paper was hung was furnished with a set of '6 neat Chinese chairs, walnut, the seats cane'. They cost £6. 12s. 0d., and five remain in the room today.

The splendid state apartments were in contrast to those in which the family lived, which retained a simpler style. In that part of the house which was not rebuilt by Flitcroft, some of the seventeenth-century rooms were given an eighteenth-century elegance by the addition of golden rococo plaster work on the ceilings. The more austere taste of the Caroline age can be seen in the room on the ground floor on one side of the grotto, which was used as the family parlour, where the chimney-piece and frieze date from the time of the fourth Earl.

None, perhaps, were more delighted with the new glory of the great house than those friends and relations of the Duke and Duchess who were invited to enjoy the *agréments* of Woburn. Richard Rigby had by 1756 become an habitué, and writing from *Library, Woburn Abbey*, expressed his enchantment to the owner, absent on military manoeuvres:

I can't refrain sending you a line from this place to tell you that it is in greater beauty if possible than I ever saw it in my life . . . I am now eating some of the best butter and drinking some of the best tea I ever tasted . . . Your harvest will be all in if this delightful weather holds . . . I think with such pens and ink as one always gets at Woburn, I have scribbled out a tolerable note. All your servants seem as glad to hear of your health as if you was return'd from the most bloody campaign. Godin is enquiring if you are not starv'd, Mrs Farrow if my Lady Dutchess has a bed to lay on. Poll flew at me to know what was become of Miss and Lemon bark'd after Tavistock. I have given them all their proper answers.

A year later Sir Charles Hanbury Williams wrote with nostalgia from his Embassy in St Petersburg that 'an airing in that delicious park and a walk in her Grace's own garden is just the exercise I require, and when it rains there is a good library and I suppose by this time the gallery is finished and the Russells in their proper places'.

The Duke of Cumberland, victor at Culloden, who had attached himself to the Duke of Bedford when they were both in opposition to the Court, brought with him his sister Amelia – least amiable of princesses. She played deep at cards and it amused her to lay bets with the Duke of Bedford on trifling matters. While others were content to play at loo for half-a-crown, the Duchess played for gold; the Princess of Wales was scandalized that her daughter played in public with the Bedfords at Bath. Possibly neither the Duke nor the Duchess was a skilled player, for he would reckon his losses and make a note of them. They were indeed modest for those times, but at the end of the year he had never gained a guinea and sometimes had to own to a loss of six hundred.

Besides the attainment of their ambition to have a fine and well-appointed house, the Duke and Duchess had other cause to think themselves happy. Their son's growth to manhood, and the developing beauty of their daughter, were daily satisfactions. The fondness of the parents for their children was reciprocated. 'Lord Tavistock says he loves to have you go abroad because he is so very glad when you come home', wrote the Duchess to her husband when their son was seven years old. As a man Tavistock found no difficulty in communicating with his father, and his affectionate letters are without the hollow dutiful phrases common at that time; their mutual trust and esteem was absolute. The Duchess, often alone at Woburn, was so perfectly happy there that she sometimes showed reluctance to leave it for Bedford House. It was her sister who urged her to present Caroline, when approaching seventeen, to the old King. 'What does it signify if you do come to town two days sooner than you intended,' wrote Lady Betty Waldegrave, 'the distress will amply be made up to you by the pleasure Car. will have in going with you preferably to any other person, one must go out of one's way sometimes to make others happy.' The reproof carried weight, and Caroline's artless behaviour at St James's was related in a letter from the Duchess to the Duke:

I got Miss presented to the Prince of Wales yesterday and she behaved as well to him as she did per contra to his grandfather; when she saw the latter coming to her, she open'd her eyes to stare at tremendous Majesty but never attempted a curtsy or stooped to receive his kiss, but when she found he persisted she almost knocked him down with her chin; I assure you it was so bad that I expect to hear that he did not like her tho' I think he could not help it she looked so very pretty and the whole drawing-room was of my opinion.

There is a postscript to that letter in Caroline's hand:

Mama desires me to add that Mr Denoyer [dancing master to the Royal family] has been with me and says that the Prince of Wales thinks me very pretty and that I have exactly Mama's smile. I was against writing you this for fear you should think I was a saucy vain puss, but Mama insisted on it.

George II was not offended by Caroline's innocent gaucherie, for soon after he took her with him in a party to Blackheath to 'eat sausages made by a famous French cook'.

During the years when the Duke of Bedford held no office he was active in debate in Parliament and his political influence could not be disregarded. The King, who disliked most of his ministers, respected Bedford and would have been glad to get him back into his service. He offered him the Privy Seal, but the Duke was determined not to serve again under Newcastle. When that nobleman resigned in 1756 and a new ministry headed by the Duke of Devonshire and Pitt was formed, the Duke of Bedford was offered and accepted the office of Lord Lieutenant of Ireland. His administration of that unmanageable country was not marked by any great triumphs, and a disaster was narrowly averted when a French force landed in the north but withdrew when opposed, losing their commander in the sea-fight which ensued. Although Bedford's personal qualities made him popular with many in Dublin, he did not escape having his effigy burnt in the streets by an unruly mob. True to his liberal principles, he advocated leniency towards the Roman Catholics, thereby easing their fears and raising their hopes. Harassed by the Anglo-Irish faction, he was conciliatory and intended to be firm, but under the baleful influence of his secretary Rigby his resolution weakened, and he resorted to the purchase of support with pensions and peerages. Rigby, whose 'festive talents' were agreeable to the Irish, obtained for himself the office of Master of the Rolls. The Duchess made herself almost universally popular by the condescension of her manners and the splendour of her entertainments at the Castle.

'She had all her life been practising the part of Queen,' observed Horace Walpole, 'dignity and dissimulation were natural to her.'

Both the Duke and Duchess preferred simple amusements to regal state and they were able to find it in company of their own choosing – though not without the censure of Mrs Delany, then living near Dublin, who, with searching eye and busy pen, was ever ready to condemn the Duchess, who, she wrote: 'will go to supper with anybody that will give her cards and a supper. I am sure I am not one of these; she dines every Sunday with Lady Barrymore on her own dinner. In the afternoon his Excellency comes, and cards and supper finish the day.'

Tavistock and Caroline accompanied their parents to Dublin, and their presence added a charm to the viceregal circle. Tavistock was commended for his gentle manners and Caroline was admired for her beauty. She joined the performers who lent their vocal talents to the newly founded Musical Academy, from which all professionals were excluded, and she was criticized for doing so by the intolerant Mrs Delany, who thought so public an appearance must 'abate that proper bashfulness which should be the characteristic of a young woman'. A sermon preached in St Patrick's cathedral was surely a greater trial for Caroline's modesty, for she was the subject of it, and the preacher spared no breath to outline her marriage prospects and detail the virtues a husband should expect to find in her.

When George II died in 1760, and the Duke of Bedford left his employment in Ireland, Caroline was eighteen years old. There can be little doubt that her parents had already decided whom they wished her to marry. The greatest match in England after the King was the young Duke of Marlborough, to whom the Duke of Bedford was guardian, and the Duchess spared no pains to secure him for her daughter in the face of other candidates for his hand; a principal aspirant being Lady Sarah Lennox. Lady Sarah had received ardent attentions from the young King, but had had to resign herself to seeing him marry a German princess. She took away Lord Newbattle from Caroline Russell, with whom he was much in love, successfully directing his passion towards herself instead, and her vanity had been flattered by the admiration of the Duke of Marlborough, but these were short-lived feminine triumphs with no sequel. 'Alas, alas,' wrote her sister, 'the Duke of Marlborough saw Sarah at Ranelagh, took no notice of her and walked all night with Lady Caroline Russell. The Duchess of Bedford lives at Ranelagh now, where she seldom or never went before. It is taken great notice of, as it is since the Duke of Marlborough's arrival that their passion for it has begun.'

When Charlotte of Mecklenberg-Strelitz married George III, the rival girls, acting as bridesmaids with eight others, carried the bride's train in the Chapel Royal. Sarah drew attention by her beauty, Caroline was admired for her demeanour. The following year, Caroline, her heart deeply engaged, married the Duke of Marlborough, with whom she lived happily for close on fifty years. Unlike her mother, whose nature softened with age, Caroline's grew harder. Queen Charlotte thought she was the proudest woman in the kingdom. Schooled in arrogance by her mother, she did not share her many other qualities that enlivened existence at Bedford House and Woburn; life at Blenheim was 'ennui itself'. In time the Duke of Marlborough withdrew from society, preferring the study of astronomy, and his wife was to persecute their youngest daughter for making a love match with an impecunious parson.

II

'Our great little man'

AT the end of the Seven Years' War the Duke of Bedford was sent as ambassador to France to negotiate the peace treaty. Lord Bute and the young King wanted peace, but Pitt and his adherents and a large party in the country were for prolonging the war which was going well for England, although it was carried on at enormous expense; it followed that the man who signed the Treaty would incur abuse from many, and the Duke was to have his full share in the years to come.

Established at Paris, he furnished with splendour the Hôtel Grinberghen in the Rue St Dominique, which he hired from the Duc de Chaulnes. Though he was able to cultivate his taste for French furniture, one piece only at Woburn can now be identified as having been in his Paris Embassy.

He was liked by the French ladies, and he made himself agreeable to the ministers with whom he had to deal – the Duc de Choiseul, and the Spanish Plenipotentiary, Marquis Grimaldi. After close bargaining, the preliminaries (which the Duke had been given power to sign) were drawn up, but the diplomacy of the French representative in London, the Duc de Nivernois (who was accompanied by that enigmatic figure, the Chevalier d'Eon), raised suspicions of French sincerity; an attempt was made by a divided English ministry to curb Bedford's powers to sign without first submitting papers to the King for his approbation – an abridgement the Duke deeply resented, and he addressed a remonstrance to the devious Bute: 'For God's sake what occasion was there for sending a minister to this Court if the whole was to be transmitted from ministry to ministry? and why was I solicited for this contemptible employment of transmitting *projects* only to my Court?' George III had some sympathy for the Duke, declaring that if power was taken from him 'a boy of ten years old would be as fit for the office of Plenipotentiary as the Duke of Bedford', but as French resistance stiffened to the terms of the Treaty, he acknowledged that 'the Duke's warmth of temper turns hillocks into mountains'. With characteristic tenacity Bedford held firm to the principles that he thought would make for a lasting peace and provide a just balance of maritime power. In the face of England's vast territorial gains, he believed in generous terms for France, and contended above all that to deprive her of her profitable fishing-grounds off Newfoundland would provoke a renewal of the war at an early date. It was a policy in opposition to Pitt, who would have stripped France of these benefits and the means to train her seamen. The Duke feared that a confederacy of naval powers against England would follow such harsh treatment of France. His views prevailed, and their acceptance was the chief cause of his unpopularity after the Peace. Attacked by gout in his hand, the Duke was heard to say that he would sign with his teeth when at last agreement on the preliminaries was reached. The Duchess made a present to George Selwin of the pen that was in the event used.

Private information that the preliminaries had been signed arrived in London before the official courier, allowing some people to profit by the rise in Government securities. It would seem that Rigby, who was in Paris, despatched his own servant to the Duke of Bedford's broker in London, who bought £200,000 of stock; an incident which, while it conforms with what is known of Rigby's character, does not comply with the accepted view of Bedford's honesty; that the Duke was pressed for money is certain, for he wrote the following year to his agent-in-chief to grant annuities and make sales to supply him with funds 'sufficient to get me thro' this ruinous embassy'.

It was six months before the Treaty was ratified, and the Duc de Choiseul is said to have vowed revenge from that moment, but he corresponded afterwards in a most amiable way with the Duke of Bedford, referring to 'la paix . . . qui est, j'ose le dire, notre enfant commun'.

The good impression made on French society by the Duke and Duchess of Bedford was further enhanced when Tavistock joined his parents in Paris. After his studies at Cambridge, he had entered the Bedfordshire Militia – it would seem against the wishes of his parents, for he was often at pains to assure them that the militia was different to the army, and that their 'suspicion of my liking for low company' was unfounded. He confessed he had a 'rage for everything that has connexion with a military life'. Excusing himself for harping on his 'hobby horse', he wrote: 'It is your own fault, my best father, for you was so good . . . to give me leave to be as particular as I pleased . . . and I am more militia mad than ever.'

He put forward his plan to inoculate his whole regiment against smallpox at his own expense, and he emphasized his desire to make his men good soldiers while not making them bad countrymen. In the face of their uneasiness his parents were, perhaps, glad to see their son set off late in 1761 to travel abroad. From Rome – where he was painted by Batoni in the scarlet uniform of the Militia – he wrote to his friend Thomas Robinson describing his awakening interest in art and architecture. 'I am engaged in a pretty deep affair, the buying of some of the best things in the Barberini Palace.' With the help of Gavin Hamilton he secured a Caracci – 'Christ in the garden of Gethsamene' – which hangs now at Woburn. Another acquisition which can be seen in one of Sir Joshua Reynolds' portraits of Tavistock was a bronze figure of Hercules.

He returned to England the next year and, pausing in Paris on his way home, he gave a dinner to some compatriots to celebrate the King of England's birthday. Laurence Sterne, then travelling in France, was among his guests. Healths were drunk, the wine was plentiful, and the complacent and brilliant author of *Tristram Shandy* showed himself in a characteristic vein of humour. Louis Dutens, a Huguenot refugee, lately in charge of English affairs at Turin, found himself placed next to Sterne, with whom he was not acquainted. The conversation turning on Turin, where some of the party were shortly going, Sterne asked his neighbour if he knew a certain M. Dutens in that town. The laughter of the other guests at this question prompted Dutens to reply that he knew him intimately – '*un original*', he remarked. Sterne, encouraged by the mirth of the company and still unaware of his neighbour's identity, was carried away by his fertile imagination to draw a bizarre portrait from hearsay and fancy of this unknown character, and to fabricate stories about him. When Dutens had left the party his name was revealed to Sterne with suggestions that reparation would be demanded by the subject of his high-spirited drollery. Hurrying next day to apologize for his exuberance, Sterne found that Dutens bore him no grudge and they parted on good terms.

After the Duke and Duchess had left England for their embassy in France, Tavistock wrote affectionately to his father from Woburn in November:

It is impossible to be at this place and not write to Paris when everything I see reminds me so much of you. Woburn is still green and in great beauty, but there is an air of solititude and emptiness that gives it a far different appearance from when you are all here . . . My company all went yesterday . . . the greatest damage we have done you here is eating up some of your porkers (for sheep and oxen we were not able to master), drinking up all your old Burgundy and burning great quantities of your billeting.

While making a show of cheerfulness to his father, he confided to his friend (to whom he had vowed while in Italy that he would keep clear of love 'for if it once gets hold of me I can no longer answer for myself') the present anguished state of his feelings:

O my dear Robinson, since we last met strange things have happened to your poor friend. I have lost the greatest prospect of happiness I ever formed to myself, but in lieu of it I have gained a certain philosophical apathy, a sang-froid upon the events of this world that partly recompense the severity of my loss. You may guess that love alone can have wrought such a change of sentiments.

Staying with his sister at Blenheim he had fallen passionately in love with the Duke of Marlborough's sister Elizabeth, wife of the Earl of Pembroke, and his love had been returned. Lord Pembroke, a coarse, bad-tempered man, had some months before gone off with a young woman abroad, inviting his wife to join them in a *ménage à trois*. Deterred by her family from embarking on so mad a course, it was not surprising that Lady Pembroke, who was all tenderness and affection, should have responded under the stress of emotion to Tavistock's declaration of love, but their passionate feelings for each other had no future; good sense prevailed, and a year later her penitent husband returned and she was reconciled to him. In old age she was to arouse the passions of the insane George III.

While the Duke of Bedford occupied the unpretentious Hôtel Grinberghen on the corner of the Boulevard St Germain, Tavistock had his own establishment in the same quarter of Paris. True to his character for sensible economy, the Duke's mode of life found no favour with one visiting Englishman. The young Edward Gibbon, as yet hardly recognized as an author, made himself known to the Duke and was civilly received, but his hope of enjoying ducal hospitality was unfulfilled. 'I have presented myself at his door once every week or ten days without ever being let in or hearing a syllable from him,' he complained to his family. 'Indeed, I have often blushed for him, for I find that his stateliness and avarice make him the joke of Paris.' The Duke perhaps preferred the company of his equals. The Duchesse de Choiseul became his friend and wrote him long letters in exquisite French full of aphorisms and sentiment, that read now like carefully constructed literary compositions. When she heard his eyesight had declined she wrote larger but not more legibly.

At twenty-four Tavistock's pleasant face laid no claim to notable good looks – an early fullness of the jaw foretold the heavier features of his father, but the sweetness of his manner, his intelligence, and his lovable disposition secured him the affection of French ladies. His liking for them was qualified.

Lord Tavistock to Hon. Thomas Robinson

March 16 1763
Hotel de Beaupréau
Rue de l'Université

. . . I have a very numerous acquaintance among the first people of the place . . . tho' upon the whole I prefer the life of London infinitely, bar politicks. The coterie to which I more properly belong is that of the Prince de Conty. He is a prince of the blood, très grand seigneur and not at all in good humour with the Court. His house is open to almost all the world and I much doubt if your opposition in England, patriotic as you are, understand courting and gaining popularity so well as he does. He is sensible, pretty much informed, generous, affable, and the freest manner of doing the honours I ever met with; there are some few etiquettes and forms which one is obliged to shew him as being of the house of Bourbon, which rather take off from what would other-wise be almost perfection in the point of society. Twice a week he gives concerts and assemblys which are open to all the world, the private parties are still more agreeable. At Easter begins one of the four *voyages* he makes in a year to his country house and to which I am invited.

. . . Suppers are very frequent, the dinners less so, and the eating is excellent and studied – indeed that and dress and other such innocent topics are the substance of almost all the conversation – scandal and gallantry, however much they may be practised, are never talked of, the former no one can more easily dispense with than myself, but a certain degree of freedom of conversation and double entendre are absolutely necessary to hinder the same thing being repeated every minute. I never saw anything so general as the reserve of the women in respect to everything that can excite the passions, I do not reckon indelicacy of the number; in that indeed they are beyond all measure. Somebody here said the other day that their ears were the only chaste part about them . . . You are made to please here and to be amused yourself. The absurdities of the French nationality are the best lesson to make one forget one's own.

For my own part my heart continues in the same situation as when I saw you last. I have loved too well ever to love again. I lye with a fille du théatre who is tolerably entertaining, and a good peice, but that costs some money. I have just furnished my house and am beginning pour donner à manger, and flatter myself it will be in tolerable perfection by the time you eat your first dinner here.

While disclaiming to his friend any desire to embark on a fashionable intrigue, Tavistock had singled out from the worldly company that frequented the Prince de Conti's apartments in the Temple, one French-woman as being superior to the rest – the Comtesse de Boufflers, who for many years had been the Prince's mistress, and wished very much to be his wife. Approaching forty, Madame de Boufflers passed for thirty, having kept the fresh brilliance of a girl. She was separated from her husband, and, living in rooms of her own in the Temple, she acted discreetly as hostess at the assemblies of her royal lover. Madame du Deffand, who disliked her, called her 'la divine comtesse', or 'l'Idole du Temple'. Well fitted by her intelligence and eloquence to move among the literary and intellectual friends and dependents of the Prince, Madame de Boufflers was herself the correspondent of Rousseau and Hume; the last was to become her devoted admirer. Attaching himself to this exceptional woman, Tavistock discerned beneath the worldly exterior the merits of her character, her good sense, and her delicacy of feeling. 'She is unique', he told Robinson. The warmth of her sentiment for the composed, sensitive, and charming young English nobleman cannot be doubted; it is likely that he confided to her his late unhappy love affair. She was an ardent anglophile, and when she planned her first visit to England Tavistock proposed to go with her. Conjecturing that news of his attachment to this celebrated woman had probably been carried to England, he wrote in advance to his father (who had been called to London): 'I am well aware that as I have chose this time to have the pleasure of seeing

Mme de Boufflers at her first arrival, the good-natured people in London will amuse themselves at our expence, but if she despises their discourses as much as I do, this will have very little effect.' The death of the Duchess of Bedford's sister, the Countess of Upper Ossory, prevented him carrying out his intention. 'I cannot', he told Robinson, 'think of leaving my mother quite alone in her present state of distress.'

Madame de Boufflers's visit to London has been wittily described by Horace Walpole – her determination to see everything and to be pleased with everything. From Strawberry Hill he wrote: 'She rises every morning so fatigued with the toils of the preceeding day, that she has not strength, if she had inclination, to observe the least or the finest thing she sees. She came hither today to a great breakfast I made for her, with her eyes a foot deep in her head, her hands dangling, and scarce able to support her knitting bag.' From Boswell we hear of her visit to Samuel Johnson in that other Temple, and the Doctor's tardy and ungainly attempt at gallantry.

During the time the Duke of Bedford acted as ambassador, he was called on but once to cross the Channel for consultation in London. It is from Casanova that we hear of an encounter on that occasion with the stubborn nobleman that is in keeping with the characters of both travellers. Casanova arriving at Calais hires the only packet available to take him to Dover, and pays six guineas in advance. Hardly has he got his things on board when the Duke of Bedford's courier appears and declares that the ship has been reserved by letter for the English Ambassador. The master of the ship equivocates; Casanova declines to withdraw. Bedford arrives himself in the town and sends a messenger begging Casanova to yield the boat to him. Casanova claims a place in it for himself and his servants before he will agree. The Duke stipulates that he must be allowed to pay the fee of six guineas. The Italian replies that the fee is already paid: 'I do not re-sell that which I have bought.' The Duke calls on him in person and says they must go shares. After exchanging civilities they shake hands and Bedford goes out, leaving unobserved three guineas on the table. 'An hour afterwards,' writes Casanova, 'I returned the call and then told the master to take the Duke and his carriages on board.'

There is no evidence that the Duchess of Bedford enjoyed the eight months she spent in France; in the early days she was bored and voiced her preference for England. While her genial husband and her son endeared themselves to the French in the salons of Madame Geoffrin and Madame Du Deffand, and in the Prince de Conti's rooms, her haughtiness may have passed for bad manners and her emphatic utterances have seemed

Francis, Marquess of Tavistock
by Batoni

Elizabeth Keppel, Marchioness of
Tavistock by Reynolds

The fifth Duke of Bedford by Hoppner

to lack wit. Before her presentation at Versailles she was assured by the Duchesse de Choiseul that she would find the King and Queen kind and not unapproachable. 'Je puis le croire,' replied the Duchess of Bedford, with Dublin in her mind, 'je viens de jouer ce rôle là moi-même.' When she left France with the Duke in 1763, Louis XV presented her with a magnificent Sèvres dinner service of one hundred and eighty-three pieces. Exquisitely decorated with birds and flowers within a border of deep blue and gold, it was one of the glories of the Sèvres factory, as it is of Woburn now. The Duke received a snuff box from the King, which may have been the one picked from his pocket at the Opera in London a few years later.

In the spring of 1764 Tavistock returned to Paris by himself. He spent a week at l'Ile Adam, the Prince de Conti's country house, where ninety or a hundred persons might gather at a time 'without', he wrote, 'being at all in each others way, for every one forms his own party for the day, whether it is for the chasse, the promenade, the Opera, the play, dancing, gaming, etc.'

Might it have been that the young man wished to speak to Madame de Boufflers about the most serious decision of his life? Their conversations taking place, perhaps, in a setting similar to those scenes we recognize in the paintings of Watteau or Hubert Robert, where striped pavilions and pedimented temples merge into the blue depths of the trees, and human beings are held in suspended animation and timeless pleasure.

His choice of a wife was disclosed that summer. 'Lord Tavistock has flung his handkerchief,' wrote Walpole, 'and except for a few jealous sultans and some *sultanas valides* who had marketable daughters every body is pleased that the lot has fallen on Lady Elizabeth Keppel.' As one of Queen Charlotte's bridesmaids, Walpole had not admired the daughter of the Earl of Albemarle, complaining that she had 'neither features nor air', but now he was all sentiment and satisfaction. Let him continue the story, for he tells it charmingly. Lady Elizabeth had been invited to go and see the Duchess of Marlborough: 'When she arrived at Marlborough House she found nobody but the Duchess and Lord Tavistock. The Duchess cried "Lord! They have left the window open in the next room!" – went to shut it and shut in the lovers too, where they remained for three hours . . . she has behaved in the prettiest manner in the world, and would not appear at a vast assembly at Northumberland House . . . nor at a great hay-making at Mrs Pitt's. Yesterday they all went to Woburn and tomorrow the ceremony is to be performed, for the Duke has not a moment's patience till she is breeding.'

'I dare not say how happy I am', wrote Tavistock to his 'best father' the day after the wedding, and to Robinson, the confidant of his previous love affair, he described his present happiness: 'I feel for her an attachment equally binding with the most violent love, tho' it wants its enchanting fire and delirium . . . I have a tenderness for her of which I did not think my heart was capable, but is very different from what I felt for Lady – .' He wishes his friend to know that he has told his wife of his former attachment: 'she wept for my misfortunes; she seemed entirely satisfied with my conduct and equally so with that of Lady – , whose love for me was the only thing I concealed from her. I think I shall not see much of London this year.' It was to be a supremely happy and tragically short marriage. Madame de Boufflers wrote to the Duke of her '*joie infinie*', and that she flattered herself that she had contributed to an event that she knew he desired more than anything in the world.

Successful in peace-making, the Duke returned from Paris protesting that he was reluctant to undertake further public service – that he wished to live in the country.

'I can't help interesting myself in politics since you take a part in them,' declared Tavistock, who since he was twenty-one had represented the town of Bedford in Parliament, 'tho' I own my aversion to politicians is stronger than ever, and I cannot help most earnestly wishing to see you serving your country as a private person.' The Duke of Bedford's friends, Sandwich, Gower, Rigby and others – the Bloomsbury Gang – who depended on his influence to get them lucrative posts in Government, felt otherwise, and it would have been surprising if Bedford had been able to abstain from engaging in the manoeuvres that put one lot of Whigs in power and turned others out. When his royal master, 'buffeted by the blasts of faction', called on him for help in making an administration he advised the King to send for Pitt; but Pitt when appealed to put an absolute veto on the Duke of Bedford. Nettled by the rebuff, the Duke unwillingly accepted the Presidency of the Council, and with Grenville acting as First Lord of the Treasury he formed what was known as 'the Bedford Ministry', a condition of taking office being that Lord Bute should be excluded from the counsel of the King.

Governed as he was by strong feelings and a hot temper, the Regency

Bill and the Wilkes affair were to inflame the Duke of Bedford's passions during the ensuing years. For wishing to exclude the King's mother, the Princess Dowager, from the first, since she was the close friend of Bute, he offended his sovereign, and for criticizing the City magistrates for their weak handling of the Wilkes riots he was long remembered as the enemy of 'Wilkes and Liberty'.

The passage in the Commons of a Bill to increase the duties on imported silks had raised the hopes of the unemployed Spitalfields weavers, but when the Bill reached the Lords, the Duke – who was against restrictions on trade – opposed it, speaking with some harshness of the weavers, and it was thrown out. A tumultuous mob threatened the House of Lords, and the Duke, who two years before had been hissed in the streets for making peace with France, was now assaulted in his coach and hissed and pelted by an angry body of weavers. He behaved with courage and resolution when a well-aimed stone caught the hand he put up to shield his head, and cut it to the bone. During the night of 18 May a riotous mob, with few weavers among it, appeared in Bloomsbury Square and began to pull down the outer wall of Bedford House. Lady Tavistock, who was near the time of her lying-in, had been sent away, but the Duchess insisted on remaining with her husband. A squadron of cavalry was quartered in the gardens of Bedford House, and troops were discreetly assembled at strategic points in other parts of the town. As may be seen in letters of that period, the siege of Bedford House was the principal news of the moment. The King was kept informed by his Secretary at War of what was happening, and the little Duke, fulminating with rage, sent out every few hours explosive letters to Lord Sandwich.

Duke of Bedford to Lord Sandwich

Bedford House
½ past 2

. . . I cannot support this house from attack both in front and Rear considering our great extent towards the fields and the badness of the walls without 170 men of infantry at least, and our cavalry to be reinforced . . . If this can't be done I must send my wife out of town and necessarily attend her myself and leave my house to be sacked and plundered.

Using Rigby as his secretary, he wrote again:

at ½ before eleven
Sunday night
19 May 1765

. . . A most riotous and tumultuous crowd assembled again this afternoon in Bloomsbury Square and all ye environs of my house, they
began first by only bellowing, shouting and making all kinds of noise . . .
till at last they became more violent and outrageous to such a degree as
to insult ye coaches and chairs of great numbers of my friends who
were so kind as to come to see me this evening. Particularly they broke
the coach glasses of Lady Bolingbroke, Lord Grosvenor . . . as well as
Lord Eglinton, who was himself struck in his coach with a stone thrown
into it. The Justice of the Peace, Mr Welsh, who attended here, out of
tenderness would not read the Proclamation, but ordered a party of
the Horse Guards to ride amongst them and be particularily cautious
not to strike any of them . . . All is pretty quiet at present, tho' when I
am to be relieved from these scandalous insults and most infamous
outrages, I vow to God I am at a loss to know . . .

At length the Riot Act was read, the Horse Guards charged and the crowd
ran; there were, luckily, few injuries and no deaths. The Duke and
Duchess were both convinced that Lord Bute had set the mob on against
them.

The antipathy between George III and his ministers provoked a crisis
soon after these events. 'Tho' unable to remove them', the King noted in
a private memorandum, 'I could not be so wanting to myself as to omit
every time I saw them shewing them by the coldness of my manner the
real dislike I had of them; this drove the Duke of Bedford to take the most
improper step of coming to me . . . and taking a paper out of his pocket,
which he read.' The paper produced from the Duke's deep pocket was a
prepared minute stating the complaint of the ministers that they had lost
the King's favour, and their belief that Bute's influence was still paramount
with him. Three accounts of this interview from the pen of George III
give the lie to the assertion of Junius that the King, overcome by the Duke
of Bedford's insults and brutal manner, had been left in convulsions. It
was not so. When the President of the Council had left him, the King sat
down and wrote two letters; one to his uncle Cumberland, one to the
Lord Chancellor. To his uncle he emphasized his objection to the Duke of
Bedford's casual manner: 'he drew a paper out of his pocket and read it . . .

I with difficulty kept my temper, but did master it.' To Lord Northington he wrote of the Duke's 'harangue'. 'You will easily conceive what indignation I felt at so offensive a declaration, yet I mastered my temper and we parted with cool civility.' There were no hysterics; it was a triumph of self-control. The Duke of Bedford, when he got home, put a short postscript to *The Minutes of Matters to be mentioned to the King*: 'To all this the King made no other answer than declaring Lord Bute was not consulted and that he had never done me ill offices with the King'. We may be certain that he was unconscious of having lectured his sovereign or treated him with any lack of courtesy. A month later George III dismissed his ministers and the Duke of Bedford did not hold office again, though he continued to use his influence on behalf of his friends.

Retirement to Woburn had at all times been a refreshment to him; how much more so now after the annoyance of these stormy events; with what contentment he must have turned his horse's head to the north from Bedford House towards the fields beyond Bloomsbury. Riding as far as St Albans he would be met by a chaise sent from Woburn to carry him the last part of the way home. Tavistock and his wife were settled at Houghton Park a few miles away, and there later in the summer the Duke had the satisfaction of seeing his first grandson occupy a cradle in the nursery.

Houghton, an architecturally distinguished house, had been built in Jacobean times for that Countess of Pembroke who was 'Sidney's sister, Pembroke's mother'. Surrounded by a park, it stood on a hill near Ampthill, overlooking the flat midlands. Today the house with its four square angle turrets and its italianate three-tiered loggia is a roofless shell. It is a melancholy monument, and a reminder of how transitory is human happiness.

Madame de Boufflers came to England in July. While fearing that she would be in the way, she had expressed a wish to pass the time at Woburn and with the Tavistocks at Houghton. She wanted, no doubt, the gratification of seeing with her own eyes the felicity of the young man to whom she was so unequivocally attached. She perhaps took the Duke back to France with her, for there is a letter from him to the Duchess from Paris, written in high spirits and partly in French.

. . . Pendant que je me régale ici avec des pêches, vous mangez des misérables bilberies là bas où vous êtes, pour mes cerneaux, vous n'avez que des misérables

noisettes; à l'égard de moi-même on me donne des baisers, au lieu des coups de pierre dont on me saluait à Londres.

Tavistock, as a farmer, was occupied with the management of his estate, sharing with his father his anxieties for the harvest, and his ideas of the philanthropy proper to a great landowner. When corn was very dear he bought in a stock and sold it cheaply to the poor people, recommending that his father should do the same. Despite the Duke's increasing gout, failing eyesight, and the rankle of political jealousies, it was a period of domestic happiness. New ties had been formed, and new affections had enlarged the circle of this united family; promise of its continuity had been fulfilled by the birth of an heir. The faithful Rigby went between the two households, as much at home in one as in the other; he gave his advice on the laying out of a garden at Houghton, and at the Abbey his irrepressible good-humoured banter and chaff was centred on the Duchess of Bedford's nieces, Miss Mary and Miss Betty Wrottesley, and Lady Mary Fitzpatrick – girls, who from sad circumstances had no other fixed homes, and had been taken under the wing of the Duchess. Mary Wrottesley was one of the Queen's Maids of Honour, and had apartments at Court; Betty, with her black eyes and drawling voice – living with the Duchess since the separation of her parents – had caught something of her aunt's manner, and in the fashionable world her light arrogance was resented by other Misses who had not the benefit of ducal protection. The presence of these young women added much to the cheerfulness of their elders after Caroline Russell's marriage. As part of the Duchess's entourage at Paris, the rival merits of Lady Mary and Miss Betty had been debated, and by Madame Geoffrin, who scolded the Duke for not getting them husbands, they were remembered kindly as *'ces deux jolies nymphes'*. Mary and Betty Wrottesley were painted by Gainsborough at the time when the Duchess sat to him for her portrait. There is a sweetness in Miss Mary's face which is not to be found in Miss Betty's.

Scattered throughout the house, paintings acquaint us with the features of these inmates of Woburn Abbey. In the Breakfast Room there is a group of portraits by Sir Joshua Reynolds that are linked – as the sitters were in life by family or friendship – by a common colour scheme of blue and shades of white. Since the flesh tints also conform to the artist's chosen principle, the robust health of the persons represented makes a curiously wan show.

Here is the Duchess of Bedford quizzing us as she lays aside her French novel; her dress is covered with a profusion of blue silk bows and immense lace ruffles fall from her elbows. Across the room we see her daughter Caroline, richly dressed in white satin with a blue pelisse over her shoulders; a pink rose is tucked into her bosom and she holds on her knees a very small Blenheim spaniel – an offering perhaps from the Duke of Marlborough. Since her eyes do not meet ours we cannot judge the quality of her expression. Of the two male portraits by Reynolds, one is of Lord Tavistock and the other of his brother-in-law Admiral the Honourable Augustus Keppel. The young Marquess, modest and manly, wears the habit of the Dunstable Hunt – a white coat, blue-cuffed, with a blue waistcoat. In the uniform of the bluff and massive naval officer, the colours are reversed, the coat is blue with white cuffs, the waistcoat being white. It was rumoured that Keppel was to marry Mary Wrottesley, but she dying when she was twenty-nine, he remained a bachelor all his life. Dominating the room is the full-length portrait of Lady Elizabeth Keppel by Reynolds. In contrast to the cold shades of the other pictures, this one captivates by its warmth and rich but subdued hues. Wearing the dress in which she was a bridesmaid to Queen Charlotte, and attended by a kneeling dusky female figure, Elizabeth raises her arms to decorate with garlands a statue of Hymen. The white and silver of her dress, the sequined bodice, the spangled gauze of the over-skirt, the diamonds in her hair strike no chill, so delicately has the artist imbued the painting with the young woman's vital humanity and joy. There can be little surprise that Sir Thomas Lawrence was to think it the most beautiful female portrait he had ever seen.

Poor Elizabeth! Passionately in love with her husband, her happy marriage lasted less than three years; in that time she bore two sons and was expecting a third child when in March 1767 Tavistock was carried home after an accident in the hunting-field. Thrown from his horse, he received a kick on the head from its hoof that fractured his skull. While he lay insensible, horrifying operations were carried out to remove splinters of bone from his brain; but nothing availed and two weeks later he was dead.

The Duke of Bedford's grief was so violent that it was thought he could not survive the blow. Horace Walpole tells of how the wretched father's head broke out in boils – 'which shows the effort he made to suppress his agony, and which probably saved his life'. A month of blank pages in the Duke's journal is a moving testimony to his suffering. In his short life of twenty-seven years Tavistock had shown the fine qualities of his character, his integrity, humility, and good sense, and he had endeared himself to all who knew him. He was universally lamented. In her uncharitable way Madame Du Deffand wrote from Paris that Madame de Boufflers '*mène un deuil de Milord Tavistock, qui fait hausser les épaules*'. David Hume commented in a letter to '*la divine comtesse*' that:

> It was very happy for the Duke . . . that there were public transactions in Parliament, in which his friends urged him to take part. The natural fervour of his character insensibly engaged him in the scene . . . He has not however recovered that terrible shock, and the Duchess, to whom the world did not ascribe so great a degree of sensibility, is still more inconsolable.

The broken-hearted young widow survived her husband no more than a year and a half. She bore a third son and then sank gently into a decline. A physician who attended her at Bedford House, feeling her pulse, begged her to open her hand. With gentle force he overcame her reluctance and saw that she held in her closed hand a miniature of her husband. When he reproached her for hindering her recovery by thus dwelling on her grief, she confessed that the picture had been in her hand or in her bosom ever since the day of Tavistock's death, and would remain so 'until I drop off after him into the welcome grave'.

The mild climate of Portugal being thought beneficial for debility and weak lungs, she undertook a journey to Lisbon; her sister went with her, and she travelled in her brother Keppel's warship. It was 'a blowing passage' of twelve days. So low had she been reduced by the doctors' ill-judged treatment of her malady that she had no chance of recovery, and soon after reaching Lisbon she quietly died. The Duke entered in his journal of 19 November 1768:

> Received the melancholy news of dear Lady Tavistock's death. Miss Wrottesley and I went to see Lady Albemarle in the evening.

He had himself little more than two years to live, and the view we form of him is of a man stricken but indomitable. Operated on for cataract, his subsequent changed appearance shocked his friends. 'His eyes are a ghastly object. He seems blind himself and makes everyone else so that looks at him', wrote Selwyn. 'They have no speculation in them, as Shakespeare says; what should be white is red, and there is no sight or crystal, only a black spot . . . he looks like a man in a tragedy, as in King Lear, that has had his eyes put out with a *fer rouge*.' Gainsborough, who finished a portrait of the Duke at Bath a few months later, handled his task with consummate skill, evading the harsh realities. The brilliant scarlet of the Duke's coat enhances the pale gravity of the ravaged face, the eyes so darkly blank that we may guess they are almost without sight. An elderly peer who sat for Reynolds once said of his own portrait: 'He has made an old man look as if he was in pain, which old men generally are, and so far he is right.' Gainsborough's picture of the ageing Duke is a fine portrayal of dignified suffering. After the death of his son he sold a picture by Gavin Hamilton, of Hector dragged at the wheels of Achilles' chariot, being unable to endure the sight of it.

When the Duke and Duchess were apart – and they often were – her brisk and affectionate letters to him have a recurring theme – her liking for young people, and her never-failing delight in Woburn. In the company of her nieces and grandsons – for Houghton had been allocated to Lord Ossory and henceforth the three little Russell boys, Francis, John, and William, lived with their grandparents – she was always happy to return to Woburn from London or from a visit to her brother at Trentham.

My dear Love, I feel quite impatient to communicate to you the pleasure I feel in being returned to this comfortable place (such nectarines), fine it cannot be thought, as the King of Denmark was on Sunday last at the George in Woburn for two hours and never looked into the park; our German cook dressed his dinner, and had much conversation with him, which ended in his giving him five guineas. Some of the suite lay all night at the inn and came here in the morning . . . I have no correspondents nor expect any visitors. My Misses and I will be quite *savantes* when you return.

We hear of 'Chuff', the eldest little boy, being 'a good-humoured little angel' and 'more delightful than ever'. In the hot weather they 'breakfasted upon the pavement', and felt cheated when it was cold, 'which is a very great misfortune to my little companions and me, for we have lived out of doors and not found the hay too long'. About this time the Duke recorded in his journal an incident that is expressive of the benevolence of both him and his wife and illustrates the warmth of her feelings for children.

This night as the servants were bringing in things for supper and were going to shut ye door out of ye Park, a little girl about three years old was found sitting on the steps with a letter tied round her neck directed to my wife. The girl said she had been left there by her Father – which child is brought up by my wife.

'A Letter to the Duke of Bedford' which Lord Brougham was to call 'the most scurrilous of any that were printed under the name of Junius', appeared that year in the *Public Advertiser*, and much pain it must have given to the Duke, for as well as taunting him with accusations of dishonesty, parsimony, rapacity, profligacy, and his brutal treatment of the King, it charged him with being insensible to the death of his son. Even today the malignity of this attack makes hateful reading, and rouses a loathing of the political writer who sheltered behind a pseudonym. The marriage of Betty Wrottesley to the profligate Duke of Grafton, First Lord of the Treasury, who had divorced his first wife, was the occasion for a public letter addressed by Junius to the bridegroom, reviling him for his public and private conduct, and observing that while his bride was the niece of the Duchess of Bedford, Grafton's late wife had married Gertrude's nephew, the Earl of Upper Ossory. 'But ties of this tender nature cannot be drawn too close, and it may possibly be part of the Duke of Bedford's ambition after making *her* an honest woman, to work a miracle of the same sort upon your Grace.'

This change of partners in marriage was successful and made for greater happiness all round. 'I must do the Duchess of Bedford justice to say that a Spartan dame never launched more excellent wives than she has done,' remarked Horace Walpole with candour and unusual generosity, and the Duke of Grafton in his memoirs was to pay tribute to the qualities of his second wife, the mother of nine children.

Sir Philip Francis, who is generally believed to have been Junius, lived on terms of great intimacy in his middle age with the fourth Duke of Bedford's grandsons, the fifth Duke and his brother John. The latter, when old, stated that except in the course of casual conversation the subject of the Junius letters had never been touched on, but confessed he thought 'there was strong internal evidence of Sir Philip being Junius'. Francis's widow once remarked that she had always had the impression that her husband, who was a great adherent of the Russells in his later days, was oppressed by a consciousness that in early life he had done the family a great wrong.

After Betty Wrottesley's marriage, which took place at Woburn Abbey, the Duke of Bedford went down to the West Country to look at his estates in Devonshire. He was Lord Lieutenant of the County, and his journey took him to Exeter, where he inspected old Bedford House, well known to the second Earl of Bedford, and he paid a visit to the earlier home of his ancestors, Berwick in Dorset, which he found 'but a dismal place'. He was given 'a fine farmer-like dinner' by a tenant, and 'a hearty welcome'. It may have partly compensated for a rude assault made on him as he came through Honiton, where a vast concourse of people had gathered outside the inn door to hiss and groan at him; there were cries of 'Wilkes and Liberty', and 'the Peace-maker', and so forth. As he rode out of the high street 'near twenty bulldogs were halloed at my horse, but by the grace of God, no one actually seized him, though I had two for a long time just under his nose. The mob then threw stones, a great many of these hit me, though without any damage to myself. Upon this I galloped forward. My chaise which followed . . . was pelted with stones and two of the glasses and a panel broken.' It was unjust treatment for an elderly man who had always acted in what he thought were the best interests of his country. As he spurred his horse on he may have cast a thought back to the violence of the weavers' riots, and recollected, too, an unmerited attack made on him many years before, when as a young married man he had been assaulted on Lichfield racecourse while he was staying with his father-in-law, the renegade Lord Gower. A Jacobite mob had set on the party from Trentham, and the Duke and Richard Rigby had not escaped being horse-whipped by a local attorney. A 'drubbing' it was called, and the story of it had spread far, serving as a jest at the Duke's expense, even within the Closet of the King.

His remarkable physical energy did not desert him until six months before his death. His practical interest in his crops and his herds, his gardens and his woods continued unabated. Finding it increasingly difficult to mount his horse, he had mounting-blocks put up in twenty places on the Woburn estate.

When he was nearly blind and partially paralysed, his charity was called on in the last month of his life to relieve the poor victims of serious floods in the Cambridgeshire fens round Thorney; he gave with a generous hand and with special thought for the children. There are entries in his memorandum books about agricultural affairs until a few days before his death in January 1771.

If we may believe the blue-stocking, Mrs Montagu, 'he departed singing the 104th psalm'. And what more fitting last words than this hymn of praise proclaiming the abounding wonders of the earth, from the lips of one who in a busy life had been most happy planting cedars of Lebanon, directing the course of the springs that the beasts of the field might drink thereof, and had taken pains that there should be grass for the cattle and green herbs for the service of men.

12

'He made two blades of Grass grow where one did before'

GERTRUDE was fifty-five when her husband died. Widowhood was not a state she could be expected to enjoy, for her zest for life was unimpaired and she still had lively passions, or an inordinate amount of vanity. Her critics were quick to note and mock her weaknesses and indiscretions. Happy with the Duke of Bedford, it seems she would have liked to make another venture into matrimony after his death, but reason did not direct her choice. Mrs Delany called her an 'old hoyden', and reported a flirtation with Lord Hertford, – 'to the great amusement of beholders'. In 1775 Edward Gibbon wrote that: 'The Duchess of Bedford made regular proposals to the young Earl of Cholmondeley, and was as regularly refused. Poor as he was (he replied to Mr. Fitzpatrick her Embassador) he was not quite poor enough to accept them.' Lord Cholmondeley was her junior by thirty years. When a few years later it was known that Lord March – a very young man – intended to marry, Lady Sarah Bunbury remarked that she was afraid 'he won't marry Miss Pelham or the Duchess of Bedford, either of which would do very well'. Two months before her death in 1794 the *Oracle* assured its readers that she was about to give her hand to 'the gallant Lothario Mr. Canning'.

The dinners the Duchess now gave were dull, and George Selwyn found the food less good than what he got in other houses. The Duchess had never liked wine, and her aversion to it and his hope of one day making her drunk was a recurring joke with Richard Rigby. Perhaps as a widow she curtailed the supply of claret and brandy. Selwyn would have remembered the splendid ostentation of former days when a masterpiece of the confectioner's art was produced to grace her dinner table – 'the Wilton Bridge in sugar, almost as big as the life'. It was a time when a great man's cook must emulate or outdo a rival's inventions and skill. At a party given by Frederick, Prince of Wales, an iced cake representing the fortifications of Carlisle was demolished by sugar cannon balls thrown by Maids of Honour, and the Duke of Bedford's cook would have heard too of a dessert at Northumberland House, which took the form 'of a *chasse* at Herenhausen'.

If Gertrude's social power and talents were now restricted she was of considerable consequence in her family, having in her charge a number of young people. To her had been left the responsibility of bringing up the three orphaned grandsons, and she had the care of several nieces; the younger daughters of her sister Lady Mary Wrottesley; and the two girls the Countess of Upper Ossory had borne her second husband – Richard Vernon, who was known at White's Club as 'the father of the Turf'.

The eldest grandson, Francis, was six years old when he became the fifth Duke of Bedford, and during his long minority Gertrude and Mr Palmer, the agent-in-chief and joint guardian of the boys with the Duchess, administered affairs with good sense, imagination and strict economy, and money was regularly put by. A profitable scheme for building over the fields of the Bloomsbury estate was set on foot; Bedford Square was laid out, and the long street driven north from the east corner was appropriately named Gower Street, after the Duchess's brother.

She had been left the use of Bedford House and Woburn Abbey until the beloved 'Chuff' came of age, and every year she moved her flock backwards and forwards between the two houses. One of her least friendly critics acknowledged that 'with all her faults she shines in education', but Gertrude was perhaps better at bringing up girls than boys, for she was never able to instil in the three grandsons her own proper regard for economy, and the devotion of the brothers to each other has been attributed to a shared dislike of their vigorous, outspoken, and dominating grandmother.

In 1777 Selwyn saw the little Duke and his next brother when they came from Westminster School to dine at Bedford House. Five years later he had another look at him at Lord Gower's, and was 'surprised beyond measure', he told a correspondent, by the appearance of the lad now studying at Trinity College, Cambridge: 'his long lank black hair covering his face, shoulders, neck and everything disguised him so that I have yet to know his figure. I can but guess at his person. Why this singularity at seventeen years of age? *cela n'indique pas un esprit solide.* Lord Gower laughed and said "You perhaps do not know who it is?" Indeed I did not. *Je devine seulement que sa figure n'est pas laide.* His *chevelure* was like that I see in a picture of the great Condé. If there is anything of that hid under this disguise *je lui passerai cette singularité*.'

Boys since then have made a gesture in defiance of authority by the dressing of the hair on their heads and faces; the attempted concealment of immature features acting as the defence of a vulnerable and half-formed nature. Later on, for having a head of straight unpowdered hair, the young duke was refused admission as a candidate for election to Brooks's Club; a rebuff that made its mark, for after a time, the *Morning Post* reported that 'the Duke of Bedford has at last begun to have hair *bien poudré et ajusté*'. Selwyn was hoaxed by the youth's strange appearance, for though taciturn and reserved there was no want of solidity in him, and his strength of character was soon to make itself apparent. The boy must sometimes have pondered on the power his rank and riches would confer on him when he reached manhood and became independent of the control exercised by his grandmother and Mr Palmer. The lack of a father or a grandfather to guide him and to whom he must render the respect due from a boy, was perhaps a deprivation deeply felt, and a reason for his early and devoted attachment to Charles James Fox, sixteen years older than himself; Mr Palmer in his position of command was after all only a servant.

Of all the later Dukes of Bedford, Francis the fifth duke is the most difficult to know, for when he died he ordered that all his papers should be destroyed, and so to gain some knowledge of him we have to sift the testimony of his contemporaries, weigh the vulgar and unreliable paragraphs that appeared in the fashionable publications of the times, examine the satirical cartoons in which he was depicted, and from his speeches in Parliament and his own actions measure his worth.

The awkward boy who at nineteen was sent abroad with a tutor for two years became the assured and magnificent companion of the Prince of Wales and Charles James Fox. He was endowed with a good and wide understanding; upright and truthful, he had a very kind nature. Generous without ostentation, his acts of munificence were governed by sound judgement, and though he was inordinately extravagant and pleasure-loving, he was never frivolous, and when his interest was engaged he was energetic and determined. Liking the company of women – an engraving had already appeared in the *Town and Country Magazine* in 1784 of 'Miss St-ns-n and the Bloomsbury Youth' – he was possibly prejudiced against marriage by feeling himself a target for the schemes of every mother with a marriageable daughter. He learnt to be wary and remained a bachelor, choosing his female company where he pleased, in the upper and lower levels of society, binding himself to none but by affection.

While he was on his first travels abroad Francis became acquainted with Lady Maynard, who as the notorious Nancy Parsons, or Mrs Horton (or Haughton), had passed from the protection of one well-known man to another. As the Duke of Grafton's mistress her appearance with him in his box at the opera – he was Prime Minister – when Queen Charlotte was present, had scandalized London, and served to put an edge on the cutting paragraphs of Junius.

Grafton deserted her when he divorced his wife and married Elizabeth Wrottesley at Woburn in 1769. Nancy passed to new lovers until the young Duke of Dorset took her for himself and carried her off abroad. When in a year or two he parted from her, she found a man who was willing to offer her marriage. 'The Duke of Grafton's Mrs. Horton! The Duke of Dorset's Mrs. Horton! Everybody's Mrs. Horton!' pronounced Horace Walpole when he heard of Nancy's marriage to Lord Maynard, a man of twenty-five, while she was computed to be well over forty; and it was maliciously observed that when she was at the height of her career her husband was not yet born.

She was the daughter of a prosperous Bond Street tailor, and claimed to have been married to a West India merchant. If she was common, as Walpole thought, she was intelligent and good-humoured, and had been well educated in Paris and elsewhere. The secret of her ascendancy may lie in two lines that were current at the time:

'Tis not her charms, 'tis her ingenious mind
That did a Grafton, doth a Dorset bind.

A delightful companion to the sophisticated and the assured, she practised an art that was peculiarly appealing to younger men – 'the art of seeming to take an interest in them, listening to them with complacency . . . making them appear important in their own eyes'. Here perhaps lay her fascination for the young Duke, for he attached himself to the Maynards, and dismissing, we must suppose, his tutor, set up house with them near Paris, moving on with them to Nancy, and later to Nice; and but for fleeting visits to England he remained abroad until after the festivities for his coming of age had taken place at Woburn and in Bloomsbury in his absence. 'Where is the Duke?' asked the *Morning Post*. 'Why comes he not? In minority or majority is it all the same. Does Nancy still control him?' This interest in his affairs was also noticeable in France; it was reported that the joint establishment was run with 'rigid economy', an expression that might have brought a wry smile to the face of Mr Palmer, who in 1784 paid out for the Duke's personal expenditure more than £9000, which in 1786 rose to £13,000.

Lord Maynard had no scruples about leaving his wife alone with the young man from time to time, returning to her side when Francis had to absent himself. In later life the Duke declared that at the age of twenty-four he had hardly ever opened a book: Nancy, perhaps, did her best to remedy the deficiencies of her companion's education, for it was reported in the *Public Advertiser* that 'the old woman' read him 'love odes, and sonnets, pastorals and madrigals, teaching him to get Ovid by heart, etc.' It may have been she who pointed to the need for certain objects that would contribute to their domestic comfort, but it was Francis who wrote out in his own hand a list of common things that were to be sent out from England by the cheapest conveyance: 'A warming pan, two porridge pots, three brass candlesticks, a rolling-pin, a gridiron, four saucepans, five Welsh porringers, one spit, two dozen pewter plates, a pint jack, and a frying pan.' And a carriage was ordered from England and despatched to Nice.

And how, we may ask, did the Duchess of Bedford view the approach of her grandson's majority in July 1786 – the moment when she must give up to him beloved Woburn and Bedford House? Horace Walpole heard that:

> The Duke of Bedford has ordered Mr. Palmer to have all his palaces ready for him – which is considered as an expulsion of the Queen Dowager. If it is only to make room for another antique, old woman for old woman, I should think one's own grandmother might be preferable to one that for many reasons might be grandmother of half London.

Francis must have expected a wrangle with the Duchess over his inheritance for he wrote from Plombières in August 1786 to his cousin the Earl of Upper Ossory:

> I was very much surprised at receiving a letter from the Duchess confirming that she meant to give me up Woburn in October . . . I intended

being in England by this time had Woburn been given up. It has made me put off my journey about a fortnight so I shall not be there until the beginning of September. I shall avoid going to Woburn after my first visit as I am sure the Duchess will do nothing but plead me to let her live there and if not to let her take away half the furniture.

It was characteristic of Gertrude to remark (so it was said) when she heard of her grandson's liaison, that 'she blessed his prudence in forming an amour which could not be productive of children and the expenses in consequence thereof'.

When the Duke did arrive in England he came with Lord Maynard, having left his youngest brother, William, to escort Nancy from France two weeks later. Francis made no secret that he would continue his *ménage à trois*, but there is no evidence that Lady Maynard was ever installed as the mistress of Woburn. She was not displeased with her sentimental education of the young man on whom the attention of society was now turned, for she told a friend:

The Duke of Bedford is so shy that he appears unhappy in society. He is so reserved that he will get into a corner. There is no doubt he would have fallen into low company who would have taught him to game and drink, and would have kept him among themselves. Now his behaviour is suitable to his rank.

She confessed ingenuously that there were advantages for herself and her husband from their association with a very rich man:

for we are able to appear more suitable to our situation than we could otherwise do.

There were rumours that the Duke (despite having two fine houses) would buy Gunnersbury, vacant since the death of Princess Amelia; that he would buy a house near Brooks's Club (Horace Walpole sneered that either of these would be convenient for the Maynards); instead he became the tenant of a small estate in Essex belonging to Lord Maynard, and in London he was seen everywhere in the company of his lordship and his wife.

'I have not observed', said Dr Johnson, 'that men of very large fortunes enjoy anything extraordinary that makes happiness. What has the Duke of Bedford?'

Johnson was not the most consistent of men. Pressed once to answer if money would not purchase occupation, he had to concede that it would: 'Sir, money *will* purchase occupation. It will purchase all the conveniences of life; it will purchase variety of company, it will purchase all sorts of entertainment.'

Becoming a friend of the Prince of Wales, and moving in the company of the Whigs who looked to Fox as their leader, the Duke of Bedford's temperament revealed a capacity to take full advantage of those conveniences bestowed on him by his wealth, and when, having tired of politics, he developed a passionate interest in agriculture, he had the means and the situation to encourage the experiments that did so much to improve English farming and livestock. He never lacked occupation. Initially too shy to speak in the House of Lords for fear of showing his ignorance of correct English, he soon gained self-confidence, but his fluency and clarity of statement were not enlightened by wit, and he showed a tendency to underrate the intelligence of his opponents.

Sharing the entertainments and pastimes of his boon companions, he raced his horses at Newmarket and Epsom, winning the Derby three times; he gambled at Brooks's and at Devonshire House; he kept a pack of hounds at Woburn, and as the landlord of the Covent Garden estate his 'energetic and capacious mind' embraced the affairs of Drury Lane and Covent Garden Theatres. Intimate at Carlton House, he was adored in the Devonshire House circle; and at that other centre of the Whig beau monde – Holland House – his hostess, who admitted that 'his manner to *all* is rude, and to his acquaintance must be intolerable', found his society amongst the greatest of her pleasures. 'No man', wrote Lady Holland, 'so just, so generous, so true.' And Charles James Fox recognized his awkwardness in social intercourse when he wrote: 'the Duke of Bedford has a very good understanding . . . I wish I could add popular manners'.

At the age of twenty-six he had grown to be a very handsome man. As he drove to Court for the King's birthday, the magnificence of his apparel and the splendour of his equipage – six footmen in liveries 'worth an argosie' walked on either side of his coach – led to the belief that he was the Prince of Wales, and the guard stood to arms when he arrived. Such an exhibition of opulence, which in some men could be attributed to swaggering vanity, in Francis might be seen rather as a straightforward youthful regard for style and an inherent love of quality. His good looks and the brilliant display attracted the attention of the King's eldest daughter, Charlotte, the Princess Royal, and perhaps also occasioned a tremor in her heart, for ten days after the Levée she had an impassioned interview with her eldest brother. Complaining of her confined life and of being subjected to the violence and caprice of her mother's temper, she begged him to urge that a marriage be arranged for her, or else that she might at least have a separate establishment. She was twenty-seven years old. Detailing to his younger brother all that his sister had said, the Prince of Wales wrote:

> She then entered into an argument with me where the impropriety wd be supposing no arrangement cd take place abroad for her, were an alliance to be thought of for her with *our friend the Duke of Bedford*, and to tell you the truth, my dearest Frederick, I think she seems more anxious for this than any foreign match in the world . . . I told her I thought yt if I knew my father, wh. I thought I did pretty well, yt he never would think of giving his consent to anything of the kind.

None knew his father better. George III would not have forgotten his antipathy to the young man's stubborn, uncomplaisant grandfather. The impatient and oppressed princess had to wait another six years before she was married to the widowed future King of Wurtemberg.

The newspapers, eager to report what the Duke of Bedford wore at Court or on other occasions, noted that when he was first introduced into the House of Lords 'his dress was at once neat and elegant' of brown cloth lined with blue satin. A Court dress was more ostentatious: coat and breeches of violet silk 'richly laced', with silver cuffs and a waistcoat of silverstuff, 'the richest that can be conceived'. It fell to that arbiter of taste and elegance, George Brummel, to voice a criticism of the Duke's sartorial style, when Francis invited the Beau to admire a new coat he was wearing. 'Brummel examined him from head to foot . . . "Turn round" said the Beau – his Grace did so, and the examination continued in front. When it was concluded Brummel stepped forward and feeling the lapel delicately with his thumb and finger said in a most earnest and amusing manner, "Bedford, do you call this thing a coat?"'

Although Francis continued to seek the company of Lady Maynard for several years, another woman figured less publicly in his life, and she too seems not to have been in her first youth. His attachment to Nancy may have been an innocent relationship, the presence of Mrs Hill at the

Abbey indicates one that almost certainly was not. Sir Gilbert Elliot, who rode about the park at Woburn in April 1789, admiring the plantations of evergreens – the fourth Duke's creation – looked also into the stables and the new kennels, regretting that there was no admission to the house, which was only shown on Mondays. 'The Duke is altering and enlarging it at a great expense, although nobody ever inhabits it but Mrs. Hill, an old Madame.' Sir Gilbert may have gossiped with the stable boys for he also noted that there were forty horses in the stables, 'sometimes 60', but that the Duke 'rides generally the same horse or two himself, has but two or three or four servants out with him hunting, and never mounts any friend'. Downman's drawing of Mrs Hill is inscribed: 'I did another drawing for the Duke of Bedford. She was much admired on horseback.' That other drawing has, alas, disappeared. Hospitable though he was, Francis could find recreation independent of his fashionable friends, and a canter round Woburn park with a handsome woman was legitimately a welcome diversion from listening to the Prince of Wales bragging about his racehorses or the Duchess of Devonshire bewailing her gambling debts.

The alterations that Francis was making at Woburn were carried out by Henry Holland, with whose work at Carlton House and Brooks's Club he was familiar. Holland remodelled part of the south side of the Abbey, transforming the insignificant rooms that had served as offices into an enfilade of splendid living-rooms, whose gilded elegance is one of the delights of the house today. The principal room in the range was a long library; two pairs of Corinthian columns at each end formed ante-rooms lined with bookcases similar to those in the main room. The leather-bound books – ornaments in themselves – set off the serene refinement of Holland's mouldings and cornices, and their genial colours were reflected in the gilt pier glasses placed between the windows. An 'inner library' at the east end reached through double doors was embellished with a marble chimney-piece for which Richard Westmacott carved the curious and charming frieze of children playing among water-lilies and nautili. The old library at the south-west corner of the house was altered to become an 'eating room', and here after 1790 were hung twenty-one paintings by Canaletto that had been purchased by the fourth Duke for Bedford House. Henceforth the cold north rooms that had been the family's living-apartments for more than one hundred and fifty years were abandoned in favour of the new ones into which the sun poured through windows that reached from the ceiling to the floor.

Transferring the entrance from the west front to the east side of the house, Holland built a portico with steps leading up to the principal floor, and a new range of bedrooms; the old stables that had strangely survived in the medieval crypt being finally swept away. A great riding-house, and a tennis court of the same dimensions as that at Hampton Court, were built between Flitcroft's stable blocks, and were the setting for indoor exercise and strenuous games of tennis between the Duke and his friends. Admiration must be felt for Charles Fox – considering his girth – who at the age of forty-five pitted himself against the twenty-eight-year-old Duke, and it can be no surprise to learn from him that he was beaten: 'I am sorry to tell you that the Duke has overtaken me at tennis and beat me, even. Last year I gave him near fifteen.'

Most delightful of all Holland's creations, and the goal of a perambulation for the Duke's guests, was a picturesque Chinese Dairy, whose oriental forms were reflected in a small lake, while porcelain bowls and dishes were displayed on its shelves within. A long covered way curved from the house to the little building, passing a magnificent new greenhouse that sheltered tender aromatic shrubs, and continuing beyond the stable blocks, ensured that visitors arrived at the Dairy without damp feet. Later on the greenhouse was adapted to become a sculpture gallery; Holland designed a small Temple of Liberty within the east end, and here were placed marble busts of Fox and the Duke's Whig intimates.

When the Prince of Wales came to see what his own architect had achieved at Woburn, he came as a familiar friend and not as a royal personage visiting a subject. As his coach approached the park from the London road, he would have seen and passed through Holland's new entrance gates – a triple arch of dove-coloured stone surmounted by the carved ducal arms, with the Russell crest above – a goat, *passant*.

While Holland was engaged on building works at Woburn the French Revolution broke out. The Bastille fell and Fox wrote: 'How much the greatest event it is that has ever happened in the world and how much the best.' Bedford, who had been on terms of some intimacy with the Duke of Orleans during his exile in England – he was reputed to share the favours of Madame de Buffon, the latter's mistress – now saw his friend return to France to take part in the destruction of the French king, and to earn himself the title of Philippe Egalité. After the revolution, when the possessions of the Duke of Orleans (for he had not himself escaped the guillotine) were put up for sale, the Duke of Bedford purchased many fine pieces of furniture for his collection, which are now at Woburn.

1793 saw the execution of Louis XVI and the declaration of war on England by the Convention. Fox, as a result of his sympathy with the revolution, found the number of his supporters diminish, but the Duke of Bedford, believing that the principles that made the Glorious Revolution of 1688 in England were being followed out in France, did not desert his leader; and counted among the English Jacobins he was caricatured by Cruikshank as a Sans Culotte in the company of Fox and Whitbread. Danton came to England in 1791 wishing to test the climate of opinion. If he met the Duke of Bedford at this time, he would not have found him in the company of men such as Priestly or Paine, the leaders of the English revolutionary party, with whom the Duke had little in common; but nearly one hundred years later a French historian claimed that in the spring of 1793 the Duke paid Danton a visit in France, and that some time before 31 May, he made his way in the company of Desfieux to Bâle – the centre of diplomatic activity. The Duke's own papers were destroyed when he died, and although no evidence of this mission occurs in the memoirs of his contemporaries or among the papers of Danton, it is not impossible that such a journey was undertaken.

In a year or two the Duke was to be called on as one of two unmarried dukes to support the Prince at his wedding to Caroline of Brunswick, and he told his brother afterwards how hard it had been to bear the weight of the drunken, weeping bridegroom, and to keep him on his feet.

1795, the year of the Prince's marriage, encompassed other matters of importance for the Duke, significant of the independence of his opinions and the increasing range of his interests. He spoke frequently in the House of Lords about the war with the French, urging the need to negotiate for peace – if it were consistent with the interest and security of England – regardless of what form of government prevailed in France. He was always listened to with attention and sometimes with applause, but he was signally unsuccessful in carrying any motion he proposed. Strenuously opposed to the war, he was, however, aware of the danger to his country, and he surprised Ministers by his contribution of £100,000 to the expenses of it. Hostile to the policy of Pitt, he expressed great admiration for his oratory, speaking of it as 'the purest, most correct, forcible and eloquent language, spoke in the most harmonious voice and animated manner'. The Duke's actions were sometimes equivocal. Pitt's decision, following a bad harvest, to tax powder, which was made from flour, prompted Francis to gather a little group of friends at Woburn, where they took part in a ceremonious washing out of the powder from their hair, agreeing to forgo the use of it in future, and the Duke ordered his footmen to go unpowdered for three months. We are left uncertain whether the gesture was a mark of sympathy for the poor who might be short of bread, or a desire to withhold revenue from Pitt.

Francis himself had long had a preference for a cropped, unpowdered head, and his appearance was described as 'striking and manly'; and so we may see him in Hoppner's full-length portrait.

1795 was the year in which Fox at last made Mrs Armistead his wife. At St Ann's Hill the Duke of Bedford was one of their most welcome and frequent visitors, and Mr and Mrs Fox from time to time were his guests at Woburn, where sitting in the long gallery after dinner Fox had a tendency to fall asleep; the Duke's nephew, little Johnny Russell, was sometimes sent to crawl on his hands and knees under the settee on which the statesman reposed, to tickle his calves to stop him snoring.

That same little boy, more than fifty years later, became the biographer of Fox, and in assessing the character of Fox's disciple, Francis, fifth Duke of Bedford, Earl Russell confidently assured later generations of Russells that there was no part of his uncle's parliamentary career that need give his family any cause for regret 'excepting only his remarks on Mr. Burke's pension'.

When Edmund Burke retired from Parliament, worn out by public service and the unchecked power of his feelings, he received a pension from the Crown. Towards the end of 1795 Lord Lauderdale attacked the grant in the House of Lords, complaining that Burke had been given 'an enormous pension for endeavouring to inculate doctrines that tended to extinguish the principles of freedom'. He was seconded by the Duke of Bedford. 'It will appear odd', wrote Burke to a friend, 'but it is true, that I never read the attacks made on me by the Duke of Bedford and Lord Lauderdale, but had them merely from a verbal . . . relator.' Turning over in his mind what he had heard, the insult assumed giant proportions, and a few months later he published his famous *Letter to a Noble Lord*. In this sixpenny pamphlet he castigated the Duke for the insolence of a very rich man presuming to censure the well-earned reward of a lifetime spent in the service of his country. Had not the Duke's ancestor received grants from Henry VIII that were 'so enormous, as not only to outrage the economy, but even to stagger credibility. The Duke of Bedford is the Leviathan among all creatures of the Crown. He tumbles about his unwieldy bulk; he plays and frolics in the ocean of the Royal bounty. Huge as he is, and whilst "he is floating many a rood" he is still a creature. His ribs, his fins, his whalebone, his blubber, the very spiracles through which he spouts a torrent of brine against his origin, and covers me all over with the spray, – every thing of him and about him is from the Throne. Is it for *him* to question the Royal favour?' In superb language, Burke's anger and sarcasm flowed over thirty-five pages. For a man widely thought of as magnanimous and compassionate, the Duke of Bedford's seconding of Lauderdale's attack on Burke appears ungenerous and, unhappily, has been freely remembered and held against him. His intimacy with Lord Lauderdale had been ironically remarked on at that time, and we must suppose that hidden fibres in his gentle nature vibrated to the manipulations of the fiery and disputatious Scottish peer.

On the day following the debate on Burke's pension, there took place a 'very numerous assemblage of people' in Westminster Hall. The meeting was addressed by Fox, Sheridan and the Duke as leaders in a protest against proposed bills for the suppression of all seditious meetings. It was commented that the sight of Lord Lansdowne and the Duke of Bedford haranguing the mob was reminiscent of early days of the French Revolution.

A spirited defence of the Duke of Bedford's attack on Burke's pension appeared from the pen of one who 'thrown by fortune at so great a distance in life as to make it almost impossible to be personally acquainted with him', apologized for being obliged to use the Duke's name. The writer proceeded to censure Burke for his 'Billingsgate abuse' of Bedford and his 'innocent ancestors'. The withering scorn of his indictment of Burke's *Letter* embraced all aspects of the statesman's political career, accusing him of being a hypocrite and an apostate from his early principles. 'I deny that his Grace did "attack you" in mentioning your pension, he only attacked administration for their lavish distribution of the public money in an hour of the deepest and widest national distress. It was an attack on the Ministers, which his duty as a lord of Parliament suggested to him to make, and not on you.'

Another partisan who had been annoyed by Burke's pamphlet relieved his feelings in *A Vindication of the Duke of Bedford's attack upon Mr. Burke's Pension in reply to a Letter from the Right Hon. Edmund Burke to a Noble Lord.* 'Mr. Burke has surprised us: he has again *varied his means*; and after having hooted and hunted down the democracy, has turned round on a sudden, and opened on the aristocracy.' After many pages discussing the propriety of Burke's slippery defence of his pension, the writer almost capitulates with a tribute to the magic power of the great man's rhetoric.

159

'It is difficult . . . to recover from the rapture and delirium into which Mr. Burke's works always throw us. The wizard has such potent charms about him, that I could almost wish to remain for ever spell-bound by him. The vigour and elegance of his periods enchant me – I admire, though I cannot approve the energy of his invective.'

Jacobin though he might appear to be in politics, the Duke was aristocratical in other matters. He was showing an increasing interest in his Woburn estate; the improvement of crop cultivation and the breeding of livestock – questions that were occupying the minds and time of other landowners, among whom notably was Thomas Coke of Holkham.

The Board of Agriculture had been set up in 1793, and the Duke of Bedford was made one of its members. Since Arthur Young was secretary to the Board, a community of interests brought him and the Duke frequently together in harmonious understanding. Young, who himself was unsuccessful as a practical farmer, was a pioneer of the innovations that were to change English farming at the end of the eighteenth and the beginning of the nineteenth century, and he had the talent to write well about it; his contributions to the *Annals of Agriculture*, a periodical he instituted and edited, are lively reading, whether he is writing about turnips, manure, or the state of agriculture in France, where he had travelled widely. He could not conceal his impatience with the people whose opinions differed from his own, and who were tardy in adopting the methods he advised to improve their husbandry. He once had the temerity to criticize the royal hogs to the King's face, and recorded in his journal Farmer George's mild remonstrance. In the Duke of Bedford he found a willing partner in experiment. With his wealth, extensive acres and large flocks, the Duke was in a position to test new methods of growing crops and raising stock, and when he cultivated an area with wild chicory – the seeds of which Arthur Young had brought from France – keeping 'ten large sheep per acre on a field of it', Young was delighted.

Apart from their wool, sheep were important for the quality of the mutton they provided; for what gentleman, in those days, missed sitting down once or twice daily to a dish of mutton chops as part of his substantial diet? The breeding of sheep became the most prominent of the Duke's farming interests; experimenting with four breeds, which were given identical treatment, he published in the *Annals of Agriculture* an analysis of how each breed responded to the same conditions and handling, giving particulars of the comparative weight of wool, meat, and offal in each case.

Between breeders of sheep it was disputed whether a South Down or a New Leicester produced the tastiest meat – the South Down being most in favour. A dinner was given for an interested company, at which two legs of mutton were served; one from a South Down and one from a New Leicester, each cut and dressed in an identical manner. The distinguished diners were invited to pronounce which was the superior joint, and to name its origin. The majority declared for what they believed to be the South Down and were told of their error. 'The flesh of the Leicester', wrote Arthur Young, 'was of a closer texture, but rather paler. The gravy of the South Down of a higher flavour.' Thus did the connoisseurs amuse themselves, and they were in a position to ignore the protests of conservative country gentry, who complained that 'Whiggish sheep' were spoiling the old breeds.

When the fifth Duke of Bedford established the annual sheep-shearing at Woburn, he was following in the steps of Thomas Coke, who each year held a similar agricultural assembly at Holkham. All kinds of people interested in the cultivation of the land gathered at these Woburn meetings, from labourers and yeoman farmers to men of high rank; they came from all over England, and sometimes from the Continent, to see what was new in agricultural machinery, and to watch the skilled shearing, the weighing of the cattle, and the ploughing matches, and to compete for the many prizes that were offered by the Duke. It appears that above all he wished to improve farming in his own county, for prizes and premiums were offered specially to Bedfordshire farmers who could show their best produce.

The background to this animated scene at Woburn was the buildings newly constructed by Henry Holland, comprising all that was necessary for an efficient home farm. During the five days in June when the sheep-shearing took place, the roads and lanes leading to the Abbey grounds were blocked with farmers' gigs, gentlemen's phaetons, and men on horseback. When it became impossible to go forward the eager country folk took to their feet to reach their destination. The Duke's own horses were sometimes brought in to supplement the short supply of local post-horses on the London Road.

For these meetings the Abbey was filled with distinguished visitors, and the day began at 9 a.m. with a cheerful 'public breakfast' for the Duke's guests in the great hall below the state-rooms, which since Holland's rebuilding of the east wing was no longer the entrance hall; between the pairs of columns long tables were set up and to this meal persons who had no seats at table apparently were admitted as onlookers. Two hours later horses were mounted and the Duke led the way to the Park Farm where the crowds were examining implements and animals: with good fortune a hog weighing one hundred stone might be on view.

Returning to the Abbey at three, the Duke's company sat down to dinner at three tables fanning out from a top table at which Francis presided, with perhaps Sir Joseph Banks, President of the Royal Society, on one side of him, and the President of the Board of Agriculture, Sir John Sinclair, on the other. At one such dinner Arthur Young was gratified at being directed by the Duke to preside at the lower table, although it was to exclude some pushing guest as well as to honour Young. Poor Young! He needed the kind attentions he received, for after the death of his youngest daughter in 1796 despair overcame him and he was a sad prey to religious mania. No longer could he join these jolly gatherings without being tormented by his conscience and condemning the luxury that surrounded him. It was indeed a strange contrast to his life at home, where it was his custom to rise at 4 a.m. on a spring morning, and walk up to his neck into his garden pond before having recourse after that chill immersion to prayer and study until his breakfast time. Approaching Woburn from his own farm in Suffolk, he ruminated on his change of heart.

How few years are passed since I should have pushed on eagerly to Woburn! This time twelve month I dined with the Duke on Sunday. The party not very numerous, but chiefly of rank; the entertainment more splendid than usual there. He expects me today, but I have more pleasure in resting, going twice to church and eating a morsel of cold lamb at a very humble inn, than partaking of gaiety and dissipation at a great table which might as well be spread for a company of heathens as English lords and men of fashion.

But push on he did and wrote:

To Woburn Abbey. Here is wealth and grandeur and worldly greatness; but I am sick of it as soon as I enter these splendid walls.

As we shall see later on, it was noticed by other critics, too, that the Duke of Bedford paid little attention to religious observances. This lack of piety – not unusual among his contemporaries – was redeemed by the upright quality of his character, which combined with a certain aloofness in his personality commanded the attention of his friends, and made them – particularly his women friends – wish to earn his respect and enjoy his affection. We find Lady Bessborough telling her young lover, Lord Granville Leveson Gower, how much she feared losing the Duke's regard.

> I have always found him the truest and most steady of friends, and what is almost unheard of in *a man*, disinterestedly so. If he is formidable to me, it is only from the good opinion I have of him, and which makes me dread forfeiting his esteem or giving him pain, for next to my Brother I know no one for whom I have so much affection and esteem. I will not deny that he *lectur'd* me a good deal while we were at Woburn, but with so much kindness, so much good sense, and I am ashamed to own it, so much truth, that I could only hide my diminish'd head and confess the justice of his assertions.

The Duke of Bedford, we must suppose, had lectured her on her un-curbed infatuation with a lover twelve years younger than herself. This enchanting and remarkable woman had been captivated by the beauty of the new library at Woburn.

> I never saw so delightful a room as the Library; it is very large, all the finest editions magnificently bound. Over the book cases some very fine pictures (portraits), most of them Titians, Rembrandts &c., three great looking glasses, all the ornaments white and golden, and the furniture blue leather. The upper part of the book cases are let into the wall, and a marble slab forms the base over the folios . . . I believe Lord B. leaves me here tête-à-tête with the Duke.

Warm-hearted, intelligent and well read, she was a woman in whose company Francis would have delighted, and when her gambling debts reached a giddy amount he acted as one of the trustees of a fund to settle them. To her sister, the Duchess of Devonshire, always in financial straits induced by her compulsive gambling, he lent a large sum, and gave her a memorandum of the transaction between them – 'that there may be no possible mistake. I propose to lend you £6000 at 5 per cent interest, on condition that you set apart £300 a year as a sinking fund to discharge the debt.' Before Francis died, Georgiana told Mr Coutts, her banker, that the Duke had waived the full repayment of the debt.

After the dispersal of the serious and hardy agriculturists at the end of the sheep-shearings the Duke would fill his house with other and more intimate friends, whose conversation was not of sheep and turnips, but of politics seasoned, when women were present, with gossip and light-hearted raillery. Frivolities such as Mrs Montagu would have described as 'divertimenti fit for children of 6 foot high', might occupy the space of a wet day, and one of these was reported in the *Morning Chronicle*:

> . . . the Honourable Charles Fitzroy, who undertook, for a considerable sum of money, to run 25 miles in four hours. On account of the weather, the spacious and extensive gallery round the Abbey was fixed on for the race; the distance carefully measured, and the number of times round it to complete 25 miles was calculated. Soon after twelve o'clock he started; for about three hours and a half he continued his course with great regularity, and it was supposed with speed and ease sufficient to have completed it within the time; after which he found himself so completely exhausted as to force him to give up the attempt. His exertions excited very considerable interest with his Grace's noble guests, and many bets were made on the event.

In July a week was annually allotted to an all-male party, and if the absence of women did not entirely please Sheridan, who was a regular guest, he was able to tell his wife Hecca how much he missed her, who his companions were, and that the Duke was proposing shortly a ladies' party.

> . . . We really keep such good hours here that my best time to write to you is when we separate at night. In the morning there is plenty to do – we dine at half-past four – and always walk out before coffee – and the post goes at six. Then I have been playing every day at Tennis, tho' I can't play the least – but all strong exercise agrees with me. In short the party is very well put together; and I see a number of old Friends in very good spirits, and apparently very glad at my coming – and as to Wine I assure you we are moderation itself, and I am particularly well, and should like it all very well if I had Hecca under the roof – Yet either I or they are alter'd for it is not to me anything really Jolly or pleasant. I must tell you whom we consist of.

1. C. Fox
2. Fitzpatrick
3. Hare
4. Lord John Townshend
   (all pleasant as possible)

5. Sheridan (stupid)
6. Erskine (in great spirits)
7. Francis (laughed at)
8. Lord Thurlow

9. Richardson
10. Adair
11. Lord John Russell
    (my particular favourite)
12. E. Faulkener

13. Dudley North (very pleasant)
14. Lord R. Spencer
15. Lord Holland
16. Duke of Bedford

Then there is the Riding House, Tennis Court, Billiards, Farm, Fishing, &., &., and if you will come on 10th September, the Duke will have your own party and Lady John will meet you. He is very friendly and good-natur'd.

The Duke relished the company of Sheridan, for at the end of the visit he drove him back to London in his sociable, an open four-wheeled carriage. When a nearly identical group of Whigs met at Woburn in July 1800 Sheridan again reassured his wife that there was 'in wine all moderation'. Deprived of the company of women and limited in liquor, he found an alternative pleasure in making:

a rare Levy on all for my Library. The Duke of Devonshire gives me the finest edition of all Rousseau. There's for you Ma'am. Nothing can be more compleat than the Library here, and the favor is beyond anything I had conceived . . . but what would make me like two or three days very well would be to have you in a sly corner or in a hollow tree, so that I could stroll on my short whites and see my roses and Emeralds, when I liked, and bring you some of the nice things that abound here.

The presence of Sir Philip Francis at both these gatherings indicates the footing on which he stood at Woburn. As a founder of the revolutionary 'Society of the Friends of the People' he had seen enrolled among its members Lord John Russell, the Duke's younger brother; there is no reason to suppose that the brothers suspected him of being the notorious Junius, who had impugned the character of their grandfather, for no such identification occurred in print until 1816. Sir Philip, in his memoirs, records a conversation that reveals a remarkable degree of altruism in the behaviour of the Duke of Bedford that is pleasing to those who find so much that is attractive and admirable in his character.

I was staying at Woburn without any party being there; and noticed that the park was full of strollers from the neighbourhood, and they came even close to the windows. I said to his Grace, 'I wonder that you, who love retirement, do not shut up your grounds – at least on particular days, or limit it to particular people. It is never private, which I am sure must annoy you.' The Duke's answer was, 'I find myself without any merit or exertion of my own, in a situation where I have the power of doing many kind or unkind actions to my fellow-creatures. I consider myself a steward to do the best I can with the money placed in my hands, no doubt, for the benefit of others. A rich man can use very little of his riches on himself, and he should use them to promote as much general good as possible. If I were to shut up this place, many people who enjoy it as much as I do would be shut out of much innocent enjoyment and healthy amusement. All those people we see come as freely as you or I, and probably have much more pleasure in it. If I were to close my gates, from a selfishness of feeling, I, who have a thousand gratifications in my power, should deprive these poor people perhaps of their only one or greatest.

In those spacious days it was usually possible for a respectable person to be admitted as a sight-seer to the interior of a great house by sending in his name. Many years before, Sir Philip had been snubbed at Woburn's door when travelling with friends through Bedfordshire. He wrote: 'The Duchess of Bedford be d———d to her wd not let us see Woburn Abbey, which we all greatly regret.'

In 1794 the old Duchess of Bedford died unlamented. Her uncertain temper and her indiscreet behaviour had made her a figure of fun to many in her last years. In 1791 a perplexing scandal occupied the gossips for some weeks; Gertrude took up a young woman called Gunnilda Gunning, of a modest Irish family, and tried to promote her marriage with Lord Blandford – her grandson, and the Duke of Marlborough's heir. Forged letters, tales of bribery, denials and protestations confused and concealed the truth, delighting Horace Walpole, who wrote that: 'Gunnilda is actually harbour'd by and lodges with the old Duchess in Pall Mall . . . The crazy old Bedford exhibits Miss every morning on the causeway in Hyde Park.' Expostulations from Blenheim followed, and

Nancy Parsons in Turkish
dress by G. Willison

Mrs Hill by J. Downman

The Woburn Sheepshearing by George Garrard (the sixth Duke in centre on horseback)

the Duchess of Marlborough attempted to open her mother's eyes to her protégée, 'but with no success; for what signify eyes when the rest of the head is gone?'

A lampoon, unequalled today for cruelty and coarseness, appeared in *The Female Jockey Club*:

Alas! poor old Gertrude! thy career is well nigh spent; nor paint nor patches, not all the cosmetics of the east, nor all the illumination of a theatre can longer animate those emblems whereupon the gloomy features of approaching mortality are impressed. After all thy amorous gallantries, thy party intrigues, to this complexion art thou come at last . . . Accustomed to public life, still thou seemest reluctant to quit the scene; night after night, presenting thy emaciated, withered form at different places of amusement, and exposing thyself to sarcastic jests . . .

Her Grace's maternal feelings at an earlier period of her life have been ably described by the celebrated Junius, and the violence of her tender passions in the more advanced stage of it, was not long since most pointedly illustrated in the *delicate* proposal made by her to a certain *gigantic* nobleman, whose *secret* perfections have long been the theme of female enthusiasm.

The partiality she manifests for a blooming buxom young lass, her constant attendant, and who has already shone with a degree of éclat in the *polite* world is said to have its origin in the above principle, and that the latter is condemned to sleep in the apartment, if not the bed of the former, under the supposition that the breath of a fresh healthy woman vivifies and invigorates the decaying principles of nature.

Soon after his grandmother's death the Duke of Bedford had the roof removed from Houghton House, where his parents had lived their brief, idyllic married life; left open to the sky it became the sad ruin we may see today. His motive is undiscoverable. The destruction shocked Lord Torrington when he rode that way and conversed with the overseer of the work in hand. As he listened to the account of how the cedar wainscot had been ripped out and the wall-paintings destroyed, he detected in the man 'the delight of a butcher at killing a sheep'.

Six years later, in 1800, Bedford House was demolished and most of the contents were sold by Messrs Christie. The twenty-four paintings by Canaletto were removed to Woburn and 'seven capital paintings after

Raphael's cartoons by Sir James Thornhill' were bought in by the Duke and given to the Royal Academy.

Was Francis assailed by premonitions of the future? Was he meditating a change in his situation? His women friends appeared to think so. At thirty-five he was unmarried but the father of two children by a Mrs Marianna Palmer of Curzon Street – a boy, Francis, and a girl, Georgiana. His attachment to Lady Melbourne – most unchaste of women, whom Lady Holland compared to Madame de Merteuil in 'Les Liaisons Danger-euses' – was well known, but Woburn still lacked a mistress. It was generally acknowledged in Whig society that the Duchess of Gordon, who had secured two dukes as husbands for her elder daughters, wished to see one of the younger girls become Duchess of Bedford. She was an un-scrupulous woman and what she wished for she usually attained. For a time the youngest daughter, Lady Georgiana Gordon, had been in love with Eugène de Beauharnais, Napoleon's stepson, but the difficulties attendant on such a marriage were insuperable, and presently it was sus-pected that she had engaged the affections of the Duke of Bedford. In the Devonshire House circle he was known affectionately as 'Loo', and in some letters written by Georgiana Devonshire to Lady Melbourne com-miserating the desertion of her lover, it is revealed how much a connection with the Gordon family was dreaded for him by his friends, towards whom he was behaving with a most unusual lack of frankness.

Chiswick, Saturday.

. . . I really could not sleep and was more disturbed than I could have supposed – for tho' I am bound by ties of affection, gratitude and regard to Loo – yet I ought not to feel as much as I do. I think I am more hurt at his having seemed to act out of his *own* good character with regard to you, (tho' I have no doubt that it was from the fear of hurting you.) It was unlike him – but he had acted strangely towards the girl. I suppose it must be so and indeed *we are all undone*. Loo's first error when he resolved against the connection was allowing himself to be surrounded by the tribe – he exposed himself at Kimbolton to the temptation of all others he was most likely to yield to – and tho' his good taste will I suppose a little disgust him with the different society he is about to mix with – yet as they will all be prepared to flatter him and as he is sometimes entertained with observing original character – of which God knows he will have enough. . . .

Whenever he thinks proper to tell me I shall say very little. I believe he must be very unhappy, – and indeed I cannot conceive his being happy, unless he becomes very different from what he *is*. I think *her* very pretty, very bewitching, and clever certainly, and I have liked some things I have seen in her. But certainly there have been stories enough to make one tremble. It is so extraordinary and so unlike him to have spoken to her before he knew he was free; that either he pretends this to lessen the surprise to you, or that he was inveigled into more than he likes to own – and what a prospect if that is so – what a futurity for Loo to be surrounded with plotting, shabby Scotts men. The very *amabilité* that some time arises from the grotesque originality of Scotch people is in a line very different from what one should have thought would be Loo's election for the Mistress of Wooburn . . . For God's sake burn this letter. I would not for worlds appear impertinent to Loo, and indeed I feel very much for him, for you, for all of us.

No possible event could have so thoroughly overthrown our society as this . . . Well, I shall get accustom'd to it I suppose, and if he is happy it will be some consolation, but I never can bear his having vex'd you, nor understand it, for I know how much he loves you.

Is there not a possibility that to get rid of the woman [Mrs Palmer] he thought it necessary to marry, and that that pointed out the fancy to him?

The question of the Duke's intentions and his prospect of happiness was never resolved. At the end of February 1802, while playing tennis in the great court at Woburn, he received an injury from a fast-flying ball which aggravated a rupture he had sustained as a boy at Westminster, when he was struck by a cricket bat. Medical aid was summoned from London and Northampton and an operation was carried out, but it soon became apparent that the Duke was dying. With great courage and composure he made his Will leaving everything to his brother John, who had been sent for. Recollecting those from whom he had received services and kindness, Francis named the individuals who were to have gifts or annuities. His servants were to be given two to three years' wages according to their length of service. Charles James Fox was bequeathed a legacy of £5000. To Lady Maynard he left an annuity of £2000. For Mrs Palmer a generous sum was secured for the support and education of their two children. And he disclosed his responsibility for three other women living in Marylebone; to each of these was allotted annuities of

£200. He died on 2 March in the arms of his distraught brother John. His last request had been that a lock of his hair should be cut off and sent to Lady Georgiana Gordon.

Crowds had come to Woburn during the four days of his illness to hear the latest news of his condition, and the funeral attracted further numbers. His instructions had been that he was to be buried 'decently not sumptuously with hired mourners', and so it was done. The journey from Woburn to Chenies was made at night, and as the hearse passed through Dunstable the townsfolk and cottagers stood in the road holding lights. It was reckoned that five thousand people gathered in the little village where the church contained the monuments of past Russells. When the church was full up some of those outside broke the windows and tried to climb in. Pickpockets abounded and made a profitable haul. It was a shameful scene. Neither the new duke nor his younger brother was present; John's grief was so violent that he was advised to stay away, and William remained with him at Streatham.

On 6 March Charles James Fox stood up in the House of Commons to pay tribute to his friend. Moving that a new writ be issued to elect a burgess for the borough of Tavistock in the room of Lord John Russell, now called up to the House of Peers as Duke of Bedford, he prefaced his motion with an eulogy on the merits and virtues of the late duke. He spoke at length, excusing himself for obtruding upon the House his feelings of private friendship: 'It is because I consider the death of the Duke of Bedford as a great calamity, because the public itself seems to consider it . . . in every part of the kingdom the impression made by it seems to be the strongest and most universal, that ever appeared upon the loss of a subject.' He remarked that there was something in the Duke's character that was peculiar and striking, and there was certainty that the progress of his life would be more than answerable to the brightest hopes conceived from its outset. He dwelt on the dangers attending prosperity in general, and high situations in particular – the corrupting influence of flattery. 'How are these dangers increased with respect to him who succeeds in his childhood to the first rank and fortune in a kingdom such as this, and who having lost his parents is never approached by any being who is not represented to him as in some degree his inferior . . . but virtue found her way, and on every side where danger was the greatest, was her triumph most complete. From the blame of selfishness no man was ever so eminently free . . . To be useful was the ruling passion of his life.'

Fox spoke too of the Duke's constancy as a friend, and how while resisting the allurements of vice, he had not lost 'that openness of heart, that warmth of feeling, that readiness of sympathy, that generosity of spirit, which have been reckoned the attributes of youth . . . Endued by nature with an unexampled firmness of character he could bring his mind to a more complete state of discipline than any man I ever knew.' And so after touching on the duke's services to agriculture, Fox came to the question of his pupil's politics. 'I feel', he said, 'a great unwillingness to be wholly silent on the subject; and at the same time much difficulty in treating it with propriety, when I consider to whom I am addressing myself, I am sensible that those principles upon which, in any other place, I should not hesitate to pronounce an unqualified eulogium, may be thought by some, perhaps by the majority of the House, rather to stand in need of apology and exculpation, than to form a proper subject for panegyric . . . No man had ever less of family pride, in the best sense, than the Duke of Bedford. But he had a great and just respect for his ancestors . . . surely in this country it is not unpardonable in a Russell to be zealously attached to the rights of the subject, and peculiarly tenacious of the popular part of the constitution . . . Whatever, therefore, may be thought of those principles to which I have alluded, the political conduct of my much lamented friend must be allowed by all to have been manly, consistent, and sincere.'

◈◈◈◈◈

13

Younger brother

THE new Duke of Bedford was but a year younger than the brother he succeeded, but he lacked the elder man's firmness of character. Placed suddenly and unexpectedly in a position of consequence and responsibility, and suffering from a new shock to his affections – he had been a widower for less than six months – he was in a highly emotional state of mind. His immediate concern in his new situation was to defend the character of his brother, and when the Duchess of Gordon put her daughter into mourning, saying there had been a private engagement, he contradicted her statement insisting that 'if the letter could be produced *one* must be found from the Duke of Bedford of a very late date declaring his regard and estimation for Lady Georgiana, but expressly saying he had no intention of marrying and thought it fair to tell her so.' The world was on the whole inclined to believe him rather than the girl's mother.

Three weeks after the fifth Duke's death, anxiety and a touching sense of his own inadequacy prompted him to write to Arthur Young expressing his passionate desire to continue his brother's good work for agriculture.

Woburn Abbey, 28 March 1802

Sir, the sudden and fatal event which deprived me of one of the kindest friends and most affectionate of brothers, agriculture of one of its firmest props, and society in general of one of its best and most useful members, coming upon me too soon after a former severe domestic calamity, left my mind in such a state of sad dejection, as to render me wholly incapable of writing to you on a subject, deeply interesting to me, because it occupied the last thoughts of my much lamented brother – his zeal for that first and most interesting of all pursuits, agriculture, did not forsake him even in the last moments of his Life, and on his death bed with an earnestness of mind expressive of his character, and with that anxious consideration for the interests of his country which occupied so many years of his well-spent life, he strongly urged me to follow up those plans of national improvement which he had begun, and from which he had formed the most sanguine hopes of success. He referred me to Mr. Cartwright and to you for explanation and details . . . I trust it will not be long before I may have the satisfaction of seeing you at Woburn, desirous as I am in every point of view to fulfill the best wishes of my departed brother, I feel that my humble efforts must be at such a vast distance from the exertions of his well regulated mind, that without the aid and advice of those most capable of assisting me I should utterly despair of attaining the objects now so near to my heart.

That year the sheep-shearings were held as usual at Woburn, and continued to take place for several years until the sixth Duke's other personal extravagances made it necessary to give them up.

There was also another matter to be attended to; one which caused him uneasiness and indignation. A small publication appeared from the pen of John Bowles, a barrister and pamphleteer, and an ardent sabbatarian – entitled *A Letter to C. J. Fox in consequence of his speech in the House of Commons on the character of the late most noble Francis Duke of Bedford*. In this pamphlet Bowles took Fox to task for having in his discourse held up the Duke as a '*great example*', as 'a *perfect model* for the *imitation* of the present age and posterity, but in which not one word is to be found, where it can be inferred that a regard for Religion, or an attention to its duties, constituted any part of the character which drew forth such unqualified praise . . . Nay, from your description of his life and death, highly wrought as it is, it is impossible to ascertain whether he was a Heathen or a Christian.' Bowles declared he had been extremely provoked by Fox's eulogy, and pointed out that the orator had been 'totally silent' on one aspect of the Duke's private life: 'his Grace's testamentary dispositions . . . which by the bequest of a large annuity recalls to our recollection some very unfavourable circumstances . . . in the former part of his Grace's life, while it seems peculiarly calculated to reflect dishonour on the marriage state.' Bowles recalled that, politically, the late Duke's 'inclination partook rather of a *bias* towards the modern rights and liberties of France than of a *leaning* towards the ancient rights and liberties of England', and as a member of the Whig Club he had been party to the jacobinical sentiment of its standing toast: 'The Sovereignty of the People'.

To the second edition of this tract was added Bowles's *Observations* on a sermon preached in the parish church of Woburn by the Rev. Edmund Cartwright on 14 March 1802. Bowles observed that the preacher spoke of the deceased nobleman 'from the *pulpit* in a strain of panegyric which could never be justly applied to any human being . . . and this in the presence of parishioners who knew that a gross inattention to Religious duties was a striking feature in the character described'; that his Grace had never joined in public worship in his parish church, and 'that he had even been the means of preventing many others from keeping that day holy. It is well-known his Grace had frequently kept his labourers from church, by paying them their wages on a Sunday, and on one occasion he employed some hundreds of them on *that* day in emptying the Great Pond at the Abbey.'

Annoyed and pained by these imputations injurious to the memory of his brother, the sixth Duke instructed William Adam, his Chief Auditor, to take the matter up with Bowles, and demand the elimination of some paragraphs in future editions; and that he should send a statement, drawn up by Adam, to the *Anti-Jacobin Review*. When Bowles quibbled Adam instituted an inquiry, and depositions were taken from labourers on the Woburn estate – loyal men, who could not write but made their mark before witnesses. They racked their memories and protested it was all a pack of lies: there had been no paying of workmen on Sunday unless there were some who by accident were not able to attend on Saturday evening. They vehemently denied being made to work on Sunday 'except once when the snow fell on the top of Woburn Abbey and wasted so fast that the pipes could not carry it off and it ran into the rooms'. One man recollected the emptying of Cowhill Pond: 'he could not remember which year, but it was the year of the mutiny of the fleet, when there were many gentlemen at Woburn Abbey but he was sure there was no fishing on a Sunday.'

The emptying and cleaning out of the ponds was always a great amusement for people staying at the Abbey; the water was run off through sluices and many of the fish could be caught and transferred to store ponds, while some were taken for the Duke's table. Young thought he dined better at Holkham than at Woburn, because, from its proximity to the Norfolk coast, there was more fish. He perhaps preferred soles to perch and carp.

The correspondence between Adam and Bowles ran on for many months, the dispute not being resolved, and was eventually printed and distributed gratis by Mr Debrett of Piccadilly. There can be little doubt that the Duke was a negligent churchman, but the whole tone of Bowles' pamphlet is imbued with a spirit of self-righteous sabbatarianism.

Francis had requested that after his death a lock of his hair should be cut off and sent with a message to Lady Georgiana Gordon; John was himself the bearer of the precious legacy, and eighteen months later he made the lovely girl of twenty-two his second wife. The Duchess of Devonshire, who had witnessed her jumping over the backs of chairs and taking part in rowdy games, had found her unacceptable as a wife for the adored 'Loo'. The wisdom of John's alliance with the Gordon family was questioned now by others. 'I hear a strange report', wrote the Bishop of Oxford to him, 'that you are going to marry a daughter of the Duchess of Gordon. It cannot be true. *God forbid*.' It turned out to be a very happy marriage, and Georgiana's boisterous spirits proved an advantage, for her husband was always shy and often silent. She had twelve children, two of whom died in infancy.

Since the later Dukes of Bedford descend from the first marriage, it is well to consider the qualities and nature of the young woman who died of consumption before her husband succeeded to the dukedom. Through her a tendency to despondency and melancholia entered the Russell family and was to reappear in successive generations.

As a young man the sixth Duke had not been sent like his elder brother to Cambridge after Westminster, but to the university of Göttingen – founded by George II, and popular with young Englishmen – where he gained a reputation for extravagance and 'imprudent gaieties'. Frequently lectured through the post by Mr Palmer and urged to attend to his books, he not unnaturally expressed a wish to travel rather than to study. Visiting Brussels he fell in love with Georgiana Byng, the daughter of the English minister, Lord Torrington. Despite the opposition of his grandmother and his guardians – for he was only twenty – he was married at Brussels in 1786 and returned with his wife to England, where Mr Palmer prudently insisted on a second wedding at St Leonard's, Streatham. The young couple lived in London and at Stratton, and later at Oakley, a charming house on the river Ouse twelve miles from Woburn, altered and improved by Holland for the Duke of Bedford. Three sons were born to them – Francis, William and John. In 1788 Lord John succeeded old Richard Rigby as one of the members for Tavistock. A desire to please her husband,

and to be of service to others was, with a loving care of her children, the chief object of Lady John's life, and she was beloved by humble people whose welfare she had at heart. Very delicate, she was often ailing; an attempt was made in 1793 to improve her health by a visit to Lisbon, and she was accompanied by her husband and the two older boys. The anguish of a rough voyage was nothing to the pain she felt at being separated from her youngest child – who was confided to the Duke of Bedford's care at Woburn; and four months spent in a climate unsuited to a person with weak lungs failed to strengthen her.

Living latterly a quiet rural existence at Oakley, often alone with her youngest boy – her 'Angel Child' John – while the elder ones were away at school, she observed nature and the changing seasons with an interested eye, sharing her pleasure with her little companion.

'John desires that I will tell you that your Calf is a *he*,' she wrote to her husband, 'which makes him very miserable as Nanny thinks that you would have kept it if it had been *a Lady*. He is in great joy at having found a Snow drop and is so convinced there are Primroses that the snow being gone he is sure they are under the leaves and with his spade he is going to remove them. He is now by me reading the Newspapers as seriously as possible – this shows that he will not only be like you in looks but Manners. Heaven grant him a Mind as honourable!'

Thirty years later the little boy's early love of gardening may have been recollected by the grown man, who, taking office for the first time – as Paymaster General in Lord Grey's administration – proposed, in the face of much opposition, that the old soldiers of Chelsea Hospital should be given a plot where they might grow vegetables or flowers, each according to his whim. 'It was', he said, 'the only official act of any consequence that I performed.' It is due to that young politician with his foot as yet only on the bottom rung of the ladder that today a Chelsea pensioner may still, if he wishes, have a piece of ground to cultivate.

Lady John studied botany to please her husband and put up boxes for the birds to nest in to please herself. Too mild to complain of loneliness, she addressed Lord John as 'the best of men' or 'my best friend'. Intelligent, high-minded and domestic, her shrewd estimate of politics and people sharpened her fluent pen in the letters she wrote him during the last three years of her life when they were often apart, and her touching and eager anticipation of his return home was always tempered with her hope that he was enjoying himself, whether he were in the House of Commons, in a male Whig party at Woburn, or shooting woodcock at Holkham. In one spirited letter only, did she accuse him of neglect. The selfishness with which Charles Greville was to charge him many years later was already present.

Oppressed by wretched health, and often in low spirits on her couch, she may have been at times a depressing companion. When she died – still a young woman – in 1801, her brother-in-law wrote: 'My Brother . . . bears his loss with a noble Fortitude, and tho' the wound is deep, from the anxious eye of Friendship he cannot conceal that his heart is torn with anguish.' Francis praised her many virtues and 'almost unexampled Diffidence'. 'I never saw her do anything which she had not previously in her own Mind decided was that which would best please him.'

14

Prodigal Splendour

UNTIL the death of his brother, the sixth Duke of Bedford's principal interest had been politics; in his new situation his horizons were much enlarged and his capacity for involvement and enjoyment stretched in many directions. As an affable host, a keen farmer, a collector of the fine arts with a preference for sculpture, an informed botanist and ardent horticulturist, he was now in a position to indulge many and various tastes, pursuing his pleasure with a quiet and cultivated enthusiasm. He made Woburn one of the most magnificent establishments in the country and took pains to bring the preservation of game on his estate to such perfection that 'there was no *bassesse* the fashionable world would not commit to shoot at Woburn' – although he did not himself enjoy the great organized *battues*, infinitely preferring to take his gun and wander down the hedgerows by himself.

At the time of his first marriage it had been noted that he was a man who 'had 8 hundred a year with a disposition to spend 8 thousand'. Succeeding to the dukedom his means increased, and when money was within his reach 'he had not the power or the resolution to hold his hand'. Employing Repton to improve his park and grounds, commissioning his son to buy in Rome notable marbles for his sculpture gallery, filling his glass-houses with rare plants, and carrying on his brother's experiments in farming, he spent with a lavish hand – to the despair of the men charged to look after his affairs, who were severely tested 'to raise the wind' to pay for his extravagance. Arthur Young predicted sourly when he stayed at Woburn for the sheep-shearings in 1804, that 'an extravagant Duchess, Paris toys, a great farm, little economy and immense debts, will prove a canker in the rose-bud of his garden of life'. He noted that 'several apartments were newly furnished and many very expensive articles, clocks etc. from Paris' were to be seen.

With a town house in St James's Square (in 1828 he moved to one of the new houses in Belgrave Square), the Duke bought a villa for his wife on Campden Hill in Kensington, and built a *cottage orné* for her above the Tamar in Devonshire. In the late summer he would transport his young family to a rented house in Scotland, and the winter months often saw him established with his wife and numerous children in a house at Brighton. In 1830 he rebuilt Covent Garden Market.

The Duke was regarded as 'respectable in debate' in the House of Lords, but Lord Holland complained that 'every man remarks how seldom he utters, and he is so unobtrusive that without any disposition in him to conceal his views and opinions, it is often difficult for others to ascertain them', and the Duke himself wrote of his reluctance to raise his voice. 'I know that I ought to speak . . . and it is a vexatious thing to be fully aware of what one's duty is, and at the same time feel an utter inability to act up to it.' In the short-lived Ministry of all the Talents he was sent to Ireland in 1806 as Viceroy. In a letter to Lord Holland from Dublin he affirmed that 'conciliation and kindness as general principles are those by which we can secure the attachment and affections of the people of Ireland and when circumstances compel me for a time to depart from these principles, it will not be without feelings of the deepest regret, mixed with serious apprehension for the consequences'. He left Ireland too soon to experience the disappointment felt by many of his predecessors and those who followed him, that kindness did not settle the affairs of that country. A despatch in which he recommended the admission of Roman Catholics into the Army and the employment of Roman Catholic gentlemen as sheriffs was instrumental in bringing down the Administration that had appointed him.

After the death of Fox he took a diminishing part in the affairs of Parliament, and was fond of saying that he knew nothing about politics, which was manifestly untrue; he looked to Lord Grey as his leader, and when his own son Lord John was charged to bring in the Reform Bill, he asserted proudly: 'I consider myself as almost the Father of Parliamentary Reform having advocated it for nearly forty years.' His long personal attachment to Lord Holland was strong, but he had no regard for him as a politician, finding him 'void of that essential quality in a statesman – judgement'. When Lord Holland as a young man persuaded Lady Webster to leave her husband and marry him, the Duke of Bedford did all in his power to reconcile the world to the divorced young woman who became the mistress of Holland House, the distinguished centre of Whig intellect and conversation. Lady Holland's gratitude to the Duke for her re-establishment in society showed itself in her unchangeable affection for him, and his letters to her are invested with the uninhibited frankness of an old friend. He allowed her to influence him in his attitude towards Napoleon, whom she admired without qualification. 'I cannot agree with you in wishing any success to the man', he wrote in March 1815 after the flight from Elba, but once Napoleon was defeated and confined to St Helena, he was as eager as she was to mitigate his exile by sending him books or anything that might please him. Occasional acerbities appear in their correspondence when she made a dogmatical statement, or found fault in her unfortunate and ungracious way with some favour accorded to her; then he would take her sharply to task, prove her unjust or wrong to his own satisfaction, and resume his letter with complete urbanity. He was the most good-humoured of men, and since they were neighbours in Kensington and in Bedfordshire – for Lord Holland had inherited from his uncle Lord Ossory the Ampthill estate – they saw much of each other, and Lady Holland's fundamental kindness was extended in a maternal way to the Duke's sons, William and John.

From his fortieth year the Duke may be seen as the central pivot of a growing family, nor did he with advancing age become detached from the affairs of his many children, nor ever lose his authority with them, nor cease to show an interest in their views, their careers and their well-being. When Lord William, the second son, served as a cavalry officer and A.D.C. to Wellington in the Peninsular War, his approving father received from him vivid accounts of the battles in which he took part. In due course he learned from his son John of his enterprising visit to Napoleon on Elba in 1814, when the great man tweaked him by the ear, and discussed the Russell family. 'He had', noted Lord John, 'a dusky grey eye, which would be called vicious in a horse.'

The Duke had a ready pen himself and wrote long letters in a graceful flowing hand; they give the impression that his attention and feelings were wholly engaged by the matter in question, whether he were congratulating or admonishing his correspondent. His style was terse and incisive, and he used, as naturally as he must have done in speech, Latin tags and French phrases as well as quotations from the Bible and Shakespeare.

A prolonged journey between 1813 and 1815 took him and the Duchess to Spain, Portugal and Italy. They were accompanied by some of their young children, and as a precaution a cow was included in the travelling party, its care and transport adding notably to the difficulties of the journey. By the spring of 1815 they had reached Rome, where the Duke, like other cognoscenti, was able to acquire antique sculptures for his collection, and he commissioned from Canova the marble group of the Three Graces, which a few years later was set up in a specially constructed alcove at one end of the sculpture gallery at Woburn, facing the Temple of Liberty, in which were enshrined busts of Francis, fifth Duke, Fox and other of his Whig associates. In 1802, the sixth Duke had hoped, he told Lord Holland, that Canova would execute a statue of his brother for this shrine of Liberty, but the sculptor, being fully occupied with commissions for the Pope, had been unable to accept the commission.

Charles Greville had many ungenerous things to say about the Duke of Bedford – that he was a weak and selfish sensualist without friends; that he only wished to gratify others if his own pleasures were not interrupted. Yet no one enjoyed the hospitality and comfort of Woburn more than the diarist, who could be sure of meeting congenial company at the Abbey and dining off the best that a French chef could put upon the table. The Duke made no bones about being a gourmand, but he was not gross, and he could restrain himself when Lady Holland sent him a turtle from Jamaica, if the gift chanced to conflict with what he called one of his 'Banyan days' – a day of fasting. After 1822 he was subject to attacks of apoplexy, brought on it may be feared as much by too practical an interest in the pleasures of the table as by his restless pursuit of change of scene. But fine fare was a legitimate interest for one who could appraise the quality of venison from his own herd of deer, and discern the difference between the meat of a doe and a havier – a gelded fallow deer. Lady Holland was equally greedy, but subject to indigestion and liver attacks; due, suggested the Duke, to her inability to resist the excellent *entrées* and *entremets* served up in her own house and at the tables of her friends. He was perfectly content to eat simple food in the company of his family in unassuming surroundings. 'I hate great dinners,' he said, 'and never give them.' Indeed his shyness makes it probable that he was happiest alone with his wife and children, but he entertained in a princely manner at Woburn, and his good manners made him an agreeable host. He relished his guests' admiration of the beauties of his property, and he liked to show off his own improvements to the house and grounds. 'It was *I*', he told his son, 'who carried the approach from the London entrance to the west front, assisted by Repton . . . I defy you to construct a better approach . . . than I have done. Repton was a coxcomb, but he had infinitely more genius than one half of his critics and detractors.' 'Talleyrand', he declared, 'used to carry everyone to the Saloon window to look at the Basin Pond. "*Tenez, c'est beau,*" he used to say, "*on ne peut pas disputer le goût.*"'

The men and women who enjoyed his splendid hospitality, and found well-appointed writing tables in the bedrooms allotted to them, eagerly took up a pen to confide to their journals or relate to their friends the pleasures (and sometimes the pains) experienced during the days they spent in the great house. The rowdiness permitted in 1812 at Woburn – instigated by the Duchess, mother of six children and recently delivered of a daughter – was recorded by Frances, Lady Shelley, in her diary:

As soon as we left the dining room the Duchess went to her nursing employment (after a little edifying conversation on the subject) and we dispersed . . . through an *enfilade* of six rooms. The gentlemen soon joined us and in the first Shelley got a companion for billiards. In the next Lady Asgill established herself in an attitude lying on the sofa with Sir Thomas Graham at her feet. In the next Lady Jane [Montagu] and Miss Russell at a harp and pianoforte (both out of tune) playing the Creation. Alas, it was chaos still. In the gallery a few pairs were dispersed on the sofas . . . Scarcely was I seated when the Duchess entered; and collecting her romping force of girls and young men, they all seized cushions and began pelting the whist players. They defended themselves by throwing the cards and candles at her head; but the Duchess succeeded in throwing over the card table, and a regular battle ensued, with cushions, oranges and apples. The romp was at last ended by Lady Jane being nearly blinded by an apple that hit her in the eye.

A few years later an American, George Ticknor, was invited to join a party at Woburn for the last days of the shooting season. He liked his plain, unpretending host, whose conversation was worth listening to, and he recorded his interest in a curious aristocratic English ritual that took place at the end of dinner when the cloth had been removed, and 'the gamekeeper appeared dressed in all his paraphernalia' and rendered his account: four hundred and four hares, partridges and pheasants had fallen to eleven guns. The observant guest was glad to see that though a good deal of wine was consumed no one was the worse for it.

There were some who, accepting the shyness and silence of the Duke,

The sixth Duke of
Bedford from an
etching by J. Wiffen
after a drawing by
Ingres

The seventh Duke of Bedford
from a print

Lord John Russell by Sir Francis Grant

found the conversation of the Duchess too free and bold, and her behaviour to her guests was often at variance with their expectations, depending on her health as much as on her temperament; those who feared to find her lofty and cross being charmed by her friendliness, while others, expecting attention and civility, were chilled and affronted by her distant manners. Emily Eden's account of a visit to Woburn exemplifies one aspect of the Duchess's conduct, while Lady Granville's witty comments illustrate the other.

'There never was a house in which writing flourished so little as it does here', wrote the young Miss Eden in 1821, 'partly because I have been drawing a great deal, and also because they dine at half past six instead of the rational hour of seven . . . After all I like this visit. It was clever of me to expect the Duchess would be cross, because of course that insures her being more good-natured than anybody ever was. I am only oppressed at being made so much of. Such a magnificent room, because she was determined I should have the first of the new furniture and the advantage of her society in the mornings, though in general she makes it a rule to stay in her own room in the mornings . . . and once safe with her the house is pleasant enough.

Lady Granville a few months earlier had accepted an affront with good humour and analysed her feelings in a letter to her sister. She confessed she was not very much charmed with Woburn, nor with the Duchess, who had neglected her and had been 'uncommonly cold and uncommonly civil'. In spite of a delightful room and company she was used to – the Duke of York, Punch Greville, the Jerseys, M. de Flahault, and many others – Lady Granville declared she would not be able to refrain from screaming with joy when she drove off at the end of the visit. 'I am inclined to say to everybody with the utmost sincerity "Yes, it is delightful, only can't I possibly get away?"' and she further wrote:

We left Woburn yesterday having spent there a week of as much pleasure as is compatible with seeing it end without regret; the *locale* itself is a great source of enjoyment. There is so much space, so much comfort, such *luxe* and ease. The society generally very good, much to amuse and nothing to annoy . . . I believe it was being obliged to dress up very smart and sitting often at dinner between Lords Tavistock and Worcester.

Frequent pregnancies and her decision to nurse her babies herself made the Duchess at times too unwell to appear at dinner when there was a party in the house. Her husband wrote blandly of her fainting twice during the course of a meal when she made an effort to appear. There was no party at all at Woburn when a warm-hearted Irishman was invited to stay there in 1821, and his elation at being treated with friendly condescension by the family allowed him to see everything through rose-coloured spectacles. Thomas Moore, who had an uninhibited admiration for the well-bred, had been presented to the Duke of Bedford in Dublin. Writing to his mother of his satisfaction at the introduction, he confessed that 'all these things are but *feathers in the cap*, but they are feathers I like to shake in the eyes of some envious people.' At Woburn the Duchess talked to him of farming technicalities and the price of pigs, and mimicked very amusingly a recent guest – the Duke of York; Lord Tavistock invited him to Oakley; Mr Wiffen, 'a Quaker poet', took his profile and Lord John's with a camera lucida, and the Duke of Bedford made him sing repeatedly Moore's own compositions – 'The Boys of Kilkenny' and 'Here's the Bower', declaring that they were his two favourite songs, and the poet was urged to make Woburn 'his inn', since he 'must sleep somewhere' on his journeys up and down the country. His cup was full when after an evening of music the Duchess expressed the wish that "I could transfer my genius to her for six weeks" and I answered "most willingly if Woburn was placed at my disposal for the same time."'

While the vitality of the Duchess and the buoyancy of her spirits contributed much to the Duke's happiness, the deviousness of her character was responsible for many squabbles within the family that were alien and distasteful to his equable temperament.

She had been kind and attentive to her three young stepsons, who each in turn had passed through Westminster School, the eldest going to Cambridge, and the second into the army, while little John, too delicate to stand more than one term of the brutal life of a public school, was by her care removed and taught at home until he was placed with a tutor at Edinburgh. But as these three reached manhood, and Francis and William acquired wives, they grew to mistrust her empire over their father and learned that she could be an unscrupulous enemy, lying and prevaricating to achieve her ends. She may have sensed that her husband had a preference for the extremely intelligent sons of his first marriage. Although he was as affectionate and thoughtful for the children borne him by his second wife he was perhaps less careful of their education; the elder half-brothers found 'the Gordon brood' rough and unruly. 'I love my children warmly, and every mark of affection from them pleases me,' the Duke wrote. The three eldest were devoted to him, noting his weaknesses with compassion, relishing his company, and relying on his prompt help in their needs. Francis, Marquess of Tavistock, married to Lady Anna Maria Stanhope and living at Oakley, was always ready to discuss with his father the politics that the Duke disclaimed most untruly having any interest in, and if he tried to avert his eyes from his parent's reckless squandering of money, and the diminishing prospects of his own inheritance, he did so without rancour, and his wife was nearly always in the good books of the Duchess. It was the marriage of his second son to the beautiful, clever and arrogant Elizabeth Rawdon, whom Byron had admired, that produced serious trouble, for William had been very fond of the woman who had replaced his own mother, until his wife opened his eyes to her jealous and dissembling nature, and induced him to withdraw his affection and respect.

In 1823 the Duchess, who was described by her hostile daughter-in-law as '*coquette comme la lune*', fell in love with Edwin Landseer; she was forty-two, and the painter was half her age. The long affair ended only with her death in 1853. Although the fashionable papers carried both sly and overt paragraphs on their relationship, the Duke was a complaisant husband - he had his own sentimental *amourettes* with Lady Sandwich and Lady Elizabeth Vernon – and his elder sons accepted with resignation and kindly forbearance an ambiguous situation in which it was not unusual for them to hear of their stepmother alone with Landseer at a lodge in the Highlands, or to find the painter in solitary company with the Duke at Woburn; Landseer's admiration for the deer roaming the park forming an instinctive bond with his host. Saddened and irritated by the barely restrained hostility of Lord and Lady William to the Duchess – William referred to her as 'my father's worse half' and Lady William called her behind her back 'a red-faced vixen' – the Duke was stoutly loyal to her, shutting his ears to gossip, and tense situations were relieved by the absence from England for long periods of his son and daughter-in-law, but his reprimands for their discourtesies were set forth in clear and measured terms.

'The Duchess and I', he told his captious son, 'have always felt and acted the same to you and Lady William . . . and the Duchess's conduct towards you and yours has uniformly been kind and generous and affectionate . . . and now let the matter drop, and be buried in oblivion. It has been the cause of too much worry, both to the Duchess and myself, and in my state of health I feel it to be more than my head can bear.' Lord John, urging his brother not to quarrel with Woburn, wrote: 'She throws stones at us to get back nuts.' The dissensions at Woburn were widely known, and everyone was sorry for poor gentle William who, torn between his love for his haughty wife and the continual but unreliable overtures of peace and affection offered him by the Duchess, was sometimes not certain how he stood with either of them. His story has been told elsewhere.

While the Duchess was still bearing sons the William Russells had made their own contribution to what Lord Holland called 'a better race than the Atridae'. 'The race of Russell is so good that it cannot be too numerous. It is the best tribe that we have', wrote Lady Holland to William in a flattering mood, while Sydney Smith proclaimed: 'The manufacture of Russells is a public and important concern.' The Tavistocks had an only child – a boy, whose constitution was not strong; the William Russells bred three sons, and it was the eldest of these, Hastings, who as it turned out was to succeed eventually to the dukedom.

'Russell pens are small daggers not goose quills,' observed Lady Holland with truth. When the Duke of Bedford and his three elder sons wrote to each other at great length about politics their correspondence was often carried on in a spirit of recrimination and acrimony, each believing that his opinions alone were in the true Whig tradition. Refusing to support Canning in 1827, the Duke welcomed the government of the Duke of Wellington, who he thought would 'prove the best Minister this country has seen for the last fifty years (with the exception of Lord Grenville's short career). It was Canning's object to destroy the Whigs. The Duke of Wellington is now the best practical Whig I know with the exception of Lord Grey. He will bring in Catholic Emancipation in another year.'

Religious liberty had always been a principal tenet of the Russell creed, and when the Catholic Bill came up in 1830, we find all the Russells imploring Lord William to return from abroad in order, as an M.P., to vote on the right side. The Duke's elder sons observed with patience and good humour their father's alignment with the Tories, yet finding it hard to reconcile the shift in his allegiance with his passion for reform.

As Premier the Duke of Wellington was often invited to shoot at Woburn – 'where he shoots very ill', declared Lord John Russell. Mrs Arbuthnot watched with some disgust a friendship with the Duke of Bedford grow closer; she had a long-standing prejudice against him and had taxed Wellington in 1821 with inviting the Duke and other members of the Opposition to meet the King at his house, and was hardly mollified when Wellington rejoined that 'they had been remarkably civil to him, were constantly asking him to their houses, and that he was glad to make some return'. That the Great Duke admired Woburn we know from an anecdote repeated during a political crisis in 1834, when the Duke of Bedford was reported to have said that as the choice was between despotism and anarchy he preferred anarchy. Wellington hearing this, said: 'I can tell Johnny Bedford that if we have anarchy, I'll have Woburn.'

Resistance to reform was Wellington's undoing, and in 1830 the Whigs returned to power under Lord Grey, after forty-six years in opposition. When the Duke of Bedford received the Garter from Grey, Mrs Arbuthnot was indignant, and thought it was 'a great shabbiness' in the Duke; 'that he pretended to take it because he knew the Duke of Wellington meant it, which is not true ... I never thought the support of the Duke of Bedford worth one pin.' Lord Tavistock wrote at this time to his brother: 'My father got the Garter from Lord Grey and has given him his Proxy, but it is evident between ourselves that his heart is in another quarter. He is to have a party of X Ministers at Woburn next week – none of his old friends invited (not even John).'

Surveying the Woburn scene from near at hand, and often present at the parties assembled there, Lord Tavistock was in a position to notice significant changes that took place, to ponder on the idiosyncrasies of his father's other sons, and to communicate his observations to his absent brother. Their half-sister had recently been married to the Marquess of Abercorn.

Lord Tavistock to Lord William Russell

Woburn Abbey,
December 28th 1832

. . . We came here yesterday and found the Premier, and a large party of young Tory Lords to meet him. It always strikes me as extraordinary what a change of society takes place here every year. How many of these changes have we witnessed from the days of the Duke of Manchester up to the present? Even the intervening sets, Punch Greville etc. are all forgotten. The great object now seems to be to make everything as agreeable as possible to Abercorn, who between ourselves told Russell the other day that he found Woburn very dull!! A strange speech for a man just married and for whom everything has been done, even to a sitting-room for his wife.

Charles has now the management of everything; the shooting, stable department, and the invitations, and it is curious to see how completely he rules my Father. He seems to do everything very well, with the exception of being a little too selfish and arbitrary. Edward is here quite well, and able to hunt and shoot. Frank also with the 'unters and ack', all as strange as himself. He was sent to a private tutor to 'study'. When he returned, my Father asked him what he had been reading. History; ancient or modern? He didn't know, but believed it was ancient. What was it? The History of England, but it was a *long while ago*!

Frank Russell was twenty-four years old. The characters and capacities of their half-brothers never stood very high in the estimation of the elder sons of the Duke; entering the army or the navy or Parliament, they rose to modest eminence in the service of their country.

Wriothesley, the eldest of 'the Gordon crop', chose the Church as his profession, and his veering towards Methodism distressed and disturbed his father who wrote: 'He is thoroughly amiable and has high principles of honour, but he has a weak mind and is easily led by designing people. Heaven guard him from the Calvinists, Methodists and Evangelicals, unfortunately so much the fashion now, amongst our young clericals . . . don't imagine I want him to be a gay and pleasure-hunting parson – quite the reverse, he must steer his boat between the Scylla and Charybdis of the Church and endeavour to be a good, pious, moral and benevolent divine without folly or fanaticism.' And this Wriothesley was to do – acting as the much loved incumbent of Chenies for over 50 years. He married his first cousin Eliza, who had been brought up at Woburn. She was the daughter of 'old' Lord William Russell, the younger brother of the fifth and sixth Dukes; a shallow man – 'an unquiet spirit' – and for a time an ineffectual Whig Member of Parliament, Lord William spent his widowed years much abroad in flirtatious idleness. In his old age when he frequented Woburn, the Duchess wrote, not unkindly, of him chattering to himself up and down the passages. He was murdered in his Mayfair house in 1840 by his Swiss valet Courvoisier, who was about to be dismissed.

The Duke's piety was of a straightforward low church, early Victorian kind. 'I dislike travelling on Sunday during church time if I can avoid it,' he informed his daughter-in-law, excusing the delay of his arrival at Woburn, 'but do not say this to Lady Holland for she would not comprehend it.' Madame de Dino noticed that Sunday at Woburn was generally more serious than other days but not kept very strictly, for M. de Talleyrand was made to play at cards. Regular in his attendance at Woburn church on a Sunday morning, the Duke, when he took the Sacrament, firmly brought to an end a traditional practice by which no one approached the altar rails until the 'Duke's pew' had communicated and returned to their place.

With the Whigs in power the Russells were again united in their pursuit of reform, and when Lord John was charged to introduce the Bill in the Commons, the approval and admiration of his father and brothers was great, though coupled with a fear that his strength might not be equal to the task; Lord John himself observed during the protracted struggle: 'It will kill me as well as the close boroughs.'

He had been elected as member for Tavistock while he was still under age, and during the years of Tory government had largely devoted himself to writing and travel. He was perhaps his father's favourite child, as he had been his mother's, but the Duke was often perplexed by his son's unpredictable comings and goings; he would disappear without notice to the Continent, and be heard of visiting in Italy the wife of a Genoese nobleman to whom he was attached, or lodging in Paris, where he had gone to test the climate of political opinion. With the passing of the Reform Bill in 1832 his rise to fame was rapid, and he became something of a hero to the masses. Lord Tavistock heard that: 'Cobbett says that John is more famous than Robin Hood's little John, and that at "one fell swoop" the whole race of Boro Mongers will be exterminated by little Jack the Giant Killer.' In his family above all he was regarded as a wonder – a misfortune, perhaps, that may have contributed to some of his faults; and the quantity of unsolicited advice that he received from his two brothers may have been the root of his vacillations so noticeable in his later political life.

His marriage in 1835, when he was forty-three, to Lady Ribblesdale, a widow with four children, was accepted in his family without enthusiasm. She was 'a pretty little goose of a woman', and made him very happy, but three years later she died, having borne him two daughters. The Russells thought that he would have stood higher with the public had he retained this single state, but in 1841 he married Lady Frances Elliot, twenty-five years his junior; and she too was to add her advice on his political conduct to that which he already received from other members of his family.

William IV regarded Lord John as a dangerous radical, and being hot-tempered he did not check his tongue. 'What you have heard of his dislike to John is perfectly true,' Tavistock informed his brother William. 'On one occasion when he [Lord John] was taken ill at Lord Stanley's dinner and an exaggerated report was made to the King about it, he said in front of eleven persons (two Bishops among them) "If you will answer for his death, I will answer for his d—n—n!"' The King had no liking for the father of his Minister either and when he found that the Duke had sub-scribed to a fund for O'Connell he gave orders that his bust should be removed from the corridor at Windsor. One of Queen Victoria's first acts was to have it restored to its place, a deed that was found deeply gratifying by the Duke's eldest son, when he was invited to the Castle.

Although the Duke was restless and moved frequently from one of his houses to another, he was never without interesting and agreeable occupation at Woburn. Experimenting on his farm with the nutritive value of grasses, he published in 1816, with the aid of his gardener Sinclair, *Hortus Gramineus Woburnensis*. Other volumes covering the cultivation of willows, pines, heaths, and shrubs at Woburn followed in due course. His knowledge of such scientific subjects allowed him to enjoy on terms of equality the friendship of Sir Joseph Banks, Sir James Smith, George Bentham, and Sir William Hooker. The Swiss botanist, de Candolle, named a genus of plants discovered by La Pérouse in New Holland, bearing a resemblance to the willows, though in natural affinities removed from them – Bedfordia as a compliment to '*l'illustre propriétaire de Woburn, qui a rendu de si grands services à l'agriculture et à la botanique, et qui s'est placé au rang des Botanistes par son bel ouvrage sur les Saules.*'

The Duke ascribed his early interest in botany to the encouragement of Dr Abbott, the vicar of Oakley, who in 1798 published *Flora Bedfordiensis* – 'and whose Botanical enthusiasm used to afford me both instruction and amusement'. He learnt his lesson well, but it was not one he managed to transmit to his children, who, as he was ready to point out to them, remained ignorant of plant physiology as well as the division of species, and were unaware that a flower submitted to him for identification with-out leaves could not be properly named. Lord William did his best to keep up with his father's interest in the science, and from his diplomatic post in Portugal touchingly enclosed in his letters to him dried flowers with his own guess at identity; he was liable to be snubbed for his pains:

'the only botanical hint you gave me was incorrect; the yellow flower was not *trifolium* but *oxalis* – the leaves are trefoil, but in flower totally dissimilar to the trifolium tribe, the *oxalis* is in English the cuckoo bread'.

The Duke was more encouraging when he sent a message to William's four-year-old son: 'Tell Odo I am delighted to find he is collecting acorns for me in the Penha Verde gardens, that I shall sow them . . . and call it Odo plantation. I wish you to send me the acorns of all the genus *quercus* or *ilex*, natives of Portugal, as I am now about to form an arboretum . . . and pray do not forget a collection of *ranunculi*, and carnations and *picotées*. Gardening is my hobbyhorse, and chief occupation and amusement.' In his seventieth year his passion for horticulture gathered momentum. He sent his gardener, James Forbes, to Germany to see what might be acquired from the royal gardens of Prussia and Wurtemburg, and was generous in offering plants of his own in exchange. New greenhouses were built at Woburn for his ever-expanding accumulation of rare and delicate plants. His collection of cacti was recognized by William Hooker, the regius professor of botany at Glasgow, as the second finest in England. 'In the stoves at Woburn the great columnar kind of *Cereus*, thirty feet high . . . contrast admirably with the strangely broad and depressed forms of *Melocactus* and *Echinocactus* groups', he wrote. Between the Duke and Hooker close ties had been formed, and when it was proposed to establish a Royal Botanic Garden at Kew or in the Regent's Park, the Duke played a major part in the discussions, and he consistently supported Hooker's anxious wish to be the director of the new garden; but he had no patience with the Regent's Park scheme where only eighteen acres were available. 'The situation is quite unfit for the purpose, the soil is as bad as possible, and the spot so near the City as to be within the anti-vegetating influence of the fog and smoke of the eastern end of the Metropolis.' He begged Hooker not to associate himself with it. 'I look with hope and confident expectations to the prospect of seeing Kew Gardens and the whole of the surrounding demesne converted into a great national establishment, which may not only rival but be superior to the Jardin des Plantes at Paris.' He did not live long enough to see his friend successfully appointed as the first head of that great scientific institution.

'I am always at your commands to assist in any botanical enterprise,' he assured Hooker in 1834, and when a botanist, George Gardner, was despatched to collect plants in Brazil, he contributed £100 to the young man's outfit – 'or a larger sum if you judge it expedient'. His own son Edward, who was commanding a ship-of-war off the coast of South

America, contrived to send home plants to gratify his insatiable father, but it was on Gardner that the Duke's expectations were firmly fixed. 'If you have occasion to write to Mr. Gardner', he urged Hooker, 'pray mention the *Orchidium Russellianum* in his letter to you. He said he was within 15 miles of its habitat. There is but one plant of it in England and it is a very small one.'

'I send His Grace two boxes of orchids and cacti', wrote Gardner, and from the Organ mountains of Brazil he told of his discoveries:

> . . . through dense masses of large bamboos with stems often more than ½ foot thick and 60 or 70 feet high, we had to cut our way up . . . till we came to a small waterfall and camped for the night. On the trunks of the trees I saw abundance of *Epiphyllum truncatum* beautifully in flower and higher up the mountain the next morning I found a lovely new species . . . It gives me great pleasure to dedicate this discovery to my liberal patron His Grace the Duke of Bedford; and I hope you will agree with me in thinking it worthy to bear such an illustrious name. In my list you will find it marked *Cereus Russellianus*. Flower regular, arising from the truncated extremities of the branch, two inches and a half long, of a delicate deep pink colour.

During the four years he was away Gardner collected and sent home dried specimens as well as plants, and when Hooker, it seems, expressed dissatisfaction with his work, he was indignant:

> You seem to think I have been idle. I can only say that since I came to Brazil I have wrought harder than any slave in the country, as anyone who has collected and dried 15,000 specimens of plants within 11 months in a tropical country will admit. My labours may have been misdirected, but no one can say it is my disposition to be idle.

At a later date the despatch of a valuable addition to the Duke's 'princely collection' of cacti was notified to Hooker by the Consul-General in Mexico – 'a most remarkable *Mammilaria* of such extraordinary dimensions, as to weigh 2 cwt; and which required the united strength of 8 Indians to convey to the wagon, on which it was brought from a distance of one hundred miles to Mexico'.

The Duke had been subject since middle age to apoplectic seizures of varying severity; the final stroke came in October 1839 when he was staying at The Doune, near Rothiemurchus in Inverness-shire – the house he hired every summer and where he so much enjoyed the Highland air. He was seated very early in the morning at his writing table, an unfinished letter to Sir William Hooker was before him when the pen slipped from his hand. He had begun to tell his friend that he still fondly clung to his wish to see him head of the Royal Botanic Gardens at Kew. Hooker was to comment that the Duke's handwriting 'beautiful at all times . . . was never more beautiful nor firm than at the fatal moment'. And writing to a botanical friend he dwelt on his enjoyment of the late Duke's company.

I shall not easily forget the very pleasant days we spent with him at Woburn two years ago. To have been admitted into the unrestrained society of such a man in his private hours and to have seen him regardless of his elevated station, condescending to enter with the heartiest zeal into whatever concerned the park, the gardens, the marbles, the pictures, the library, and the other treasures of his princely seat, was one of those gratifications that are justly to be accounted privileges . . . Neither you nor I shall soon forget how his eyes glistened and his cheeks for a moment lost the sickly pallor of ill health, when one morning he produced the éloge of his brother . . . as delivered by Charles Fox, and bade us observe the volume in the handwriting of the illustrious Statesman himself, as one of the treasures of the library.

꧁꧂

15

A High-minded Whig, a Recluse, and a Cynic

'IT will be necessary to shut up the old Abbey for a time', wrote the new Duke to his brother William, then serving as ambassador to the Prussian court at Berlin. The debts and encumbrances on the estate which had been created by the extravagance of the fifth and sixth Dukes must be attended to, he insisted; a large estate might bear two extravagant possessors, but the third must be prudent in order to save it. 'It must be my part, therefore, to repair the breaches that have been made, or the family importance and influence in the Country will sink into ruin.' He had a very strong sense of duty, he was hard-working, and he was determined to succeed. The most humble of men, he ascribed any virtues he had to his mother Georgiana Byng. Politics and sport had occupied his time while he was still Lord Tavistock. He sat in the House of Commons as the member for Bedfordshire until 1833, when he was called to the Upper House under the barony of Howland: his integrity and his sound political judgement had established him as a man to whom 'the secrets of both camps' might be entrusted. An ardent foxhunter, he had kept his own pack of hounds at Oakley, and he raced his horses at Newmarket and Epsom. His early middle years were overshadowed by wretched health and for some time it was thought that his lungs might be affected; an increasing loss of weight alarmed his family, but his fundamental constitution was sound and he had an indomitable spirit. He drove himself mercilessly whether for the public good or for private pleasure; impatiently disregarding his physical condition, he broke his bones in the hunting field and lost his money ruefully on the racecourse. 'He scarcely ever seems to have a horse to run, and when he does he is beat', observed his father.

Assuming the responsibilities of his new position as Duke of Bedford he applied himself with high-minded energy to the task in front of him, and he told his brother that he rose at five in the morning to sit at his table trying to grasp the many problems he faced. He was often irritated by the readiness with which William proffered his advice from abroad, for his brother's conduct of his own affairs had not been marked by much good sense. William had always grumbled to his father – as younger sons were wont to do – about primogeniture, and had dwelt with rancour on his own meagre lot compared to the great inheritance his elder brother might expect. 'With respect to elder and younger brothers,' the new head of the family now told him with that fluency and ease of expression which has been characteristic of the letters of many Russells, 'be assured that all positions in life have their due share of good and ill . . . You are little aware of the cares and worries and plagues I have had to go thro in ye course of the last year, and were it not that it wld be wicked to complain of my lot, and not to be grateful for it, I shd say that a man with fewer of these cares and responsibilities is a happier man. I know that the happiest years I have passed were at Oakley, free from all duties and cares that have since fallen upon me.'

He owed all his domestic happiness to his placid, gracious, and good-humoured wife, Anna Maria Stanhope, a daughter of the Earl of Harrington. Creevey called her 'a gaby' and her foolish remarks were noted and repeated among her contemporaries. Platitudes and banal expressions filled her letters, and in an intellectual family, she did not know what reading meant. But it was significant that she marked in her prayer book the Epistle for the fifth Sunday after Trinity, for she put into practice St Peter's injunction to be compassionate and courteous, to love life and eschew evil, in such a manner that she was beloved by humble women, who reached to touch her garments as she passed, and received favours at her hands without feeling patronized. She was appointed in 1837 one of the young Queen's ladies, and acting as head of the female part of the Royal Household she was much criticized for the part she played in the scandal centred on Lady Flora Hastings – Lady of the Bedchamber to the Duchess of Kent – who from a change in her figure was suspected of being pregnant though unmarried, but who was in fact suffering from a disease of the liver from which she died two months later. It was Lady Tavistock's lack of good sense rather than feeling that sent her to consult the Prime Minister, Lord Melbourne, before she spoke to Lady Flora herself, and she was later exonerated from heartlessness.

Conscious of his carefree, self-indulgent father's prodigality in the administration of his estates, the seventh Duke, during the twenty-two years of his reign, addressed himself to putting what was wrong right. He bought, sold, built, drained and planted, and with the help and advice of able men brought his property back from the verge of decay to be a pattern of good management and prosperity. Believing that the habits and morals of the poor would be improved by being well housed he built for his agricultural labourers cottages that were so convenient – even luxurious – that a country gentleman being shown them exclaimed: 'These are not cottages, these are villas.'

He lacked his father's happy enjoyment of a variety of interests, and was driven by his desire to do well rather than to enjoy what he did. He gave his father's outstanding collection of orchids to Queen Victoria, and she presented it to Kew. 'Although I am fond of plants and flowers', he told Sir William Hooker, 'and delight in the ordinary pleasures of a garden, I do not profess to understand Botany, or to take the same interest my father did in the higher branches of that rational and useful science. In this respect and in many others I feel myself to be a very unworthy successor to him.' His sense of unworthiness was perfectly genuine, and we must accept his word that he allowed himself to delight in so ordinary a pleasure as a garden – his wife's taste 'in grouping the most beautiful flowers in nature, with the prettiest patterns and the most beautiful masses of colour' being unequalled – a tribute paid her by her son after her death.

Easily gratified by marks of regard from others, the Duke was without vanity. His wife avowed that his character was portrayed in the fifteenth psalm.

Lord, who shall dwell in thy tabernacle, or who shall rest upon thy holy hill?
Even he that leadeth an uncorrupt life and doeth the thing which is right, and speaketh the truth from the heart.
He that hath used no deceit from his tongue, nor done evil to his neighbour and hath not slandered his neighbour.
He that setteth not by himself, but is lowly in his own eyes and maketh much of them that fear the Lord.
He that sweareth unto his neighbour and disappointeth him not though it were his own hindrance.
He that hath not given his money upon usury nor taken reward against the innocent.
Who so doeth these things shall never fail.

She may be credited with a certain bias, but it was a tribute to which many who knew him would have subscribed. He was perhaps lacking in humour, nor greatly aware of his capacity to bore or irritate by his earnest conviction that what he talked about was as interesting to others as to himself. Lady Granville found him an uncongenial neighbour at the dinner table; the mature Miss Eden was so much annoyed by his repetition of a political apothegm that she wrote him 'short savage notes. I hope I have rather enlightened that slightly damaged article his mind. It is a good old mind, too, in its little bald shell', and his sister-in-law, Lady William Russell, complained that when he was not talking about 'country interests, grazing cattle, capital sport, hounds and constituents, game and Ministers', he was like his ancestor described by Grammont: '*taciturne à donner les vapeurs.*'

Less than a year elapsed after the death of his father before the Duke and Duchess made a cursory stay at Woburn – 'just to look about us and feel our way, and establish order and regularity'. The following year a visit to Belvoir Castle was profitable, for he saw much of 'the interior management and economy of a most magnificent establishment conducted with a degree of order and regularity – combined with the truest hospitality'. The Duke of Rutland, he affirmed, 'lives like an English Duke'. And that was what he set out to do himself. The Duke of Bedford's hospitality was prodigious; a record kept of the number of people provided for at the Abbey from Lady Day 1859 for one year, shows that 1,129 persons ate at his Grace's table during that period; at the steward's room table 2,596 were accommodated, and in the servants' hall 8,217 were fed – a total of nearly 12,000 persons. With the accomplished and graceful help of his wife, whose talents were agreeably social, he undertook the dutiful performance of the obligations of his position. Once again Woburn was established as a centre of political hospitality, and the Duchess's introduction of five o'clock tea became an institution generally adopted as a feature of London and country house life.

William Russell – now separated from his clever but difficult wife – stayed at the Abbey for Christmas 1841. He often felt ill at ease and chilled by the cold manner of his brother – 'Good God, how the Duke freezes one' – but he was impressed by the style in which life was again conducted in the great house, and he took up his pen to give the widowed Lady Holland his account: 'In point of magnificence it is equal to the old days, and in point of comfort there is an evident improvement; that is, all that concerns the housekeeper's department is more *soigné*. We are 30 at table, great profusion, and an admirable *cuisine*, besides, repasts at every hour of the day. From 10 to 12 breakfast – from 2 to 3 luncheon, from 5 to 6 tea, at 7 dinner, and after balls and theatres hot suppers, otherwise cold. The Duke of Sussex appears delighted, passes the morning in his room and is no *gêne* to any one. You will be glad to hear the old Abbey has come out of the fire of its purification with more splendour than ever...'

A young member of the family remembered in later life that it was the custom when the family had dined on Christmas Day, to throw the remaining mince pies, and even cutlets and bons-bons, from the dining-room windows to an expectant crowd of townsfolk and labourers gathered outside, who scrambled for the good things from the rich man's table.

The Duchess was in her element at Christmas, when a large party of family and friends gathered at the Abbey, and she was prodigal with presents for her guests. From the tree which was illuminated not on Christmas but on New Year's Day, she distributed 'small items of jewellery' and embroidered Indian articles to the ladies, while their daughters received wreaths and bouquets of artificial flowers. Waistcoats – Garter blue or ruby-coloured (but black and gold for the Prime Minister, Lord John Russell) – were given to the men. French fans were chosen for the sisters-in-law and little girls got white muslin frocks over silk with tucks and rows of white narrow satin ribbons. One year there was a blue net cap with three square diamonds for the Dowager Duchess of Bedford, and a wreath of pomegranates and mignonette for her unmarried daughter Rachel. In the 1850s the waistcoats might be of white or thistle green silk (claret velvet for his Grace), and the ladies found themselves indebted for poplin or merino dresses, and a purple velvet cloak trimmed with black lace was bestowed on Elizabeth Anne, the widow of Lord William Russell. From this we may see that there was nothing derogatory in the gift of a gown, and that it was presumably the condescending manner in which Lady Ashburton presented Mrs Carlyle with a dress that caused so much offence, and induced Jane's inference that dresses were presents for servants. The Duchess of Bedford had a flamboyant taste in clothes herself, and her dresses were once remarked on for looking 'as if they came out of an old masquerade warehouse'.

Sometimes the essentially domestic scene was enlivened by the intrusion of public events if Lord John was staying at the Abbey. In December 1847 his recommendation that the Queen should appoint an unorthodox divine to the bishopric of Hereford raised an outcry, and it was uncertain

The eighth Duke of Bedford by Hayter

The ninth Duke of Bedford by G. Richmond

if Dr Hampden would be elected by the cathedral chapter. The Prussian Minister was staying at Woburn and observed how when the company was collected in the library in expectation and talking against time, the door was thrown open and Lord John's five-year-old son, Johnny, escorted by his aunt-like half-sister, stationed himself in the entrance 'distinctly proclaiming like a herald – "Dr. Hampden – a Bishop!" We cheered him and someone asked him if he liked Dr. Hampden. "I don't mind (was his answer) for I don't know him."' A sensible answer to a grown-up's foolish question.

On New Year's Day 1848 Monckton Milnes was also of the party, and in his spirited way he wrote a long witty epilogue to be spoken after a ballet – *Les Arbres Celestes* – performed in the room that served as a small theatre at Woburn. The closing lines had a pun on the name of the Dean of Hereford, who had resisted the consecration of Dr Hampden.

Come middle-age, Repose
And content their charms disclose
Merriment for all together
    (*to Lord John*)
You my Lord have *Merryweather*,
While in joyous union we
Dance around the Christmas Tree

After the epilogue was spoken a curtain was drawn back to reveal the Christmas tree 'with lights and gifts all over and around it'.

Professionals must have been engaged to dance on this occasion, but ever since the time of the fourth Duke the performance of plays had been a source of occupation and amusement, with a cast drawn from the family and from among the people staying in the house. In spite of his shyness the sixth Duke had readily taken a part in them, though others might be less anxious to appear upon the stage. 'We have been on the point of acting,' Emily Eden had written in 1821, 'but the Providence that guards *les fous et les ivrognes* evidently keeps an eye on Amateur actors and preserves them from actually taking the boards.' Lord William and Lord John were sometimes called on to write the prologue or the epilogue, and the programmes were printed on white satin.

In the summer of 1841 the newly married Queen Victoria and Prince Albert spent a few days at Woburn – the old state bedroom and the rooms adjoining being prepared for their reception. Lady Lyttelton accompanied the Queen, and her witty pen did justice to the occasion when the host and hostess excelled themselves in efforts and attention.

How dull! Bless me! We are eleven of us Dukes and Duchesses, and most dukefully dull indeed we are. The Queen must carry away with her a strange idea of what society and conversation mean . . . the house most comfortable and huge, and the dinner also, after a great and un-concealed effort, contrives to be *almost* as sumptuous as our daily fare at Windsor . . .

Two professional singers had been engaged for the second night, and

the Queen was pleased and did her part well, getting up when it was over and going into the music room to compliment Masson, whose downcast eyes and loyal simpering were worth seeing . . . Lady de Grey performed with Lord Melbourne a regular *pas-de-deux* argument on political economy. She was graceful and he was clever and it killed us a good twenty minutes . . .

The Queen was shown all over the house. Too shy to ask questions about the pictures and portraits she appeared like a girl just out of school, but peeping into the guests' bedrooms amused her very much. A County address was presented to her next day and she read her reply 'most enchantingly',

her pretty emphasis and half smile to the Duke, as she uttered 'the noble and patriotic house of Russell' made his eyes glisten and the good-natured Duchess had to hide a tear or two behind a geranium.

Although the Queen confessed to her Uncle Leopold that she had enjoyed her subsequent visit to Lord Cowper at Panshanger more, her host at Woburn was perfectly satisfied with the success of his endeavours.

'I believe I entertained my Sovereign in a becoming manner, so at least I was told by all my guests, and no one among them expressed himself more strongly and more warmly than the Duke of Wellington.' Ques-tioned why he had invited Wellington and Lord de Grey, and not Lord John Russell – as it looked 'Toryish' on his part – he replied: 'My answer is that this having been the Queen's first visit to the Country House of one of her subjects I considered it of the highest importance that it should not have a Party character . . . I might to be sure have made it more a Party affair, but I wished to take higher ground, and it succeeded perfectly (asking all Whigs except the two named).' Lord John Russell was absent because he had chosen that moment for his second marriage to take place in Scotland.

There was one person the Duke and Duchess would dearly have loved to have had with them at Woburn on that occasion – their only child, Lord Russell (now Marquess of Tavistock, though always known to them as 'Russell'); but they had long recognized that they could not expect their son to take any part in an important social event, and he now rarely came to Woburn.

On her wedding day in 1808, Anna Maria had been given a diamond cross by old Queen Charlotte, accompanied by a charming note: 'From one who truly wishes you never heavier crosses than the one given you by your sincere friend Charlotte.' During the course of a happy married life the Duke and Duchess of Bedford found that with the passing years they had to accept a private sorrow and to bear a heavy cross – the increasing tendency to hypochondria of their handsome, delicate and introspective son. He had been sent to Eton as a boy – a disloyalty to Westminster School that the sixth Duke had deplored. At nineteen he had been consigned to the care of William Adam for a tour of the fens and the Thorney estate, when the shrewd Scotsman had observed the lad closely, and given his father a summary report. He found, he wrote, a most ingenuous and frank disposition, but very little energy and activity of mind. No particular bent, no particular ambition, and very little information. 'It would be a great object to excite his curiosity and attention by making him acquainted with interesting subjects . . . In his situation he must gain knowledge now or not at all.' Constitutionally languid, and the object of his mother's 'anxious affection', the young man's physical energy was never stretched, but his aptitude for study led him to profound consideration of the human condition, and he found little therein to cheer him. Representing Tavistock in Parliament from his coming of age to his thirtieth year, he cut no figure in the House of Commons and withdrew for reasons of health. Lord Grey found him impenetrable, 'More silent even than a Russell, it is impossible to get a word out of him, but he seems contented and good-humoured.' When he began to eschew society and the festive worldly life in which his parents took part they were alarmed, and wished above all things that he would marry, in the hope that his health would claim less of his attention, but about the time he left Parliament he wrote his father a letter that must have given pain.

> I don't think I shall ever marry. I also think it as well to tell you that in case I should survive you, which I think is most improbable, and I trust you may live to an extreme old age in the enjoyment of the property which you seem to enjoy. But if I should survive you, and you were to leave Woburn to me, I think it as well to tell you I don't think I should live there. I think it fair to tell you this because you might like to leave it in another direction and make provision for it to be kept up.

His father treated his son's morbid depression with great kindness. 'Russell', he declared, 'reads and thinks deeply, but does not reap happiness from his studies and reflections.' The fruits of his meditations Russell confided to his father in lengthy letters or in a few lines, and the impression given is that of a man who found it impossible to stop thinking. The Duke answered his outpourings with warm interest – he had a great respect for his son's political opinions – and each preserved the letters of the other. Politics were discussed in a practical manner by the elder man, and in a more detached and philosophical vein by the younger, who confessed himself to be an enthusiastic radical, believing that happier prospects were opening upon mankind. His admiration for his uncle John was great and curiously uncritical. 'I do not think England ever had a greater statesman. Lord John is always right.' Pages might on one day be devoted to a survey of public affairs; on another he would write at length about his capricious digestion, and then on the next he would give his views on architecture and the new buildings of London. He approved the classical aspect of Belgravia and Tyburnia, and disliked the medieval style so widely popular. 'I think Palmerston was right in objecting to Gothic architecture for the new Foreign Office. Gothic buildings are gloomy and the conception of a barbaric age . . . Christ and the disciples lived in the midst of Classic architecture.' His father encouraged these musing communications. 'As you live so much alone and think so much . . . it is a good thing for you that you should give vent to them by writing the results to your mother and me.'

In 1834 Don Carlos, younger brother of Ferdinand VII of Spain, had arrived in London as a refugee. The King had died in the previous year leaving his crown to his only child, Isabella. Don Carlos, the representative of absolutism and the Catholic Church, claimed the throne for himself under the Salic Law. For a year he threw in his lot with the Portuguese reactionary Dom Miguel, who was contending in a civil war for the crown of Portugal. Defeated in their aims, the two pretenders gave themselves up to an English admiral and were taken on board an English ship-of-war. Palmerston refused to hand Carlos over to Spain and he came to London, where he rented Gloucester Lodge in Kensington and had talks with the Duke of Wellington. Refusing a pension of £30,000 offered by the Spanish ambassador if he would renounce his claim to the Spanish throne, he presently slipped away unobserved and, reaching Spain, engaged in a savage civil war, which ended only in 1839, when he escaped to France and was interned by the French authorities and eventually allowed to go to Austria.

It seems likely that the Duke and Duchess of Bedford met the Spanish pretender in the company of the Duke of Wellington, and perhaps the Duchess, who was an old friend of the Duke's, made herself particularly charming to the Spaniard, and may have talked of her concern for the future happiness of her unmarried son. The wealth and standing in England of her husband was known to all. It must have been a matter of considerable astonishment to the good Duke when his wife revealed to him the contents of a letter she received from Paris.

> Hotel de Bragance
> 10 Rue de Courcelles
> 20th March 1841

Dear Madam,

... The friendly attentions which you have shown towards me and the Princess during our residence in London, make me anxious to evince in return, the sincere interest I feel, in contributing to your happiness, and I hope I am not mistaken in thinking that I cannot do so more congenially to the feelings of so affectionate a Mother, than by proposing a union between your son the Marquis of Tavistock and one of my nieces, Her Royal Highness the Princess Isabella Bourbon Infant of Spain and daughter of T.R.H. Don Francisco di Paola and the Princess Louisa Charlotte Infante of Spain, my sister. It would make me truly happy to see my niece the Daughter-in-Law of one who holds so high a position in public opinion as yourself and I may confidently assure you that the Princess possesses all those attractions and accomplishments calculated to render the married life a happy one. The young lady is 20 years of age, most prepossessing, highly educated and extremely amiable. If you approve of my projected marriage for your son, you may *then* mention it to him, and the Duke of Bedford *enjoining them to secrecy* for your reply will direct me as to the propriety of naming it to my sister H.R.H. the Infanta, who at present is ignorant of my writing to you on the subject!! Pray excuse all errors in my epistolary style, as I write in English, but believe me that good feeling has dictated every word. Hoping soon to hear from you I am Dear Madam with sentiments of the highest consideration

Yours very faithfully

Carlos

The Duchess wrote a dignified and grateful letter of refusal:

. . . Lord Tavistock is also very grateful, but we all feel that a proposition of Marriage on his part even if favourably entertained would not secure the happiness of a Princess born in so high a rank and destined to so conspicuous a position among the Royal Families of Europe – therefore with all humility we decline this proffered honor, begging your Royal Highness to believe that we shall ever remember with affectionate gratitude your partiality to us.

The Duke joins me in hoping that we may some day have the honor of receiving your Royal Highness and the Princess at Woburn Abbey.

I have the honor to be

Your faithful servant

Anna Maria Bedford

A connection between the House of Bourbon and the House of Russell would surely have been one to startle the Whig families of England!

The little Queen of Spain was later married against her will to the Duke of Cadiz, the impotent brother of that Infanta proposed as a bride for Lord Tavistock.

In the autumn of that same year the Duke received two letters from his son that were deeply disturbing:

October 22 1841

. . . I believe the more wisdom a man has the more miserable he is . . .

I don't like to give you any reasons why I shrink from marrying, because I know a reason may always be combated, and that a reason which seems as heavy as a mill stone to one person, seems as light as a feather to another. I do not think I shall live much longer. I have little life in me now. Always and every day I am living rather as flogged along or upon pluck, than having anything approaching to enjoyment of life, always saying to myself 'Courage! Courage! Courage!' What the principle of life may be I don't know, perhaps a rich blood . . . I shrink almost with a feeling of horror of uniting a young girl full of life to a semi-corpse. I feel the machinery is nearly worn out . . .

Your affte T.

I think few people ever have passed a much more unpleasant life than I have done. People think I am a happy fellow enough, because I am not generally in the habit of complaining. I have often broken out into a cold sweat and felt sick at the stomach with misery . . . What this misery was I can't say, but misery seemed to circulate with my blood and pass like electricity through every nerve and fibre of my body, and yet there was no pain. Fancy a soul in hell, that gives a better idea of my sensations and existence than anything else.

London, Wednesday, 1841

. . . Ever since I could think, ever since I was at Eton, my mind has been discouraged. I have felt despair at finding myself in a creation in which there is so much Evil. It has tormented me without cease. I have longed for something wise and good to which I might trust. I have ransacked the thoughts of the wise and good, and have found nothing but what I have thought to be folly and injustice. I have tried often religion, and it has been repugnant even to loathing (from what seemed to me to be its nonsense and cruelty) to what ever little reason I possess. I have now tried it in another way by faith – throwing reason entirely aside. And I now think I may say I believe in it. That is to say I have stifled my reason, without respect to that subject. If people die of broken hearts and disappointment why should not many years of despair, produced by a longing after, and inability to find a good power in the universe, cause the body to be sickly? Mankind has advanced prodigiously in knowledge and mine is I believe a very common cast of thought in the present day. Especially on the Continent among the upper classes, and in England amongst the lower. I believe it has led many a man to suicide.

I have had in early youth a passionate longing after a principle of excellence and truth, therefore my disappointment has been in proportion. At last I ceased both to long and to despair, and I became callous. And now I have taken refuge in faith. I was a radical from the disgust excited in my mind, from reading of the crimes and injustice of great men, and the upper classes. I thought a great revolutionary movement was agitating society throughout the civilized world. And I hoped that a happier era was likely to arise for mankind. Since then I have thought that the mass of mankind must always be the dupes or victims of humbug, or tyranny. I hope you will always look upon my opinions with distrust and repugnance, for they are not pleasant ones. I should be glad to exchange them for yours. But a man's thoughts spring as naturally and inevitably from his nature and organisation, as particular plants do from particular soils.

The Duke submitted both these letters to his brother John, who at once arranged for a physician to see his nephew, and reported the verdict: 'that it was a case of deep hypochondria' and 'that a bad stomach, Byron and Voltaire have been the causes of the mischief'.

Although the unhappy hypochondriac lived much alone in his parents' house in Belgrave Square, he had an alternative address in Kensington, where round about his thirtieth year he had installed a mistress in a small house in Leonard Place, and where he himself was known as Mr Johnson. This simple woman can have been no intellectual companion for him, but she earned his lifelong devotion. She could not however relieve his despondency – indeed after a few years she was to add to it, for she became insane through an hereditary tendency, her principal delusion being that she had died and was now living her second life. His every endeavour was used to keep her out of an asylum. Appealing to his father for an increase in his allowance, he revealed that Lord Holland had once taken him aside to tell him that the income he received from his father was contemptible. He begged now for three hundred a year more in order that he might provide all the care and medical attention the wretched woman needed, in her own home. As an economy, he would if necessary give up his own brougham – that carriage with wooden shutters to its windows in which he was conveyed, invisible, through the streets between Belgrave Square and Kensington. The Duke was to respond generously, providing a fund to be ministered by trustees for the care of 'the insane person'. Urged to come to Woburn, where it was promised that he would find no party, only near relations, Russell made excuses. 'The long passages and rooms of Woburn hurt my leg', he wrote, complaining of his varicose veins.

> By long experience and the exercise of ingenuity I have found ways of passing the day without its seeming long. But in the country, as I can, owing to my lameness, neither take a walk in the garden, nor owing to the weakness of my sight, avail myself of a library by looking at books or prints, I find by experience I am quite without resource in the country, and without any sort of pleasure or amusement, and bound hand and foot the victim of ennui.

In 1851, as the second Census was about to be taken, 'Mr Johnson' of Leonard Place protested vigorously to his father.

> . . . Can a man force his way into every dwelling and insist upon knowing whether every individual is married or single? Every man's house is his castle. Are all veils to be torn rudely aside? Are there no such things as private marriages? (I beg to say I am not privately married).

And so on, over six double sheets of writing paper. Eschewing an easy solution to his difficulty by spending the night in Belgrave Square he duly filled up the Census form at Leonard Place, appearing as:

> William Russell, – head, commonly called Marquis of Tavistock, magistrate, unmarried, age 41.

There followed:

> Harriet Walls, visitor, unmarried, 30, annuitant, Born Bath.

A housekeeper and a nurse completed the list of occupants.

The Duke did not relinquish his wish that Russell would change his way of life, and sometimes his injured feelings would break out, as blow after blow was delivered to his pride and hopes by the clear, passionless statements of his son and heir. On New Year's Day 1853 he returned to the subject that so constantly occupied his thoughts.

> How anxiously, my dear Russell, do I wish and pray that you would let me try to bring about what I so ardently desire for your happiness and our own. You have it in your power in this way to make us supremely blest. Is that no object of desire to you? As for the person in which you are interested there cd be no difficulty about her. An ample provision with a comfortable asylum and occasional visits if you wished it. Time passes and there is none now to lose. You led me to hope sometimes that you would marry at 30 . . .

He divulged that there was staying at Woburn a girl who he and the Duchess had agreed would be the perfect wife for him – 'morally and religiously excellent, domestic, attractive, gay in grace, with the best understanding and judgement, and as great a lover of truth as you are'. It was of no avail. The name of this young female paragon remains undisclosed to us.

When Russell suggested that his father might wish to leave Woburn 'in another direction', his languor may have prohibited any curiosity or concern of his own for the future of the property, but to the Duke one direction would have been clearly indicated, and painful as it must have been to him to accept that it would be his brother's descendants and not his own who would one day inhabit the Abbey he dutifully took steps to become better acquainted with Lord and Lady William Russell's handsome, honourable and ardent eldest son. The transformation of this attractive, warm-hearted, and merry young man into the unsociable, embittered and cynical ninth Duke of Bedford makes a sad passage in the history of the Russell family and might be traced to a number of causes. His early years have been recorded at length in another book.

Through the perversity of his mother, Elizabeth Anne Rawdon, who did not care for her husband's relations, and preferred life on the Continent to a pecuniarily restricted existence in England, Hastings had been brought up principally abroad. Before he was two years old he had travelled about Germany with his parents, and the death in a shrieking delirium of his much-loved nurse at Vienna could be thought to have left a deep scar on his subconscious mind. As a little boy he was doted on by Lady Holland, a woman not naturally drawn to children. 'As to Hastings', she told her son, 'he is without exception the most pleasing, promising child I ever saw, full of *sense* besides his acquirements, with all his father's courage, manliness and gentleness. Not in the least spoiled, well-behaved and tractable.'

Lord William some years after his marriage had renounced Parliament and a career in the army – where he was doing well, for he was a good soldier – to please his intellectual and beautiful, but selfish wife, in order to idle in her wake through Italy and Switzerland, until his brothers, distressed to see him without occupation, exerted their influence and he was pressed into diplomacy. A shared interest in the education of their three sons united the William Russells for a time, but the defects of her difficult temper, and a conspicuous love affair of William's in Germany, effectually separated husband and wife, and thereafter they were rarely together. At the age of sixteen Hastings was his mother's constant companion, and became largely responsible for her and his brothers' well-being as well as having in his charge the care of the horses, the grooms, and the vehicles in which they were all transported about Europe according to the vagaries of Lady William's inclinations. Her sons delighted in her stimulating companionship, for she was extremely intelligent and well informed. They were accompanied everywhere by a French and a German tutor, and the languages of these two men were more familiar to Arthur and Odo Russell than their own native tongue.

Hastings had a cheerful temper and he wrote witty letters that were full of fun to his absent father, discoursing on drunken German grooms, equine vexations, his brothers' activities, his mother's indispositions, and his own ardent wish to enter the Army when he had finished his education. Since childhood he had had a passion for firearms. He was nominated a lieutenant in the Scots Fusilier Guards in 1838 when he was nineteen, and returned to his native land the following year to take up his military duties; his mother and brothers accompanying him. They had been away from England for five years, and they were joined in London by Lord William. The sixth Duke of Bedford had been dead two months.

While his mother remained in England Hastings showed no wish to break away from the close family circle and to be swallowed up in the fashionable world, and when she returned with his brothers to the Continent he contrived to pass his summer leave with them at Carlsbad or Vienna, in the society of the aristocratic Austrians with whom he had spent his adolescent years.

Living on his own in London, his status in the succession to a dukedom ensured that he was invited to dine and to dance, to visit and to shoot. The Duke of Bedford was avuncular without being warm, and Hastings received his advances with circumspection. The Duke wrote to his brother:

I tipped Hastings £50 on New Year's Day, thinking that a little pocket money is never unacceptable to a Sub. in the Guards. He was very amiable about it but said that not having been at school and therefore not accustomed to tips, he hardly knew whether to take it, but I told him that tips are always allowable from an Uncle to a Nephew.

Showing his desire to act in a proper manner to his brother's son he wrote from Woburn that he had hoped that Russell

would have taken Hastings by the hand, but it is not his way. I wish it was. He never calls on anybody . . . Russell I know likes Hastings, but he must learn to take people as he finds them. Russell like all of us has his merits and demerits, his good and bad qualities – among the latter is a most extraordinary and morbid feeling of diffidence which makes him think he cannot be useful or agreeable to anybody. There has been nothing I am sure to make Hastings think he would only be *tolerated* here, my invitations have been as cordial as my desire to see him here has been great . . . I was not only anxious to see him, but in a fidget from day to day at his not coming . . . I think him a very nice youth.

The good relations that were to exist between the two first cousins were still twenty years ahead.

A witness through his boyhood of the dissensions between his parents, Hastings was deeply attached to both, and his affectionate nature was often wounded by their censorious and unjust attacks on him made from a distance – 'which pains me more by letter than by word of mouth' – and which did much to lower his self-confidence in early life. At ease with his captious and contradictory father he loved him with a compassionate forbearance; the devotion and admiration he felt for his clever, dominating mother survived her displeasure and her heartless treatment when he married in 1844 Lady Elizabeth Sackville West – a marriage she at first approved and then objected to. Pausing at Brussels on her way from

Carlsbad to England, Lady William remained abroad storming about settlements and abusing her son until the wedding was over, and would not come to see him after it, directing her steps instead to Paris, where Hastings went first alone to see her and then took his wife. Seven months after the marriage he wrote disconsolately to his father that his mother's 'dislike to my wife, which is consummate, tho' not unexpected as you know, forbids my looking forward with much pleasure to anything.' For a time he could do nothing right in her eyes: 'she is constantly displeased with me. I am very sorry but do not know how to regain her favour.' He left the Army when he married, unable to afford the expense of being an officer in the Guards with little hope of promotion; the abandonment of his profession was a disappointment deeply felt by him. For a time he lived an idle life in Cambridgeshire, sharing the intense enjoyment of fox-hunting with his wife. They were visited at Bourn Hall by Lord William, who having thought the bride at her wedding 'not pretty but dignified and lady-like', now found her 'cold and close'.

The continued hostility of Hastings' mother and the fault-finding letters he received from both his capricious parents unnerved him.

> I want encouragement, and not rebuffs. Without a little vanity (self-esteem) nothing would be done in this world, and to be constantly told by one's Mother that one is an idiot, a coward and a liar is very disheartening.

From time to time he made rapid journeys across Europe to mollify them and to see his much loved brothers who, to his distress, spoke English with foreign accents after their long residence abroad.

When Lord William – unemployed since the fall of the Whig Ministry in 1841 – became ill during a lonely sojourn at Genoa five years later, it was Hastings and Elizabeth who went to him, since repeated appeals to Lady William met with no response, and nursed him tenderly for six weeks until he died in July 1846. Lady William arrived from Vienna with her boys Arthur and Odo, before the end, but there was no reconciliation with her eldest son. The great heat, grief, and resentment produced sad scenes while they were all together, and when Lady William took her two younger sons back to Vienna Lord John was the recipient of his sister-in-law's outpouring of excuses and attempted self-justification, coupled with accusations of arrogance and insolence against her first-born. Hastings, when he returned to England, unburdened his own grief and emotion to old Mrs Rawdon, his foolish but dearly-loved grandmother, the constant companion of Lady William in her German wanderings.

> I reached Chenies in the middle of the night . . . and thanked God I had reached my journey's end – for I had a great wish that he should lay at Chenies. I was also very thankful to have been able to spare Mmyo much misery by enabling her to leave Genoa as soon as she did and it is a great comfort to me to think I was allowed to nurse my Father during the whole 46 days of his illness and to pay him the last duties as I have done – tended him in sickness and washed him after death, seen him laid in his coffin and travelled safely eleven hundred miles with it and lastly and at last gone down into the vault with him and seen him placed where I hope one day to lay beside him.

His anxiety for his mother's health and his continuing exclusion from her affection was the theme of many letters to his grandmother that followed:

> I am heartbroken at MM's relentlessness but I see no way to soften it. I think that she is throwing away her own happiness by driving those most attached to her away. It has marred mine, but I have said as much and perhaps more than a son ought to say to his mother about this without attaining anything. Nothing I can say or do, depend upon it, dear Granny, will conquer MM's aversion. I can only hope for a mild word which will always bring me back to my MM whenever she shall be tired of scaring me away.

Lady William's aversion to her daughter-in-law was never overcome. Twenty years later she compared her to a housemaid or an under teacher in a boarding school. '*Elle me fait l'effet d'une mauvaise odeur.*' By then all three of her devoted sons were used to the lash of her tongue and her 'coarse and abusive language'.

A seat was found in Parliament for Hastings in 1847, and he represented Bedfordshire until 1872. 'I hope', wrote Lord John to Lady William, who had Tory sympathies, 'that Hastings will be a good Whig and not a Radical or a Tory.' He was in the years ahead to be much put out by his nephew's political veering.

Hastings' separation from his mother and brothers, now men of twenty and twenty-four who remained abroad tied to Lady William's apron strings, was a constant source of sadness and annoyance to him as it was to their uncles, who were not resigned to seeing their grown-up nephews becoming no more than 'intelligent foreigners'. In 1849 Lord John, now Prime Minister, secured that Arthur should return to England and act as his private secretary, and Odo was attached to the embassy at Vienna. Lady William herself was drawing nearer to England, but Hastings was overcome by melancholy at the passage of time. He wrote to Arthur in October:

> I am 30 today. I have no illusions, little industry and less energy. I shall never make anything very much. My chief pleasure will be to see you and Odo honourable and useful in your own country, and if I can make myself a *'point d'appui'* from whence you may begin to move the world it will be my greatest satisfaction. I am sorry not to have you with me today, but I am less lonely than I have been for nine years since you are no longer at a great distance from me and my Mmyo seems more reconciled to me.

Lady William returned to England in 1850 and her purchase of a house in London made a reconciliation between her and Hastings inevitable, and perhaps by then he was finding his wife's companionship inadequate and her intelligence may have fallen in his estimation. Among the notable and cultivated people who gathered in Lady William's drawing-room in the evenings to enjoy her brilliant conversation, her eldest son was one of the most eager to be present.

The seventh Duke died in 1861, his beloved wife having predeceased him. Appealed to from Woburn by his aunt, the Duchess of Abercorn, to visit his dying father, Lord Tavistock found himself unable to comply. 'He speaks with great tenderness of you,' she wrote, 'I wish you could have met once again in this world, and had his last blessing, But I suppose it is impossible.' Lord John wrote rather severely to his nephew that he hoped the Duke would have his reward in heaven.

Immediately after the funeral the management of all the estates was put into the hands of Hastings Russell by the middle-aged invalid who had become the eighth Duke of Bedford. Latterly when urged by an acquaintance to marry and beget an heir, he had rejoined: 'Why should I? Could I have a better son than Hastings?'

> You have trebled my income, wrote Hastings gratefully, conferred a residence in the country and appointed me your representative at

certain times, besides exhausting every question that kindness and liberality could suggest. I beg that you will never pass over any act of mine that does not give you satisfaction.

His residence in the country was to be Woburn Abbey.

In 1863 the blue-stocking Sarah Austin, in a letter to Guizot, wrote:

I went to visit my dear young friend Hastings Russell at Woburn Abbey. It is very interesting to me, who love him, to see the care, the anxious thought and conscientiousness with which he administers the vast *dominions* confided to his management. It is an oppressive charge.

'I have an ardent wish to serve you as you desire,' Hastings told his cousin, and the sincerity of his ambition was undoubted. The Duke was consulted at regular meetings, and in their correspondence 'I beg to recommend' was Hastings' submissive phrase when putting forward for the Duke's approbation any policy of action. Every year like a Chancellor of the Exchequer he prepared his budget for expenditure on the estates – alterations, repairs, new churches and schools to be built were estimated for in detail. If in later years he lamented that his days were passed in fulfilling the duties of a land-agent he had many rewards for his labour. He was able to remain in Parliament, to command the Bedfordshire Volunteers, to bring his four children up at Woburn, and to entertain there his relations and friends. Arthur, elected as the member for Tavistock in 1857, remained anchored to his mother's side, slowly making a name for himself as a savant and a philosopher. Odo rose rapidly in his profession, and during the period of Italian unification, distinguished himself as the English envoy to the Vatican, where he was on friendly terms with Pius IX, and his excellent despatches were highly praised by his uncle John Russell, the Foreign Secretary.

When it was possible for the three brothers to be together at Woburn Abbey, Hastings recaptured the happiest hours of his boyhood, when they had been united in a passion for natural history – a preference for the cold-blooded creatures of the animal kingdom prevailing. It was not unusual for Odo to go about with a small snake in his pocket. The numerous ponds at Woburn were fished and dragged by the hour with boyish enthusiasm; frogs, toads and water-tortoises in variety were procured from zoological shops and from abroad, to be released in suitable areas, and their survival or increase was noted by the brothers with scientific interest.

The tenth Duke of Bedford

e eleventh Duke of Bedford and his son Hastings,
later the twelfth Duke

Mary Tribe, Duchess of Bedford

Woburn Abbey in the 17th century (*above*) and Woburn Abbey, the west front today (*below*)

Such harmony between the brothers was not always maintained. Hastings' growing obsession with money became a noticeable feature of his character, viewed by Arthur, the brother closest to him, with astonishment and distress, and his increasing irritability, caustic remarks, and his impatience in discussion impaired the old happy relationship with his brothers. He became preoccupied with the 'uncertain prospects' of his children, his difficulty in providing for them – though the security of their future can hardly have been much in doubt. 'Do you not think it is quite hopeless for him to succeed in getting any sympathy for his misery?' asked Arthur of his confidante, Lady Salisbury, the sister of Hastings' wife, and later to become the wife of Lord Derby. Hastings' cynicism was derived perhaps, as his father's melancholy had been, from the disappointment of ambitions unfulfilled – both had abandoned the profession of their choice.

Arthur's marriage in 1865 at the age of forty, to a liberal-minded Frenchwoman, Laura de Peyronnet, evoked no affectionate response in his brother. 'Hastings takes it very well,' he told Lady Salisbury, 'but has not said one word to me (except about settlements), I suppose that could happen in no other family.'

The importance of Woburn as a house where politicians of both camps could meet was paramount under the aegis of Hastings and Lady Elizabeth, as it had been in the time of the seventh Duke and his amiable wife. The firm judgement of the Duke had helped to sort out problems for the Whig party, and Lord John had accepted reproofs from his brother when from time to time his shilly-shallying or abrupt decisions had thrown the Cabinet into confusion. In 1852 when Lord John dismissed Palmerston, the Duke transmitted to Lord Tavistock the conversation he himself had with the ruffled Foreign Secretary, who, declaring he could 'no longer serve under John in any future Government, admitted that privately . . . his sentiments are unchanged – adding "I love him and always shall"' – a sentiment to be echoed by Lord John's devoted valet: 'I love every hair of his head.'

Hastings was sometimes criticized for the unconventional way in which he invited incongruous people – the illustrious and the obscure – to meet at Woburn, but his parties were successful and allowed his guests an opportunity – which might not otherwise have occurred – to exchange ideas. He was a genial and charming host, laying himself out in little attentions to his guests, and his witty conversation, spiced with quotations from unusual books, displayed the range of his reading.

'I hope you will lock up your spoons', wrote a foolish friend, who heard that Lord John was taking John Bright to stay at Woburn. The great Radical commented that he was reminded of a factory when the many windows of the big house lit up the quadrangle at night.

The eighth Duke of Bedford died suddenly in 1872; he had known for twenty years that he had a grave heart disease. '*Le Duc est mort! Vive le Duc!*' wrote Odo from his Embassy in Berlin. 'His character may change', Arthur wrote hopefully to Odo, 'when the irritability caused by dependence on the Duke, who constantly *biffé* his plans, has ceased . . . He changed much when our Uncle died and he assumed his present great position'; but from this time to the end of his life Hastings' cynical despondency increased. As the ninth Duke of Bedford he has been represented as a lonely man perpetually thinking about money, driving daily in his brougham to the Bedford office in Bloomsbury, where he pored over his money bags. 'His love of money has become a form of insanity', wrote a friend, who knew him well. The pages of his journal, largely left blank, served to record remarks implying a contempt for riches. 'There are men who do not succumb to the numbing influence of riches.' 'Wherever there is profuse expenditure corruption as surely follows as disease follows the conditions which are favourable to it.' 'No credulity more absolute than that created by a high dividend.' On his bust by Westmacott he had inscribed in Greek a quotation from Euripides: *You are rich, but do not imagine that you understand everything else*. 'He would sometimes say that he had lived on all incomes from £200 to £200,000 and that he could do so again,' wrote Benjamin Jowett after Hastings' death. 'He always retained in his personal habits the simplicity of a poor man – wealth was rather an inconvenience to him. He had a fixed opinion that it is far easier to do harm than to do good, and that doing good is usually more than counter-balanced by attendant evil. It was a favourite expression with him, "He did as little harm as he could help."'

While anxious that his huge contributions to charity, his aid to experiments in agriculture, the improvement of schools, and other good works, besides his generous treatment of his tenants in times of agricultural depression, should not be overlooked, he preferred not to be thanked for his munificence. He was enormously generous to his brothers, but unable to make them his pecuniary gifts without an accompanying imputation of their own improvidence, and when they bred large families the name of Malthus figured in his lightly sarcastic letters.

He himself raised two sons and two daughters, but was unable to engage their affection; they were afraid of him, of his critical and scathing tongue, though two of his nephews – twins – remembered how as small children he took them by the hand to gallop merrily along the passages at Woburn crying 'Tally Ho! A-hunting we will go!' The fear he inspired in his own children mounted with the years. 'The discovery that one is disliked by one's own children must be painful and . . . it is impossible he should not perceive how all dread his arrival and hope for his early departure, and that there is an end of all mirth, freedom and enjoyment as long as he is present', wrote Arthur Russell in 1875 to Lady Derby. The unimaginative and ponderous temperament of the Duchess of Bedford was not capable of raising the cloud of gloom that encompassed their family life. In a preposterous portrait by Gordigiani she appears as the embodiment of dullness, and splendour, and Victorian material ease. The life-size statue of her by Boehm in the gardens at Woburn was originally gilded; was this a cynical joke epitomizing Hastings' contempt for his wealth?

The death of his mother in 1874 left a scar that could not be healed. He told a friend that she was never for an hour out of his mind. He had continued to delight in her company and to frequent her drawing-room in the evenings when he was in London. The civilities she received from English and foreign royalty made it necessary for him sometimes to entertain such people at Woburn, a liability welcomed by his Duchess if not by him. His mother's old friend, the Queen of Holland, was received in 1872, and the Crown Prince and Crown Princess of Germany with three daughters paid a visit to the Abbey in 1878; a special train was reserved for their use and extra assistance was engaged to help the household staff. The burden of these visits was sometimes lightened, as when the Prince and Princess of Wales, the Duke of Connaught, the King of Greece, and the Duc d'Aumale accepted a luncheon only, and 114 neighbours were invited to meet them for tea.

The purchase of Norris Castle in the Isle of Wight, and a large yacht, furnished an escape from social obligations. Norris was rarely used for entertaining and in the *Claymore* Hastings was able to cruise – usually without his family – round the coasts of Britain.

With the entry of Sackville, his eldest son, to Balliol College, he came in contact with Benjamin Jowett, and a strong friendship grew up between them. His annual visit to Woburn was one of Jowett's great pleasures, and he observed his host's character with understanding and compassion. In 1877 Lord Beaconsfield and Jowett were fellow-guests at Woburn. The

Prime Minister had expected to meet Lord Derby there, but found the party had a distinctly Whiggish flavour – Derby having been detained with a cold.

> Duke, whom I always like, and who received me with cordial cere-mony, soon suggested that I might like to go to my room but I had not had my tea, and did not want to be dismissed for two hours. Still he hung about me, and tho' once repulsed, and tho' nobody else was moving, he still 'harped upon my daughter' and would insist upon showing me to my room. It seems the State suite was prepared for me, which is very gorgeous, and he wished, I suppose, personally to witness the effect produced upon his guest. I sleep in a golden bed, with a golden ceiling, and walls covered with masterpieces of modern art – Landseer, Linton, Newton and Leslie, and in the right place the picture of the trial of Lord Russell by Hayter. Then I have a writing-room, not less magnificent, and that opens into a third long gallery room, 'where,' said the Duke, 'you are to receive the Ambassadors!', they being, I suppose, Odo and Lyons.

He wrote to the Queen next day:

> The Duke is a strange character. He enjoys his power and prosper-ity, and yet seems to hold a lower opinion of human nature than any man Lord Beaconsfield was ever acquainted with. He is a joyous cynic.

A year later it was Mr Gladstone who was entertained in princely fashion at the Abbey, and when he departed a great deodar had fallen to his axe. Earlier that year, when it appeared that he would no longer represent Greenwich in the House of Commons, the Duke had suggested in a brief note to his brother that he should cede his seat at Tavistock to Gladstone. Arthur wrote at once:

> 13 March 1878

> I do not wish to leave Parliament and have on the contrary the strongest wish to remain there, however as you seem desirous to offer a seat to Gladstone I am willing to make the sacrifice in his favour, but in favour of no one else.

Gladstone did not retire from Greenwich and the sacrifice was not made, but Arthur was angered and hurt by the suggestion.

Gladstone was Hastings' leader for many years, although the fitful inconsistency of the Duke's vote in the House of Lords bewildered and annoyed the Liberals as he veered towards the Conservatives.

Gladstone's Irish policy, which split the Liberal Party, lost him the support of Hastings and Arthur, who both adhered to the Liberal-Unionists.

After the death of Lady William Russell, Hastings expressed the wish that his own life might not be prolonged. When ten years later Odo – who had been created Lord Ampthill – died at the Berlin Embassy aged fifty-five, that day, too, became 'one of the increasing anniversaries that sadden the decline of life. Mother's birthday. Mother's death day. Odo's birthday, Odo's death day', the Duke wrote on a blotted page to Arthur.

Mr Gladstone and Lord Granville discussed whether to offer him the Berlin Embassy in succession to his brother. 'The Duke of Bedford has various points of recommendation and something of the born diplomatist, nor do I see the objection to him, if he would go', wrote the Prime Minister, but it was the Duke's son-in-law, Sir Edward Malet, recently married to Hastings' younger daughter, Lady Ermyntrude Russell, who succeeded the man that Bismarck and the Germans had loved and admired.

Hastings had a great fear of pain and a lingering death. A theme – his prayer that God would grant him euthanasia – recurred in his letters to his brother throughout the 1880s. He suffered from painful rheumatism and failing strength: 'I am able to do half a day's estate inspection – and no more', he complained in 1887. Four more sad years passed, and then he shot himself in his London house while suffering from influenza, and what he himself would have called a fit of 'the Blue Devils'.

A shrewd and compassionate summary of the Duke's character appeared from the pen of Jowett in the *Spectator*, but it was the perceptive Lord Acton who, in a letter of condolence to Arthur Russell, touched on the possible causes of Hastings' embitterment and disillusion.

March 12, 1891

... To me there is almost always an unexplained mystery in the character of any man worth analysing; and I never felt that I really understood the nature of the drawback which made one of the most distinguished men of my time comparatively obscure, and one of the most agreeable men unpopular. I could not tell whether the dislike of effort was only disregard for the reward of effort and the want of *liant*, the intense contempt for men, was the result of secret wounds or of an acquired philosophy . . . There was nobody I was so glad to meet; therefore it is not for me to say that he was uncongenial. But so many people found him so, found him bitter and hard, that it can hardly have been their own fault.

I can remember when people used to say that the Russells were heavily handicapped because they were educated at home – or rather abroad; and that they knew foreign languages so much better than anybody else that they could never be master of their own. But the official success of one brother, and the social success of the other, deprive us of these explanations. No doubt you know what I do not even conjecture, and could tell whether natural timidity, or early sorrow had to do with the immense disproportion between his powers and his success in outward life. I don't even know whether he felt that want of visible success, with its rather vulgar prizes, or grew to be satisfied with being useful in so many inconspicuous ways . . .

16

A Singular Couple

In the materialistic Victorian age it was the aim of every ambitious mother to catch the eldest son of a duke as a husband for her daughter. When he was twenty-four, Sackville, Marquess of Tavistock, allowed himself to be captured. His marriage to Adeline, the daughter of Earl Somers, was loveless and without children. Benjamin Jowett, under whose care he had been at Balliol, took a warm interest in his career and hoped great things of him in the political world and society, but he was an indifferent pupil and left Oxford with a third in history and a memory of the Master's strong tea, which he said 'nearly blew your head off'.

Ten years in Parliament representing Bedfordshire was his contribution to public life. His enormous appetite at table excited comment, and his capacity to drink great quantities of sherry without muddling his brain was noted with astonishment. During the two years he reigned at Woburn as the tenth Duke of Bedford, he and his wife succeeded with charm and kindness in pleasing their guests, but could not conceal that so enormous a house was a source of trouble to them. He suffered from diabetes and died suddenly as he was leaving the dining-room in March 1893.

It was his younger brother, Lord Herbrand Russell, who, as eleventh Duke, now entered on nearly fifty years of rule at Woburn. A professional soldier, he had fought with the Grenadier Guards in the Egyptian War, and had served as A.D.C. on the staff of Lord Dufferin in India, where at the age of twenty-seven he met and married Mary Tribe, the handsome, intelligent and athletic daughter of the Archdeacon of Lahore. It was two hundred years since the bride of a future Duke of Bedford had been chosen outside the ranks of the aristocracy, and the last such – Elizabeth Howland – had been a great heiress. Lord Herbrand's parents had received the news of their younger son's engagement with outward equanimity.

'My little boy,' the Duke had written, '13 years ago, as soon as I had the power in anticipation of your letter received today, I began to "build up" incomes for my younger children to enable them to marry when they pleased. What more can I say at this moment – in answer to that letter. B.'

'I hope', the Duchess wrote, 'your wife will not be an extravagant fine lady, and will not lead the life of the young married ladies of London.'

'Your management of the Vice-regal Household ought to teach you something of household management,' suggested the Duke some weeks later, 'without which a large household is a curse to its neighbourhood and a snare to its (empty) head.' He urged his son to leave the Army and to come home without delay. 'If you care to see me again – it would not be very safe to wait till "my next birthday" when I may or may *not* be here.'

The wedding took place at Barrackpore in January 1888, and the young couple then returned to England. Any fear the bride may have felt that she would not be well received in her husband's family was shown to be groundless; in a reassuring letter to the Archdeacon, Lord Dufferin wrote that the Duke and Duchess were 'delighted with her looks, manners and everything, and think her most charming and clever', and it was made evident to the Duchess that her daughter-in-law had no wish to be a social butterfly. Neither Lord Herbrand nor his wife had any aptitude for ordinary social life. He was precluded from enjoyment of it by over-whelming shyness, and she already suffered from the deafness – the legacy from an attack of typhoid fever in India – that was to increase with age. After a season in London, they took the lease of Cairnsmore in Galloway, where their only child was born in December. He was christened Hastings after his grandfather.

The death of the ninth Duke in 1891, followed by that of the tenth Duke two years later, altered – although not unexpectedly – the life of the Herbrand Russells. Woburn became their home, while Cairnsmore remained a well-loved retreat for the late summer.

The new Duke and Duchess were a remarkable pair, both endowed with exceptionally strong characters. Remaining deeply attached to each other, they came in time to lead very separate lives, each pursuing their interests while sharing some. They both loved animals; the Duchess had her cats and her dogs, and the Duke his well-known zoological collections, for which, until 1914, his wife kept a meticulous record of his purchases and the subsequent births and deaths among the animals. Some beasts, like wapiti, bison, and Przewalsky's wild horses, were kept in large fenced areas, but experiments were made in adapting deer of many different breeds to live together at liberty within the Park, where they roamed in company with emus, cranes, rare geese, and wild turkeys. Exchanges were made with Continental zoos and animals were imported from their native lands. The herd of Père David deer was the greatest treasure of the collection. These somewhat ungainly creatures – who still wander in the Park – had been discovered by a French missionary in the Imperial Hunting Park at Pekin. Becoming extinct elsewhere, the Woburn herd was for a time the only one in existence. All through their busy lives the Duke and Duchess enjoyed an evening stroll in the Park together, at a time when small animals, startled in the dusk, sprang with bird-like cries from the long grass, and large birds groaning like hoarse deer took to the air; an experience not easily forgotten by any lover of animals.

The Duke was above all a great and enlightened landowner with an outstanding sense of duty towards the responsibilities of his vast estates. Although he had a strong feeling for tradition it was combined with an independent outlook; he attacked the hereditary principle of the House of Lords, and he favoured land reform, though he was opposed to national-ization. By financing his own tenant farmers, he enabled them to buy their land from him.

Accustomed to vice-regal splendour, and with a memory of Government House, Calcutta – where servants were beyond counting – it was natural for him to preserve at Woburn a way of life – doomed in most of England after 1914 – that appealed to him and which he thought was suitable to his station. The indoor staff at Woburn Abbey numbered close on seventy until the death of the Duchess in 1937, but owing to his shyness and the deafness of his wife, visitors after early days were not numerous and were principally confined to relations.

The Duchess did not care for what she called 'the strict formality' of Woburn, and was never enslaved by it. Taking advantage of her husband's wealth – and he was extremely generous – she was able to pursue her many independent interests, and since she was increasingly cut off by her aural disability from her fellow-creatures, many of her occupations were solitary ones. She was a first-rate shot and skilful with a salmon rod; an expert skater and a capable needlewoman, she had also a talent for drawing flowers and insects. Part of the gardens at Endsleigh were enlarged under her direction, and canoeing parties on the Tamar gratified her love of adventure by risking shipwreck among the stickles and rocks of the swiftly flowing river: while others capsized she usually managed to keep afloat. From the early years of the century to the end of her life Mary Bedford loved watching birds, and her large private yacht carried her, her maid, and perhaps one female cousin round the coasts of England to the Outer Hebrides, Scandinavia, and the Arctic. These experiences, and a list of the rare birds she saw, were recorded with fluency and a dry humour in her diary. Embracing each new activity as a challenge to her intellect and skill, it is difficult not to believe that the occupations that engrossed her, one after another, were undertaken and excelled in at the expense of the development of her heart and emotions. She gave her husband as much affectionate attention as she could spare from her fascinating pursuits, but her son has attested that while he was a boy she was too busy to give him much of her time, and too impatient to enter into his childish pastimes. Deprived of his mother's company and encouragement, he found sympathetic companions for his lonely hours in a collection of spiders, which he kept in boxes and viewed with scientific appreciation. The Duke was devoted to his little boy and always set aside an hour in the evening to read and talk to him. They shared a love of animals. An excellent person, Miss Flora Green, who had been governess to some of the Kaiser's children, instructed young Hastings until he went to Eton, when she stayed on at the Abbey as the valued and reliable friend of the Duke and Duchess.

The inner warmth of the Duke's affectionate nature was not readily discernible under the military discipline of his exterior, but his generosity and many acts of thoughtfulness for those around him were evidence enough of his human feelings for people less well off than himself, who yet were, in some respects, more fortunate than he. When he went to London for public business or private affairs – to attend the House of Lords or preside at a meeting of the Zoological Society – and travelled by motor car from Woburn to London, he changed at Hendon into a car sent from Belgrave Square, the first chauffeur and car returning to the country; this operation was repeated in reverse on the return journey. His reason, he explained, excusing this eccentric behaviour, was that he had a feeling that it would be wrong to separate a man from his wife for a single night.

The Duchess had no great regard for the historical collections of her home, declaring that her predecessors lacked artistic tastes. 'When I say no artistic tastes I mean only respect for portraits by good painters and bits of furniture which cost a lot, but no innate artistic feeling. The furnishing of the Abbey is enough to make artistic angels weep.' Her contribution to improving matters was to banish the beautiful old mahogany *lits bateaux* and to install brass bedsteads from Maple & Co.; the cups and saucers on her tea table were decorated with rosebuds, blue ribbons and forget-me-nots.

The Army had always been very near the Duke's heart, and on the outbreak of war in 1914 he put on khaki and organized a depot for the Bedfordshire Territorial Regiment, of which he was Colonel. Every officer leaving the camp was presented with a pair of binoculars – the personal gift of the Duke of Bedford. The pacifism of his son was a cruel blow to his pride and caused a breach between them, lasting twenty years. With much to annoy him, and concerned for the good name of the family, he could nevertheless reflect with satisfaction that at the turn of century Oliver Russell, Lord Ampthill, while governing Madras had acted as Viceroy during the absence of Lord Curzon; that many of his cousins were serving in the armed forces, and that a brave police officer – Russell Pasha – was successfully combating the traffic of drugs in Egypt.

The Duchess embarked on another activity that had attracted her since her youth. In 1898 she had opened a Cottage Hospital in Woburn. A few years later it was replaced by a model hospital designed by herself, and in 1914 it became a Military Hospital, while Flitcroft's Riding School and Tennis Court were converted into another hospital with eighty beds. In her lifetime the Duchess was to give thirty-four years of devotion to hospital work; as a probationer scrubbing floors to acting as theatre nurse, she served in all departments, and it cannot be doubted that her service to her patients – who knew her as 'Sister Mary' – brought out the most human side of her character. When after the war the Abbey Hospital was closed, she reorganized her Cottage Hospital to take only surgical cases. She herself acted as surgeon's assistant in the theatre, and as radiologist, doing herself all the work of the X-ray department unassisted. Her day was regulated like that of any professional.

Often spending his day alone, the Duke took a great interest in the history of his family and in his collection of portraits. Wishing to know more of the history of the Russells, he had the good fortune to acquire the services of a talented scholar, Miss Gladys Scott Thomson, who delved into the archives preserved at Woburn. When she produced several admirable books about the family based on her researches he was delighted and under her direction established a well-furnished muniment room where many of the choicest manuscripts were put on show. Inevitably spending much of her time at the Abbey, she was unabashed by the 'strict formality' maintained by the shy and silent Duke, and guests at the ducal table were often grateful for her cheerful voice and conversation, which surmounted the heavy tread of the five or six footmen who handed the dishes and often outnumbered the people seated at table.

Yet one more hitherto unknown activity was to engross the Duchess. When she was sixty-one she made her first flight from Croydon to Woburn, and thereafter one of her chief pleasures was flying in an open aeroplane. Fortunately able to command the services of a succession of admirable and resourceful pilots – who became her friends while being her servants – she became a pioneer of long-distance flying, and with their skill and her remarkable courage and endurance she achieved in 1929 the record for a flight to India and back in eight days – breaking a further record the following year with a flight to the Cape and back. On these flights she took the controls for short periods and was expected to undertake some mechanical tasks. On such long journeys the inadequate petrol tanks of a small aeroplane resulted sometimes in an unavoidable shortage of fuel, placing the aviators in situations of extreme danger. Her witty diaries show that her only thought as she viewed without panic the prospect of inevitable death was for 'poor Herbrand'. Better known to the public as the Flying Duchess than as Sister Mary, her exploits were eagerly reported by the Press. She learnt to fly her own little aeroplane and delighted to make short solo flights from Woburn when she was able to visit alone the haunts of the wild birds she so much enjoyed watching. From Cley on the shores of the Wash (she had taken the mill and was restoring the sails) she wrote in 1936 to a Russell cousin of the loud incessant noises in her head and 'the strain of trying to hear what I cannot hear'. She had a great fear that her usefulness in hospital work might be terminated by her increasing deafness. Unconsciously presaging a danger that had significance the following year, she wrote: 'My little Moth takes me down in an hour over country which always interests me, the Wash and the Bedford Level. As I follow the Wash for its whole length I can afford to look about me and not bother with the compass, otherwise that flat east coast country wants a lot of watching or you soon find yourself lost.'

In the afternoon of 22 March 1937, she took off in good weather from the hangar in Woburn Park, meaning to view the unprecedented floods in the Fen districts, and to complete in less than one hour 200 hours of solo flying. At 4.30 p.m. she had not returned and a heavy snowstorm had set in. The police were alerted by the Duke, and the R.A.F. took part in the search for her. It was only eleven days later that a strut from her aeroplane was washed up near Yarmouth, and the remaining three appeared one by one along the east coast. It will never be known if she lost her way, as seems most likely, or whether she was tired of life, and changing course flew out to sea to find eternal rest in the ocean. The verdict remains an open one.

The last three years of the eleventh Duke's life were singularly sad ones; losing the wife he loved and admired, death soon deprived him of the companionship of the faithful Miss Green. Disappointed in his son and in his grandson, impatient of opposition, he was vexed by wrangles and disputes about their affairs. Another European war was menacing, and the prospect of Woburn as he had known it surviving such a disaster was minimal. Taxation had already forced the sale of estates that had been part of the Russell heritage for generations. His crippling shyness deterred demonstrations of sympathy. Affectionate female cousins in succession sustained him with their company and conversation at Woburn: he had always been used to ordering and running the great house himself. Friends and relations who applied to him for the favour of his private boxes at Drury Lane or Covent Garden still regularly received, with his brief note of pleasure in the donation, the pink or blue paper slips that gained admission to the theatres and that were signed in a firm clear hand 'Bedford'. When he died in August 1940 a Government Ministry was established in Flitcroft's magnificent stables and was already anticipating occupation of the Abbey itself.

Appendix

Various ways of spelling Woburn,
collected from letters and parcels by the Postmaster in 1840

Aubon	Hurbn	Hubburn	Oueeborn
Boubone	Hubrn	Holbhorn	Orooburn
Booburn	Hurbin	Hooben	Oporne
Buorn	Hoabir	Habaen	Owburn
Hubon	Houbone	Hulbon	Obering
Habon	Hubbon	Howbrn	Obborn
Hoaborn	Hucbuer	Hobuend	Olburn
Heuborn	Hobor	Howon	Obarn
Hobern	Hobart	Harborn	Obren
Heobren	Houghburn	Hoobbern	Oobourn
Hoburn	Huburnon	Hoobone	Obert
Holbern	Hotsburn	Haurbern	Obairn
Holbin	Hoham	Hoobun	Obowin
Hoolborn	Holobon	Muubborn	Roburn
Horeban	Hubman	Naburn	Roobud
Horbon	Hubeen	Noburn	Reuber
Houboun	Horbern	Norborn	Roobnd
Hourbon	Hobn	Oberon	St. Woburne
Hubarn	Hubhurn	Obon	Uborn
Huban	Houghbourn	Obron	Uburn
Hubearn	Hawburn	Obern	Uobeen
Huben	Hurbunn	Orbon	Uberer
Hubborne	Houberon	Oburin	Uuburn
Hubon	Herborn	Oumbun	Ubon
Hurben	Hawboum	Obburn	Ubun
Hurbon	Holbourn	Onbourn	Valbon

Vobam

Woubnn

Woborn

Wooburm

Whrbourn

Wobebourn

Whoebard

Woubon

Worbn

Whobeen

Wouber

Whabarn

Woabbern

Woben

Wholboon

Wosburn

Wobewn

Woubenn

Wourbunn

Wubawrn

Woubur

Waybourn

Wobuen

Woodburn

Weeburn

Woronburn

Woblowne

Walburn

Wodburn

Wehbborn

Waban

Whuband

Worborne

Wouber

Wolarn

Whobroun

Wosurin

Woorbunn

Woerben

Wbun

Wburn

Weburn

Woburn

Wobin

Woolm

Woaborn

Waberne

Wabrn

Waburne

Woobun

Wooburn

Wbren

WBun

Whe Bren

Wheorborn

Whoban

Whobern

Whoborn

Whobron

Whohousn

Whoobowen

Whorebin

Whopen

Wobburn

Woberan

Woban

Wobberon

Wobirn

Wobon

Wobourne

Waboun

Wobran

Wo Bin

Wobourn

Woeburn

Wohbourn

Wolburn

Waoburn

Woobeern

Woobun

Wooburge

Woodbarn

Woolbon

Wooburn

Woosbon

Worborn

Woowbourn

Wolborn

Wobourne

Wooborn

Wobreo

Woobern

Worbon

Woslorn

Worbebnm

Wouboarene

Wonbun

Woubrn

Woubnre

Wouburn

Wabourn

Wubon

Wobury

Wobuan

Wwoburne

Wobuorn

Whoper

Woobennd

Woowborn

Woarnb

Wobborn

Worbunn

Wwoo Burn

Woabarn

Wobans

Wooben

Wodurn

Wolbourn

Woutbon

Wooborg

Worban

Wilburn

Woodum

Woobbern

Wobin

Woodburnt

Wobwen

Warben

Wobre

Wannbourn

Wobbern

Womborne

Wodun

Wuborn

Woolboum

Woroben

Wobunn

Woven

Wolbor

Youborn

Bibliography

Unpublished Sources

Bedford Office: HMC No 8
   Papers of the 7th, 8th and 9th Dukes of Bedford.
Letters to Lord G. W. Russell. 3 vols. Privately printed 1915–20.
Letters of Lady John Russell to her husband 1798–1801. Privately printed 1913.
Diary of Lady John Russell. 1793–95.
Mary, Duchess of Bedford. John Gore 2 vols. Privately printed 1938.
The fifth Duke of Bedford. Gladys Scott Thomson.
Herbrand, 11th Duke of Bedford K.G. by one of his godsons. C. W. H. Rawlins.
Herbrand, 11th Duke of Bedford: a Memoir. Cosmo Russell.
Letters of Arthur Russell to the Countess of Derby.
British Library: Add Mss. 15,955; 31,141–2; 35,128–9; 51,345; 51,661; 51,665.
Blenheim Papers.
Royal Botanic Gardens, Kew: Papers of Sir William Hooker.
Russell papers in possession of the author.

Published Sources

Letters and papers of Henry VIII.
Calendar of State Papers Domestic:
   Henry VIII
   Elizabeth
   James I
   Charles I
Historical Manuscripts Commission.
   Various 8
   Carlisle (15th report Part VI)

Bibliography

ABBOTT, E. AND CAMPBELL, LEWIS (eds): *Life and Letters of Benjamin Jowett*. 2 vols. New York 1897

ADAM, WILLIAM: *A pamphlet printed from the MS in the possession of Mr Adam respecting the fifth Duke of Bedford*. 1803

AIRLIE, MABELL, COUNTESS OF: *Whig Society*. London 1921

AKRIGG, G. P. V.: *Jacobean Pageant*. London 1962

ANDREWS, C. BRUYN (ed.): *The Torrington Diaries*. 4 vols. London 1938

Annals of Agriculture. xxvi. 1976

ASPINALL, A. (ed.): *Correspondence of George, Prince of Wales*. London 1963–71

BALD, R. C.: *John Donne*. Oxford 1970

BAMFORD, F. AND WELLINGTON, DUKE OF (eds): *Journal of Mrs Arbuthnot*. 2 vols. London 1950

BEDFORD, HASTINGS, DUKE OF: *The Years of Transition*. London 1949

BEDFORD, JOHN, DUKE OF: *A Silver-plated Spoon*. London 1959

BEDFORD, JOHN, DUKE OF: *The Flying Duchess*. London 1968

BESSBOROUGH, EARL OF: *Georgiana, Duchess of Devonshire*. London 1955

BETHAM-EDWARDS, M. (ed.): *Autobiography of Arthur Young*. London 1891

BLEACKLEY, HORACE: *Ladies fair and frail*. London 1909

BLUNT, REGINALD (ed.): *Mrs E. Montagu. Letters and friendships*. 2 vols. London 1923

BOWLES, JOHN: *Observations on the correspondence between Mr Adam and Mr Bowles*. 1804

BOWLES, JOHN: *A Letter to the Hon. Charles James Fox in consequence of his speech in the House of Commons on the character of the late Duke of Bedford*. N.D.

BROUGHAM, HENRY, LORD: *Historical Sketches of Statesmen of the Reign of King George III*. 3 vols. London 1843

BROWNE, M. C.: *A leaf out of Burke's Book being an Epistle to that Rt Hon. Gentleman in reply to his letter to a Noble Lord on the subject of his pension*. 1796

BUNSEN, FRANCES, BARONESS: *Memoirs of Baron Bunsen*. 2 vols. London 1869

BURKE, EDMUND: *Letter to a Noble Lord*. 1796

BURNET. G.: *History of his own Times*. London 1838

CARLETON, DUDLEY, to John Chamberlain 1603–24: *Jacobean Letters*. New Brunswick 1972

CARSWELL, J. and DRAKE, L. A. (eds): *The Political Journals of George Bubb Dodding-ton*. 2 vols. London 1865

CASANOVA, J.: *Mémoires*. 12 vols. Paris 1961

CORNWALLIS, JANE, LADY: *Private correspondence 1613–1644*. London 1844

CUNNINGHAM, P. (ed.): *The Letters of Horace Walpole*. 9 vols. London 1861

DICKINSON, VIOLET (ed.): *Miss Eden's Letters*. London 1919

Bibliography

DUTENS, LOUIS: *Mémoires d'un voyageur qui se repose.* 2 vols. London 1806

ELLIS, SIR HENRY (ed.): *Original Letters Series 3.* 4 vols. London 1825–46

ENGEL, C–E. (ed.): *Mémoires du chevalier de Gramont.* Paris 1958

FABER, GEOFFREY: *Jowett.* London 1957

FISHER, H. A. L.: *History of Europe.* London 1936

FITZGERALD, B. (ed.): *Correspondence of Emily Countess of Leinster.* Dublin 1949

FORTESCUE, SIR JOHN (ed.): *Correspondence of King George III.* 6 vols. London 1927–8

FROUDE, J. F.: *History of England.* 12 vols. London 1870–2

FULLER, T.: *Worthies.* 3 vols. London 1840

GARDINER, S. R.: *History of the Great Civil War.* 3 vols. London 1886–91

Gentleman's Magazine 1802.

GODBER, JOYCE: *Bedfordshire.* Bedford 1969

GORE, JOHN: 'The Flying Duchess'. *The Quarterly Review.* January 1965

GOSSE, E.: *Life and Letters of John Donue.* 2 vols. London 1899

GRANVILLE, CASTALIA, COUNTESS: *Private Correspondence of Lord Granville Leveson Gower 1781–1821.* 2 vols. London 1916

GREEN, DAVID: *Sarah, Duchess of Marlborough.* London 1967

GREIG, J. Y. T. (ed.): *Letters of David Hume.* 2 vols. Oxford 1932

GRIMBLE, IAN: *The Harrington Family.* London 1957

HALL, EDWARD: *Chronicle.* London 1809

HARRISON, G. P.: *Jacobean Journal.* London 1941

HERBERT, EDWARD, LORD: *History of England under Henry VIII.* London 1870

HILL, G. BIRKBECK: *Letters of David Hume to William Strahan.* Oxford 1888

HILLIARD, G. S. (ed.): *Life, letters and journals of George Ticknor.* 2 vols. Boston. 1909

HOLINSHED, R.: *Chronicles.* 6 vols. 1807–8

HOLLAND, LORD: *Memoirs of the Whig Party.* 2 vols. London 1854

HUGHES, HELEN SARD: *The gentle Hertford.* New York 1940

HUSSEY, CHRISTOPHER: 'Woburn Abbey'. *Country Life,* 31 March, 8 September, 1955

ILCHESTER, COUNTESS OF, AND STAVORDALE, LORD (eds): *Life and Letters of Lady Sarah Lennox.* 2 vols. London 1901

ILCHESTER, EARL OF: *Lord Hervey and his friends.* London 1950

ILCHESTER, EARL OF: (ed.): *Journal of Elizabeth, Lady Holland.* 2 vols. London 1908

INGPEN, ROGER (ed.): *Boswell's Life of Johnson.* 2 vols. Bath 1925

JESSE, CAPTAIN W.: *Life of Beau Brummel.* 2 vols. London 1886

JOWETT, B.: 'The late Duke of Bedford'. *The Spectator.* 7 March 1891

LAUD, WILLIAM: *Works.* 7 vols. Oxford 1853–60

LEES-MILNE, JAMES: *Earls of Creation*. London 1962

LEVESON GOWER, HON. F. (ed.): *Letters of Harriet, Countess Granville, 1810–1845.* 2 vols. London 1890

LLANOVER, LADY (ed.): *Autobiography and correspondence of Mary Granville, Mrs Delany.* 6 vols. London 1861–2

LLOYD, DAVID: *Stateworthies.* 2 vols. London 1766

LUTTRELL, N.: *Brief Historical Relation of State of Affairs, 1678 to 1714.* 6 vols. Oxford 1857

MACAULAY, T. B.: *History of England.* 5 vols. London 1861

MCDOWELL, R. B. (ed.): *Correspondence of Edmund Burke*, 8 vols. Cambridge 1969

MACRAY, W. DUNN (ed.): *Clarendon's History of the Rebellion.* 6 vols. Oxford 1888

MAXWELL, SIR HERBERT (ed.): *The Creevey Papers.* 2 vols. London 1903

MINTO, COUNTESS OF (ed.): *Life and Letters of Sir Gilbert Elliot, 1st Earl of Minto.* 3 vols. London 1874

MONEYPENNY, W. F. AND BUCKLE, G. E.: *Life of Disraeli.* 6 vols. London 1920

MORRIS, C. (ed.): *The journeys of Celia Fiennes.* London 1947

MUIR, KENNETH: *Life and Letters of Sir Thomas Wyatt.* Liverpool 1963

NORTON, G. E. (ed.): *Letters of Edward Gibbon.* 5 vols. London 1956

OMAN, CAROLA: *The Gascoyen Heiress.* London 1968

PARKES, J. AND MERIVALE, H. (eds): *Memoirs of Sir Philip Francis.* 2 vols. London 1867

POPE-HENNESSY, JAMES: *Monckton Milnes: The years of promise. 1809–71.* London 1949

PRICE, CECIL (ed.): *Letters of R. B. Sheridan.* 3 vols. Oxford 1966

RADZIWILL, PRINCESS (ed.): *Memoirs of the Duchesse de Dino (1836–40).* 3 vols. London 1909–10

RAMM, AGATHA (ed.): *Political correspondence of Mr Gladstone and Lord Granville 1876–82.* Oxford 1962

RATHBONE, A. (ed.): *Letters of Lady Jane Coke to Mrs Fyre.* London 1899

ROBINET, DR: *Danton émigré.* Paris 1887

ROGERS, SAMUEL: *Pleasures of Memory.* London 1845

ROSCOE, E. S. AND CLERGUE, HELEN (eds): *George Selwyn: His Life and Letters.* London 1899

ROWSE, A. L.: *The later Churchills.* London 1958

ROWSE, A. L.: 'The Dark Lady from a woman's point of view'. *The Times*, 2,3 July 1973

RUSSELL, LORD JOHN (ed.): *Correspondence of John 4th Duke of Bedford.* 2 vols. London 1846

RUSSELL, LORD JOHN (ed.): *Letters of Rachel, Lady Russell*. London 1853

RUSSELL, LORD JOHN: *Life of William, Lord Russell*. London 1853

RUSSELL, LORD JOHN (ed.): *Memoirs, Journals and Correspondence of Thomas Moore*. 8 vols. London 1853–6.

RUSSELL, LORD JOHN: *Life and Times of C. J. Fox*. 3 vols. London 1866

SACKVILLE-WEST, V. (ed.): *Diary of Lady Anne Clifford*. London 1923

SAINTE-BEUVE, C. A.: 'Madame de Boufflers'. *Nouveaux Lundis*. Paris 1865

SCARISBRICK, J. J.: *Henry VIII*. London 1968

SCOTT STEVENSON, G.: *Charles I in captivity*. London 1927

SCOTT THOMSON, GLADYS: *Two Centuries of Family History*. London 1930

SCOTT THOMSON, GLADYS: *Life in a Noble Household 1641–1700*. London 1937

SCOTT THOMSON, GLADYS: *The Russells in Bloomsbury 1669–1771*. London 1940

SCOTT THOMSON, GLADYS: *Letters of a Grandmother 1732–35*. London 1943

SCOTT THOMSON, GLADYS: *Family Background*. London 1949

SEDGWICK, ROMNEY (ed.): *Letters from George III to Lord Bute 1756–1766*. London 1939

SEDGWICK, ROMNEY (ed.): *Lord Hervey's memoirs of the reign of George III*. 3 vols. London 1931

SMITH, C. NOWELL (ed.): *Letters of Sydney Smith*. 2 vols. London 1958

SMITH, W. J. (ed.): *Grenville Papers*. London 1853

SPRIET, PIERRE: *Samuel Daniel*. Didier 1968

STAFFORD, COUNTESS OF (ed.): *Leaves from the diaries of Henry Greville*. London 1905

STIRLING, A. M. W.: *Coke of Norfolk and his friends*. London 1908

STRACHEY, L. AND FULFORD, R. (eds): *Greville Memoirs*. 8 vols. London 1938

STREET, T. G.: *A vindication of the Duke of Bedford's attack upon Mr Burke's Pension*. 1796

STRONG, ROY: *The English Icon*. London 1969

STROUD, DOROTHY: *Henry Holland*. London 1966

TATHAM, REV. H.: *Memoir of Anna Maria, Duchess of Bedford*. London 1858

TAVISTOCK, ADELINE, AND RUSSELL, ELA: *Biographical Catalogue of the Pictures at Woburn Abbey*. 4 vols. 1890–2

WALPOLE, HORACE: *Memoirs of King George III*. Edited by G. F. Russell Barker and H. Legge. 3 vols. London 1894

WALPOLE, SPENCER: *Life of Lord John Russell*. 2 vols. London 1891

WEDGWOOD, C. V.: *The King's Peace*. London 1955

WHARNCLIFFE, LORD (ed.): *Letters and Works of Lady Mary Wortley Montagu*. London 1861

WHEATLEY, HENRY (ed.): *Memoirs of Sir N. Wraxall*. 5 vols. 1884

Bibliography

WIFFEN, J. H.: *Historical Memoirs of the House of Russell.* 2 vols. London 1833

WILLIAMS, HAROLD (ed.): *The Correspondence of Swift.* 5 vols. Oxford 1965

WILLIAMSON, G. C.: *George Clifford, Earl of Cumberland.* Cambridge, 1920

WYNDHAM, HON. MRS HUGH (ed.): *The Correspondence of Sarah Spencer, Lady Lyttelton.* London 1912

YORKE, P. C.: *Life of Lord Chancellor Hardwicke.* 3 vols. Cambridge 1913

Index

Index

Index

Index

Holbein, 13, 49
Holkham, 121, 122, 161, 174, 177
Holland, Henry, 155–6, 161, 175
Holland, Lord, 165, 179, 186, 206
Holland, Lady, 153, 168, 179, 180, 181, 189, 197, 208
Holland, Sophie, Queen of, 217
Hooker, Sir William, 190, 191, 193, 196
Horton, Mrs, *see* Maynard, Lady
Houghton House (Beds.), 117, 139, 140, 143, 167
Houghton Hall (Norfolk), 121, 122
Howard, Catherine, 19
Howland, Elizabeth, *see* Bedford, Duchess of
Howland, Mrs Elizabeth, 76, 78, 80, 82, 85, 86, 117
Howland, John, 75
Howitt, William, 5
Hudson, Thomas, 107
Hume, David, 109, 133, 142

Ile, Adam, l', 135
Ireton, Henry, 65
Ireland, 32–4, 126–7, 179
Isabella Bourbon, infanta of Spain, 203, 204
Isabella, Queen of Spain, 203, 204

Jacobins, the English, 157
James I, 4, 28, 44, 45, 48, 58
James II, 69, 71, 73, 74
Janssen (or Johnson) 98, 99
Jerningham, Sir R., 14
Jerningham, Lady, *see* Bedford, Countess of
Jersey, 3rd Earl and Countess of, 102
Jersey, 5th Earl and Countess of, 183
Jervas, Charles, 86
jewellery, 1, 35, 57, 90, 104
Joanna, Archduchess, 10, 11
Johnson, Samuel, 105, 134, 152–3
Johnson, Mr, *see* Bedford, 8th Duke of
Joll, a fool, 25
Jones, Inigo, 45, 54
Jonson, Ben, 37, 45, 46
Jowett, Benjamin, 216, 217, 219, 221
Judgement of Paris, the, 84
Junius, *see* Francis, Sir Philip

Kennedy, Sir John, 58
Kennedy, Elizabeth, 58
Kent, William, 122
Keppel, Hon. Augustus, Admiral, 110, 141, 142
Keppel, Lady Elizabeth, *see* Tavistock, Marchioness of
Kew Gardens, 191, 193
Kingston, Russell, 8, 28
Kneller, Sir Godfrey, 81, 82, 92, 100, 104
Kneller, Lady, 92

La Hogue, battle of, 74
Landseer, Edwin, 185, 218
Lanier, Emilia, 42, 43
Lansdowne, Lord, 159
Lanzknechts, 16, 21

La Pérouse, 190
Laud, Archbishop, 56, 57
Lauderdale, Earl of, 158, 159
Lawrence, Sir T., 141
Legge, Henry, 109, 113
Lely, 69
Le Neve, 5
Lennox, Lady Sarah, 127, 147
Letter to a Noble Lord, 158
Leveson Gower, Hon. Baptist, 115
Leveson Gower, Hon. Elizabeth, 115–16
Leveson Gower, Hon. Evelyn, 115–16
Leveson Gower, Hon. Frances, 114–16
Leveson Gower, Hon. Gertrude *see* Bedford, Duchess of
Leveson Gower, Lord Granville, 109, 163
Lisbon, 99, 102, 143, 176
Lisle, Lord, 18, 19
Lloyd, David, 23
Long Acre, 21
Long, Elizabeth, *see* Russell of Thornhaugh, Lady
Louis XV, 135
Louis XVI, 157
Louisa Charlotte, infanta of Spain, 203
Lovett, Sir Robert and Lady, 60, 61
Lyons, Lord, 218
Luke, Sir Samuel, 64
Lyttelton, Sarah, Lady, 199, 200

McHugh, Fiagh, 34
Malet, Sir Edward and Lady Ermyntrude, 219
March, Lord, 147
Marlborough, 1st Duke of, 87, 88, 103
Marlborough, 3rd Duke of, 103, 119
Marlborough, 4th Duke of, 127, 141, 166
Marlborough, Caroline Russell, Duchess of, 106, 108, 112, 124, 125, 126–7, 135, 141, 167
Marlborough, Sarah, Duchess of, 87, 88, 89, 90, 91, 92, 93, 96, 97, 99, 100, 101, 102, 103, 104, 108, 118
Marlowe, Christopher, 29
Mary I, 22, 23, 26
Mary II, 74
Mary of Modena, 70
Mary, Queen of Scots, 27, 28
Masques, 18, 45
Masson, Miss, 200
Mayerne, Sir Theodor, 50
Maynard, Lord, 150, 151, 152
Maynard, Lady, 150, 151, 152, 169
Melbourne, Lord, 195, 200
Melbourne, Lady, 169
Melville, Sir James, 27
Menill, Mr, 98
Merryweather, Dean, 199
Miguel, Dom, 203
Miller, Philip, 112
Monckton Milnes, Richard, 199
Moneux, Sir Humphrey, 98, 99
Montagu, Mrs E., 145, 164
Montagu, Lady Jane, 182
Montagu, Lady Mary Wortley, 91, 105, 107

Index

Index

Russell, Edward, Lord (s. of 2nd Earl), 30, 31
Russell, Edward, *see* Orford, Earl of
Russell, Lord Edward (s. of 6th Duke), 188, 191
Russell, Eliza (niece of 6th Duke), 182, 188
Russell, Lady Elizabeth (d. of 2nd Duke), *see* Essex, Countess of
Russell, Elizabeth (d. of John, Lord Russell), 31, 32
Russell, Lady Ermyntrude (d. of 9th Duke), *see* Malet
Russell, Sir Francis (s. of 2nd Earl), 30, 32, 40
Russell, Francis (s. of John, Lord Russell), 31
Russell, Francis (s. of 4th Earl), 60, 62
Russell, Francis, Lord (s. of 5th Earl), 68, 70
Russell, Francis (s. of 4th Duke), *see* Tavistock, Marquess of
Russell, Lord Francis (s. of 6th Duke), 188
Russell, George (s. of 5th Earl), 68, 78
Russell, Hastings, *see* Bedford, 9th Duke of
Russell, Henry, 6, 7, 8, 9, 10
Russell, James, 10
Russell, John (s. of Henry Russell), 10
Russell, Colonel John (s. of 4th Earl), 60, 61, 62
Russell, Lord John *see* Bedford, 4th Duke of,
Russell, Lord John *see* Bedford, 6th Duke of
Russell, Lord John (1st Earl Russell), 2, 6, 35, 158, 180, 184, 186, 187, 202, 211, 212, 213; character, 189; and his mother, 176; and gardens, 176; and Reform Bill, 179, 189; and politics, 190, 198, 199, 206, 216; and Palmerston, 215
Russell, Lady John (Hon. Georgiana Byng), 172, 175, 176, 177, 194
Russell, Lady John (Lady F. Elliot), 189
Russell, Lady John (Adelaide Ribblesdale), 189
Russell, Lady John (Lady Diana Spencer), *see* Bedford, Duchess of
Russell, Johnny (s. of 1st Earl Russell), 199
Russell, Lady Katherine (d. of 4th Earl), *see* Brooke, Lady
Russell, Katherine (d. of William, Lord Russell), *see* Rutland, Duchess of
Russell, Hon. Leopold, 6
Russell, Lady Louisa (d. of 6th Duke), *see* Abercorn, Duchess of
Russell, Lady Margaret (d. of 2nd Earl), *see* Cumberland, Countess of
Russell, Lady Margaret (d. of 5th Earl), *see* Orford, Countess of
Russell, Odo (1st Baron Ampthill), 15, 191, 209, 212, 213, 214, 216–18, 219
Russell, Oliver (2nd Baron Ampthill), 225
Russell, Rachel Wriothesley, Lady, 70, 71, 73, 75, 76, 79, 80, 81, 82, 85, 86
Russell, Rachel (d. of William Lord Russell), *see* Devonshire, Duchess of
Russell, Lady Rachel (d. of 2nd Duke), *see* Bridgewater, Duchess of
Russell, Lady Rachel (d. of 6th Duke), 198
Russell, Stephen, 7, 8
Russell, Thomas (Russell Pasha), 225
Russell, William, Lord (s. of 5th Earl), 2, 68, 108; character, 69, 70, 74; marriage, 70; Rye

House plot, 71; trial and execution, 71, 72, 73; attainder reversed, 75
Russell of Thornhaugh, William (s. of 2nd Earl), 30, 38, 39, 43, 44; in the Netherlands, 32; Lord Deputy of Ireland, 32, 33; his portrait, 35; death, 35; Chapman on, 36; and fen drainage, 55
Russell of Thornhaugh, Elizabeth Long, Lady, 35
Russell, Lord William (bro. of 5th and 6th Dukes), 142, 143, 152, 170, 188
Russell, Lord G. William Russell (s. of 6th Duke), 175, 180, 184, 185, 186, 190, 191, 194, 197, 199, 208, 209, 211
Russell, Elizabeth Anne, Lady G. W., 185, 186, 189, 197, 208, 210, 211, 212, 213, 214, 219
Russell, Lord Wriothesley (s. of 6th Duke), 188
Russell House, Strand, 19, 23
Ruthven, Lord, 28
Rutland, 2nd Duke of, 75, 81
Rutland, 5th Duke of, 197
Rutland, Katherine Russell, Duchess of, 75, 81, 85
Ruvigny, Rachel de, 70
Ryalton, Lord, 87
Rye House plot, 71
Rysbrack, 122, 123

Sacheverell, Dr, 82
Sackville, Lord John, 114–16
St John, Margaret, *see* Bedford, Countess of
Salisbury, Marchioness of, *see* Derby, Countess of
Sanderson, John, 111, 118, 120
Sandwich, 4th Earl of, 109, 111, 113, 136, 137
Sandwich, Countess of, 185
Sandys, Lord, 89
Sapcote, Anne, *see* Bedford, Countess of
Savoy, Duke of, 13
Scott Thomson, Gladys, 6, 225–6
Selwyn, George, 129, 142, 147, 148, 149
Seven Years War, 128
Sèvres dinner service, 135
Seymour family, 22
Seymour, Jane, 12, 17, 18
Shaftesbury, 9
Shakespeare, 4, 35, 142
Sheep, 160–1
Shelley, Lady Frances, 182
Sherard, Dr James, 84
Sheridan, R. B., 159, 164–5
Shirley, Lady Fanny, 97
Sidney, Sir Philip, 32
Silk weavers' riots, 137, 138
Sinclair, 190
Sinclair, Sir John, 162
Skipton Castle, 40, 41
Sloane, Sir Hans, 82, 85
smallpox, 50, 57, 66, 85, 86, 106
Smith, Sir James, 190
Smith, Sydney, 186
Somerset, Duke of, 21
Somerset, Robert Carr, Earl of, 48, 58, 59

244

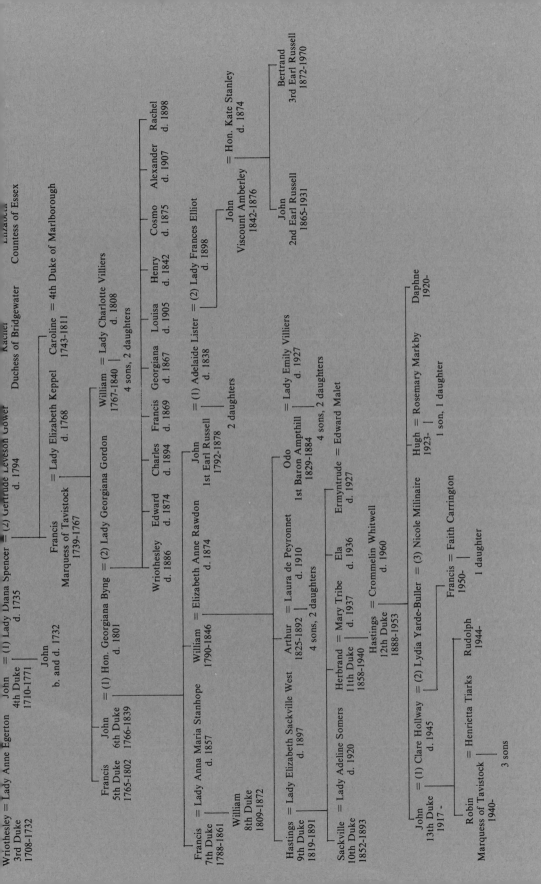

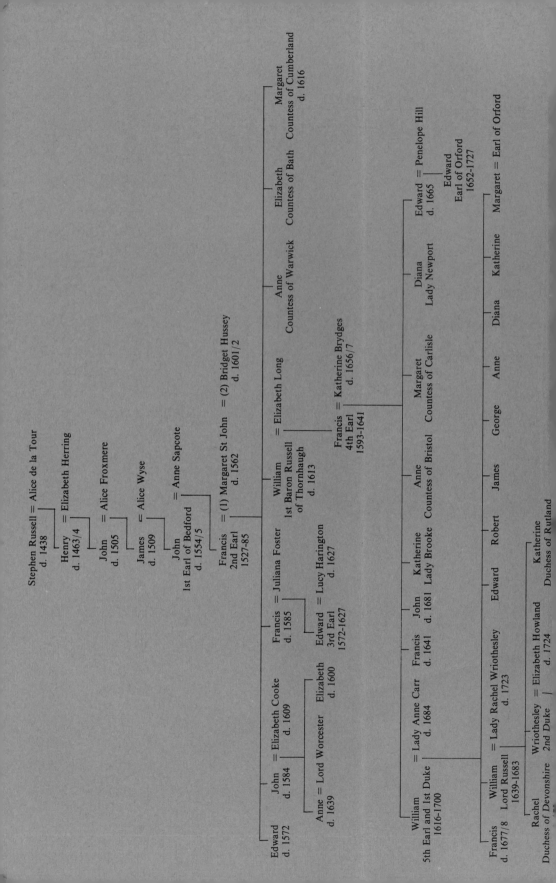

Stephen Russell = Alice de la Tour
d. 1438

Henry = Elizabeth Herring
d. 1463/4

John = Alice Froxmere
d. 1505

James = Alice Wyse
d. 1509

John = Anne Sapcote
1st Earl of Bedford
d. 1554/5

Francis = (1) Margaret St John = (2) Bridget Hussey
2nd Earl   d. 1562   d. 1601/2
1527-85

Edward
d. 1572

John = Elizabeth Cooke
d. 1584   d. 1609

Anne = Lord Worcester
d. 1639

Elizabeth
d. 1600

Francis = Juliana Foster
d. 1585

Edward = Lucy Harington
3rd Earl   d. 1627
1572-1627

William = Elizabeth Long
1st Baron Russell
of Thornhaugh
d. 1613

Anne
Countess of Warwick

Elizabeth
Countess of Bath

Margaret
Countess of Cumberland
d. 1616

Francis = Katherine Brydges
4th Earl   d. 1656/7
1593-1641

Francis
d. 1641

John
d. 1681

Katherine
Lady Brooke

Anne
Countess of Bristol

Margaret
Countess of Carlisle

Diana
Lady Newport

Edward = Penelope Hill
d. 1665

Edward
Earl of Orford
1652-1727

Margaret = Earl of Orford

William = Lady Anne Carr
5th Earl and 1st Duke   d. 1684
1616-1700

Edward

William = Lady Rachel Wriothesley
Lord Russell   d. 1723
1639-1683

Robert

James

George

Anne

Diana

Katherine

Francis
d. 1677/8

Rachel
Duchess of Devonshire

Wriothesley = Elizabeth Howland
2nd Duke   d. 1724

Katherine
Duchess of Rutland